Indian Politics & Our Thought

Indian Politics & Our Thought

Rajnath Singh

Edited by

Prabhat Jha

Ocean Books Pvt. Ltd.

ISO 9001:2015 Publishers

Published by
Ocean Books (P) Ltd.
4/19 Asaf Ali Road,
New Delhi-110 002 (INDIA)
e-mail: info@oceanbooks.in

ISBN 978-81-8430-200-4
INDIAN POLITICS & OUR THOUGHT
by Shri Rajnath Singh

Edition
2025

Price
₹ 700.00 (Rupees Seven Hundred only)

Printed at
Narula Printers, Delhi

Editorial

It is not an ordinary thing to be the national president of Bharatiya Janata Party which is at the centre of the national politics. In the current era of cut-throat competition, it is as difficult as sending a message of hope in politics as keeping oneself accountable and ethical along while being suave, restrained and sensitive. Bharatiya Janata Party is not only a political party but an ideological movement. When a political party works as a symbol of an ideological movement then the people's way of looking at the party changes.

BJP had started its ideological-political journey from Bharatiya Janasangh. This party has seen its government in many states and today also it has its government in many states. BJP is the only party which came to power while being in opposition. BJP has given a global personality as the most successful prime minister whose name is Shri Atal Bihari Vajpayee. Prior to the journey of Jansangh two personalities in the name of Dr. Syama Prasad Mookerjee and Pt. Deendayal Upadhyay emerged. Jansangh was not weakened by the untimely martyr like demise of these two personalities but instead the party was strengthened by their martyrdom. And from there like the duo of Maryada Purushottam Ram and Shri Lakshman, Shri Atal Bihari Vajpayee and Shri Lal Krishna Advani never allowed the journey to stop and the ideology which was emitted from the light of the 'lamp', the same ideology started spreading in the entire country in the shape of 'lotus'. These two untiring traveler on the journey of ideology did a lot of hard work. This rare duo has set an example in the Indian politics with their unflinching faith, indefatigable courage and limitless excellence. In the fifty years of untiring journey they steered the party several times and while one became the prime minister, the other became deputy prime minister.

Therefore those who consider BJP to be an ordinary party they perhaps forget that the name of the future party of India is Bharatiya Janata Party.

Those who get the responsibility of president of a party like this are enlightened by the light of the ideology. Born on 10 July, 1951 in village Bahabhaura, tehsil chakiya, district Chandauli of Uttar Pradesh Rajnath Singh adorned the post of party president. Before this he started his journey from Jansangh. He moved ahead by learning different aspects of politics. He never got politics as a legacy. He was elected as a member of legislative assembly for the first time in 1977. After this, after serving as BJYM national president and on other big posts in BJP he became the chief minister of Uttar Pradesh. Although he got a very short time as chief minster but he was able to make a mark as chief minister. He was also agriculture minister in the cabinet of former prime minister Shri Atal Bihari Vajpayee. He made image of a farmer leader all over the country. Today, farmers and Rajnath Singh are synonym of each other.

The ideas of such people are useful not for them but for the society. And the importance of these ideas is more significant when these are placed as national BJP president. Therefore the compilation of the presidential speeches delivered in the national council and national executive meetings by Shri Rajnath Singh when he became national president for the first time is presented in this book. The speeches of Rajnath Singh are full of ideas. Not only BJP activists but all those who take interest in politics may read this book. The effort has been made by keeping this in mind. I hope that when you will read this as national ideology of BJP then not only will you get a direction but your ideological commitment will also be strengthened.

—Prabhat Jha

(MP and BJP National Vice-President)

Contents

Re-dedication of a Young Party

20 January, 2006 (New Delhi)
National Council

Bharatiya Janata Party is now 25 years young. Recently we celebrated Silver Jubilee of its foundation. On the conclusion of the augustconvention in celebration of that occasion, the onerous responsibility of Party's National President was placed at my shoulders. I accept it in all humility. In this task I enjoy the blessings of my senior party veterans, cooperation of my colleagues, and affection of every worker. This spirit of love and affection generates a sense of coordination, collectivism and camaraderie which is the very basis of our party's strength. At a time when most of the political parties in the country have been reduced to the position of personal fiefs of a few leaders, BJP stands apart as a party which passes through a process of natural evolution and developments in the organization. I owe my present position entirely to this natural evolutionary process in the party.

BJP is a political party rich in distinct ideology possessing an army of committed and dedicated workers. Added to this is a succession of capable, industrious and talented leaders, and above all, inspiring leadership of respected Shri Atal Bihari Vajpayee and Shri Lal Krishna Advani. On this basis, I can say with confidence that together we all shall take BJP to a bright future. Our collective endeavour would accelerate the process of development and instill probity in public life. On being returned to power, our commitment would be to establish *Su-Raj* (good governance). Our ultimate aim shall be to re-establish the divine glory of Mother India in the world, as visualized by the great sage visionaries, like Shri Aurobindo, Swami Vivekananda and several other great souls.

What Politics means

As political activists we are all devoted to the service of society.

Therefore, we need to be clear in our minds about the nature and purpose of politics. *Rajniti*, the Sanskrit word for politics, is derived from conjunction of two words '*Raj*' and '*niti*'. The word *Raj* is derived from the word *Rajya* meaning state and *niti* from Sanskrit word '*nay*' meaning to lead. Therefore, *Rajniti* means a system of government that leads to the right path.

In our ancient culture, *Rajniti* is known as *Raj-Dharma*. The dignity and sobriety of the word *Rajniti* should always be clear to us. Without this depth of understanding, we will neither realise our responsibilities nor will politics get a meaningful direction.

Present Politics

The present political environment doesn't inspire faith in the minds of people but generates distrust and fear towards life. In the present political scenario, forget about *Dharma* and ethics, even the set standards of morality have collapsed. Now even public etiquettes and sense of shame seem to be vanishing. Politics today stands tarnished with the evils of selfishness, arrogance, casteism and corruption.

What is the scenario of political power in the country? We have a government at the Centre with numerous tainted ministers. Two ministers had at one time been declared proclaimed offenders; one had to resign on charges of rioting; one lost his ministry for involvement in oil scandal, and still another is involved in the controversy surrounding Bofors scandal. The ruling coalition is full of contradictions. In states they fight internecine political and electoral battles against one another but in the Centre they gang up just to oppose BJP.

In order to change this situation, we need both internal strength and strategy. But the question arises: what will be inspire us and guide us to our goals?

Our inspiration - Indianness

BJP is not merely a political party but a political movement raised on solid foundations of principles inspired by India and Indianness. Our Indianness is not merely a matter of cultural pride but a source of India's latent strength as well.

Three elements are universally considered vital for a nation's greatness.

1. Economic Power 2. Defence Power 3. Intellectual Prowess.

Possessed of these elements, USA continues to occupy the top position in the world for the last fifty years. Earlier, for some 100-100 years, 50-50 years Britain, Spain, Turkey and Rome did occupy the top positions. But in the face of adverse circumstances, these powers at the top of the world went down within ten-twenty years.

India had been at the pinnacle of prosperity in the past. The process of loot and aggression against us began with Alexander's invasion in 4th century BC. Then came Greeks, Huns, Shakas, Mongols, Turks, Arabs, Afghans, Spaniards, Portuguese, Dutch, Mughals and last of all, the British. These invasions continued till as late as the 18th century. Till that time we continued to enjoy our prosperity. While it took only 10-20 years for the economies of others to get destroyed, it took 2000 years for our invaders to make our economy collapse. But more than that, while it took at the most 50 years for other civilizations to get destroyed, even under adverse conditions India was able to withstand the onslaught and maintain its cultural essence for 2000 years. Yet, western scholars continued to praise us for our philosophy even during the worst of times.

Today, having entered the 21st century, we recall all this not just to sing eulogies of our past, but to underline the fact that in future also we will continue to acquire excellence in vital economic, military and intellectual spheres. Our inspiration is the tradition that is recognized as Indian or Hindu culture.

Hindutva

Hindutva is the symbol of Indian culture and traditions. It is also the source of economic prosperity, capacity to struggle, and intellectual prowess. *Hindutva* kindles feelings of respect for all. It arouses faith in justice and eliminates communal ill-will. It spreads the message of social equality and, above all, *Hindutva* is the symbol of nation's way of life. The Supreme Court of India has also expatiated upon *Hindutva* on these lines. *Hindutva* is therefore an inspirational and liberal thought. Those who still dub it as communal ideology should apologise to the nation for this blunder.

Integral Humanism

The liberal, all-embracing way of life that persisted in the Indian culture down the ages has been expounded as "Integral Humanism" by our great visionary ideologue Pt. Deendayal Upadhyay in tune with the present times. In it, the relation of an individual to society, nation, world, nature and God has been propounded to be natural and continuous. This thought doesn't provoke clash but only inspires harmony. The uplift of deprived, oppressed, *dalit*, neglected and backward sections is the centre point of our ideology, because without it the comprehensive development of the society cannot even be thought of. Under the philosophy of 'Integral Humanism', the concept of *Antodaya*, that is, the emancipation of the person standing on the lowest rung of the societal ladder, takes us to the fullness to our ideology.

Cultural Nationalism

Culture, and not political might, is the very foundation of any nation. To substantiate this point, I quote the example of two countries. One was Soviet Union that was a very strong power on the strength of political might which in the first half of 20th century had come to exercise control over almost half of the globe. Yet it could not withstand the impact of adversity of circumstances and within 72 years disintegrated into not one or two but 18 splinter states. The other country is Israel that stood obliterated from the map of the world for more than a thousand years but owing to cultural vivacity stormed back to life and political reality.

The feeling of nationalism remains vibrant in the normal course in the cultural stream. The *Ram Janmabhoomi* movement was the natural manifestation of this flow. The demand for removal of Article 370 and enactment of a common civil code for all citizens is the expression of feelings for national integration. It will be our earnest effort that all political parties and all communities, especially the Muslim community, come forward and rising above political contours, find out a solution to the Ram temple issue in accordance with the peoples' sentiments. Anything other than constructing a grand temple of Ram Lalla, at the site of Ram Janmabhoomi, will not be in accordance with the national spirit. It is an issue with which the faith of crores of our countrymen and the very pride of the nation is attached.

On the issue of Uniform Civil Code, I wish to remind that founder of the Constitution, Dr. Babasaheb Ambedkar had pleaded for it in the Constituent Assembly. In the last few years, even the Judiciary had stressed on the government the need to implement directions in the Constitution regarding Uniform Civil Code. In these circumstances, I feel that keeping in view the intent of constitution-makers and directions of the Supreme

Court of India, all political parties should review the matter and evolve a consensus on the subject.

With regard to Article 370, I wish to say that every political party is free to hold an independent opinion on any issue of national interest. While fully respecting this freedom of theirs I would like to request them to ponder over the spectre of terrorism raging in Kashmir for the last two decades and, at the same time, not ignore the plight of Kashmiri Hindus who have been forced to lead a life of refugees in their own country. In these circumstances, if all political parties take a sympathetic view and review their stand, it could lead to the generation of a more congenial atmosphere for finding a solution in the national interest.

The honour and proper rehabilitation of Kashmiri Pundits have been a priority for us and even today we continue to be sympathetic to the issue.

Bharatiya Jana Sangh/BJP have always been on the vanguard of upholding India's national unity and cultural awareness. We have been struggling for unity and integrity of India from the beginning. In 1953, Jana Sangh founder Dr. Syama Prasad Mookerjee laid down his life for mobilising public opinion for the cause of integration of Jammu and Kashmir with the rest of India. To underscore the profound cultural affinity and unity Kashmir has with the rest of India, in 1991 Dr. Murli Manohar Joshi undertook a *yatra* from Kanyakumari to unfurl the national flag at Srinagar's Lal Chowk ignoring the threat to his life. We have been in the forefront of struggle against tyranny and fascism during the days of the Emergency. The sacrifice and suffering of the dedicated cadres of the then Bharatiya Jana Sangh/RSS to restore democracy and civil liberties in the country can never be forgotten.

The Ram Janmabhoomi Movement shall always be reckoned as the biggest mass movement in post-independence India. The Somnath to Ayodhya *Rathyatra* under Advaniji's leadership infused a new vigour in the country. This movement imparted a new identity to India by infusing in it the concept of cultural nationalism. The movement for integration of Kashmir, struggle against the Emergency, and Ram Temple movement are milestones in the history of independent India. We are proud that Jana Sangh and BJP were harbingers of these three movements.

When the NDA government was formed at the Centre under the leadership of Shri Atal Bihari Vajpayee, he gave a new dimension to the country's self-respect by conducting the Pokhran nuclear tests in May,

1998. After India became a nuclear power state the world has started looking India with respect. Friends, time and again BJP has proved that what we say is not empty speeches or slogans for electoral gains only. We preach what we practise.

In other words, whether it is in the role of the ruling party or of the opposition, BJP has always been in the forefront to defend the political and cultural unity of the nation.

UPA Government failures

It will be more appropriate to call the ruling coalition at the Centre led by the Congress and subsisting on the crutches provided by the Communists as an immoral alliance not in the service of the nation but just to grab political power with the sole purpose of opposing BJP. The UPA government has only created more problems for the country and complicated many others.

National Security

The country is feeling concerned today because of the deteriorating national security scenario. Terrorism is on the rise in Kashmir and peace which returned to Punjab many years back is once again being threatened by terrorism raising its head in the State. In addition, Naxalite violence has already gripped and is increasingly spreading its tentacles fast in about 170 districts covering the States of Bihar, Jharkhand, Uttar Pradesh, Chhattisgarh, West Bengal, Andhra Pradesh and other parts of the country.

The situation is deteriorating in India's northeast day by day. Violence has escalated in Assam and surprisingly its Congress Chief Minister is proposing to provide safe passage to extremist organisations. In Manipur, it appears as if the administration has apparently prostrated itself before the adversary. Terrorist organisations there are forcing the BJP and other opposition parties to keep away from elections. Senior Police Officers have been murdered. An ethnic war erupted between Dimasa and Kabri Anglong tribes and the government has continued to be a mute spectator. Here also Congress is indulging in a policy of appeasement of terrorist organisations.

In the 19 months of UPA government's reign, the terrorist assaults in Ayodhya, Delhi and Bangalore have proved that this government can neither protect centres of cultural importance like Ayodhya, nor centres of political importance like Delhi, nor the developing centres of economic and technical importance, like Bangalore. During its rule terrorism is fast moving towards destroying the cultural, political and economic fabric of the country.

Demographic Aggression

The Census 2001 has revealed alarming facts about worsening religious balance in India's demography. The government tried its best to suppress these facts. The growing imbalance in religious demography in frontier districts of West Bengal and Assam is a matter of national concern. It is not what is happening in the natural course but the impact of demographic aggression from across the international border. Sadly, this enjoys the indirect patronage of the UPA government.

Infiltration from Bangladesh is on the rise. Today more than 20 million Bangladeshis have intruded into the country. The Supreme Court has likened the situation to the one of external aggression. The IMDT Act promulgated with the intention of detecting and deporting illegal immigrants in practice proved to be their greatest promoter and protector. The Act was struck down by the Supreme Court as unconstitutional. The Congress and Leftists, keeping political expediency in mind adopted a lax attitude in this regard. There would hardly have been any other country in the world that tolerates such type of infiltration. The Congress has thus, for selfish reasons, put a question mark on the security of the country.

Policy of Appeasement

Congress has a history of indulging in a policy of appeasements at the cost of national interests. Right since the partition of India to Shah Bano case only this facet of Congress has manifested itself. As a consequence, the present government has started eroding the basic structure of the Constitution. The court judgments against reservation to Muslims in Andhra Pradesh and in Aligarh Muslim University substantiate the righteousness of BJP's stand. In spite of this, the Union Human Resource Development Minister continues to harp that the government would find out some other means for giving 50 percent reservation to Muslims in post-graduate courses in AMU. This is nothing less than a blatant contempt of the Constitution.

Politicisation of Education

In ancient past, India had been the *Vishwaguru* of the world and, in the present, it is emerging as an intellectual hub of the world for the future. The importance education enjoys can, in the normal course, be appreciated from this fact. Our system of education needs to be such that it promotes nationalism. But unfortunately, the Congress and the leftists have conspired to remove the elements of nationalism from education. By describing Lords Rama and Krishna as mere imaginary characters they are trying to sever future generation's links with the nation's heritage. If Lords Rama and Krishna are imaginary beings, then can the greatness of India be real?

Not only this, the government has gone to the extent of undermining nationalism by denigrating the revolutionaries of our freedom struggle in the text books. A UPA minister committed the nefarious act of removing the historic plaque of *Swatantryaveer* Vinayak Damodar Savarkar from the Cellular Jail in Port Blair. The tendency to insult the elements of nationalism is very much visible both in thoughts and actions of this government. The institutions of higher learning are being commercialised to such an extent that it is becoming increasingly impossible for a poor student to afford education in an institution of higher education.

Village, Poor and Farmer

75 percent of India's population lives in villages. Agriculture is the mainstay of our economic development. In spite of that the Indian farmer is leading a life of want and misery. Thousands of farmers have committed suicide. The situation is so alarming that over 500 farmers from a village in Vidarbha, Maharashtra, plagued by bad debts wrote to the Honourable President of India seeking permission to end their lives. 40 percent of farmers want to quit agriculture and engage themselves in other professions. UPA government policies is completely anti-farmer. In recently concluded WTO meet at Hong Kong, UPA government buckled under the pressure of developed countries and sacrificed the interests of Indian farmers. This government apparently lacks the will power to protect the interests of farmers.

Bharatiya Janata Party is committed to ensuring the emancipation of the village, the poor and the peasantry. Farmers represent not only the bulk of country's population, they also constitute the largest chunk of producers and consumers. The economic advancement of the country can be ushered in only if we enhance the purchasing power of the farmers. Comprehensive development of rural sectors is absent at the moment. Farmer is the backbone of rural sector. The village environment creates a sense of self-reliance and social relationship in the farmer. It is therefore necessary that the condition of farmers should be improved by making greater investment in the farming sector. Industrial development of the nation is inter-linked with the agricultural development. Besides being the purveyor of food grains for the country, farmer also produces the raw material vital for industrial development of the country. Agriculture can become the pivot of this country's economy and the mainstay of building a self-reliant nation.

The NDA government had taken several initiatives for the uplift of village, poor and farmers. For the first time in the history of India the rate of interest on farm loans was reduced from 14-18 percent to 9 percent. Kissan Credit Cards were distributed and terms for farm loans were relaxed and made easy. The Agriculture Income Insurance Scheme was launched to guarantee a definite income to farmers and to insure his farm earnings, but the present UPA government has shelved these farmer friendly schemes. Therefore, I accuse that the mindset of this UPA government as antipathetic to rural areas, poor and farmers. The struggle of rural areas, the poor and the farmer is in fact the real struggle for India's uplift, for decentralisation of political power, for equality and harmony in society, and in the real sense the struggle for country's self-reliance.

I wish to call upon the activists:
Pahuncho Khet aur Khalihanon tak
Gaon, Gareeb aur Kissanon tak
(Reach out to the fields and farms, to villages, poor and farmers.)

Why protect Quattrocchi?

Nearly two decades old Bofors Scandal recently took a shameful turn when two London accounts of middle-man and close Gandhi family friend, Ottavio Quattrocchi, were allowed to be de-freezed by UPA government. It created queer and embarrassing situation for the Congress. First, it was stated that PMO had no information about it, and later, it was given out that Law Ministry has no links with it. Whatever it is, it looks strange that Additional Solicitor General of Government of India should go to Britain to give a clean chit to a person against whom a case is pending in Delhi High Court and Interpol has issued a Red Corner Notice against him. It has happened for the first time in the history of India that an investigating agency has taken upon itself the function of a Judge. When the case is sub-judice in court, has the Law Ministry the power to decide whether there is sufficient evidence against the accused or not? But without a sense of shame the UPA mounted pressure on the CBI to change its original stand and cleared the decks for withdrawal of $4 million Bofors kickback money parked in two London bank accounts.

Bharatiya Janata Party feels that the amount Quattrocchi has withdrawn from his London account is the hard-earned money of Indian taxpayers. Therefore, it must be brought back to India. Speaking from an undisclosed location, Quattrocchi has alleged that a particular political party of India was targetting him for his proximity to the Gandhi family. We acknowledge that Quattrocchi is referring to BJP. But with all the courage and determination at our command we declare that BJP will target every person who tries to siphon off Indian money abroad. The Prime Minister and Smt. Sonia Gandhi must clarify why the country was taken for a ride.

The Common Man

The phenomenon of uncontrolled rise in prices has become synonymous with the advent of Congress governments. Today the prices of petrol, diesel, LPG, cereals and fertilizers are spiraling. These have been raised upward six or seven times during last 19 months. Even in spite of skyrocketing prices, nothing like LPG, fertilizer and the like is available easily in the market. Black market in essential commodities is thriving in the country to the discomfort of the common man and to the prosperity of the black-marketeers and hoarders who seem to be the main supporters of the present government.

The interest rates on small savings by common man have been reduced. So have the interest rates on Provident Funds for government employees gone down. On the contrary, interest rates on loans for house construction have been hiked.

The government went a step further. It curtailed the quota of ration for those living below the poverty line, which for the time being had to be rolled back under intense political pressure. This has laid bare the anti-people and anti-poor face of this government.

By launching Employment Guarantee Scheme without a matching budgetary provision, the Congress has played a cruel joke with the unemployed youth. Now it has become amply clear that be it the poor farmer or the unemployed youth, the government employee or the common man, everybody is the victim of the wrong policies of this government.

Therefore, I declare from this platform that we find this government inimical to the poor and the farmer.

During the last General Elections the Congress had raised the slogan- "*Congress Ka Haath, Aam Admi ke saath*" (The Hand of Congress is with the common man). It is now beyond proof today that the Hand of Congress is not helping the common man but is actually thrashing him.

Collapse of Constitutional Order

Because of the wrong policies of the UPA government, the situation in the country has deteriorated. By misusing power with ulterior designs, the constitutional order stands very much disturbed. UPA has indulged in blatant misuse of constitutional institutions to serve its selfish ends. This process commenced with the creation of two power centres in the government. In practical terms, it was a devaluation of the office of Prime Minister. An extra-constitutional power centre was created under the name of Chairman of National Advisory Council. Several MPs with criminal backgrounds were inducted into the Union Council of Ministers.

The government indulged in more grievous blunders subsequently. The way a BJP government was pulled down in Goa and people verdict was hijacked in Bihar and Jharkhand through gubernatorial manipulations is well known to the entire country. While the Supreme Court held the dissolution of Bihar assembly as 'Unconstitutional', it described the conduct of Jharkhand governor as 'fraud' on the Constitution. With these actions the dignity of the office of Governor has been lowered. It is becoming increasingly evident that the intentions of this government run from behind the stage by an extra-constitutional authority are intended to undermine authority of the Constitution.

A Union Minister, in a press conference, abused the Election Commission of India as being not only partial but casteist too. Two Cabinet Ministers called each other's names from public platforms. Twice, Union Ministers were found fugitives. Never had the dignity of Union Cabinet plummeted so low in independent India as it is under UPA.

The incident of MPs accepting bribe is utterly reprehensible. It should be taken to mean a matter involving the dignity of Parliament. Corruption charges have been levelled against individual MPs even before. In a recently published book *Mitrokhin Archives-II*, compiled by a former KGB archivist, Vasili Mitrokhin, it has been revealed that the entire Congress and Communist Party was guilty of accepting foreign money as bribe. In Volcker

Report, it is not only Natwar Singh, but the name of Congress Party figures prominently as a beneficiary in the oil scam. The charge of accepting bribe for ideology and making compromise with nation's sovereignty has been levelled against Congress and Communist Party. We already know that the ideology of Communism had come from abroad on the strength of foreign money. The Communists who oppose Foreign Direct Investment in industry and commerce, had been welcoming foreign direct investment in their ideology!

Our Neighbours

The foreign policy adopted by NDA Government under the able leadership of Atalji resulted in emergence of India as a potent economic and military power on the global scene. But this government has failed to safeguard our national interests even with our neighbours.

Pakistan

The peace process with Pakistan was a courageous pioneering step by Atalji with a commitment to peace. We need to cultivate friendly relations not only with Pakistan, but with all our neighbours. But at present every suggestion emanates from Pakistan and India is just giving its reactions. It will be a great blunder on the part of the present government if we lose the initiative at improving relations started by our Government. Why is the Government not taking people into confidence on this issue? Government must learn to stand firm.

Bangladesh

The BJP is very much concerned with the incidences going on in Bangladesh. Bangladesh has become a new resort for the terrorists, drug mafia and the smugglers of weapons. If the problem of infiltration, rising crime and the mushrooming of *Madarsas* in Bangladesh along the Indian border, all are taken together, this gives a very serious picture. This is a very sensitive issue pertaining to our internal security. UPA Government should try to find out some solution before this problem takes a gigantic proportion.

Nepal

The harmony of intimate relations between India and Nepal is historical and spans centuries. We can see the glimpse of this intimacy in the various fields from education to trade and commerce and even representation in the Army. The basis of this relationship is the cultural and civilisational affinity. During the last few months this mutual relationship has turned sour. The government of India has stopped the supply of arms and ammunition to Nepal for fighting against the Maoist insurgency. In the mean time, China has supplied some arms to Nepal. Pakistan is also inclined to have friendship with Nepal.

NDA Government adopted an appropriate policy towards Nepal, which is not the case with this Government. Constitutional monarchy symbolises the people's sentiments and the Nepali ethos. The democratic system is required for the modern development and economic and social advancement of Nepal. The lack of any of these two can create imbalance leading to uncertainty in Nepal. The government of India must keep an eye on it. The rising influence and terror of Maoist forces cannot be left apart as an internal matter of Nepal. This is bound to inflict far reaching consequences on our internal security. It will be better if all the political parties in Nepal take part in the democratic process initiated at the level of local bodies by H.E. King. The Government of India should try to create an atmosphere conducive to this process. As the Maoist forces are indulging in violence since several years, so their approach cannot be termed as truly democratic. Therefore any step of non-cooperation with the Government of Nepal on the issue of countering the Maoist forces is not in the national interest. It is required that the UPA Government should rectify its policy and remove the present restrictions on arms supply to Nepal. Government and should ensure to maintain our natural and intimate relations with Nepal. The policy of India towards Nepal cannot be considered only as a matter of foreign policy as it involves many consequences on the future of our internal security.

Dubious Agreement

There is lack of transparency in the nuclear agreement reached between India and USA. There is ample scope for suspicion on this account. UPA government is committing a series of blunders in the vital area of national security. Have we compromised with the independence of our nuclear policy? The Prime Minister claims that the deal has been struck from a position of equality, but the statements made by US officials do not substantiate PM's claim and fail to convince people. It is an anomalous situation in which US Parliament has been provided with full details of the agreement while the Indian Parliament has been kept in the dark.

After the end of cold war, India's relations improved with the rest of the world, including the US during the NDA rule. It is a matter of proud achievement for the nation. However, the manner in which the UPA Government is cultivating its relations with the US administration, the domination of American interests, policies, and strategies is becoming increasingly prominent. Because of these wrongs of UPA, India is now losing fast the advantage it had gained in the wake of Pokhran test in 1998. The BJP warns the Government not to do anything under pressure which disturbs the balance of our relations with US presently on an equal footing. It should not compromise with our integrity and sovereignty.

Social Harmony

BJP considers every person from the Himalayas to the Indian Ocean as an Indian. India is his origin and that is his caste. We all are one and constitute one nation with a unified culture and only one nationality. In spite of this fact, with an eye on vote bank many political parties indulge in petty politics of caste. BJP stands committed to empowerment of socially and economically underprivileged, those left out of the national mainstream as a result of neglect by state and society, and extending special opportunities to Scheduled castes and groups as pledged by our constitution makers. BJP believes in the oneness of the people. We favour extending special opportunities to them and other economically backward people in matters of nation-building. When I was Chief Minister of UP I had charted out a programme for identification of extremely backward people and *dalits* to give them special benefits and opportunities. But the pseudo standard bearers of social justice nullified all our efforts and achievements in that direction.

The NDA government

The work done by respected Atalji during six years of NDA rule was outstanding and unprecedented with regard to India's development. History will definitely take note of the fact of the finesse with which respected Atalji successfully carried forward an alliance of 26 parties. We have shattered the Congress myth that it alone can run a government smoothly and for long. We altered not only the polarisation of politics in the country but established ourselves as the most dependable and effective party in coalition politics.

The present government is reaping the fruits of the policies in economy, foreign affairs, military prowess, rural development, emancipation of farmers and youth in the country launched by NDA regime. We can proudly claim that we had solidified the foundation to make India a superpower and can claim with conviction that we alone can take this initiative to its logical conclusion.

We have some plans for ushering in a bright future for the country.

BJP favours Women's Reservation Bill

We believe that to create a mighty and prosperous India, it is necessary to empower women. It is imperative to increase representation of women at every level. There is a need to give them greater responsibilities in matters of the nation and organisation and inspire them to perform their roles well. That is why BJP strongly supports 33 percent reservation for women in Parliament and we want the Women's Reservation Bill to be adopted in Parliament at the earliest. We are relentlessly striving to increase women's representation in BJP. There is a need to give women greater representation down from *mandal* level up to top-most echelons of the party.

State funding of elections

Bharatiya Janata Party from the very beginning has believed and accepted the principle that it would be appropriate for the Government exchequer to bear all expenditure related to elections. Advaniji has often taken initiative in this matter. It is our firm belief that the main reason that promotes the prevalent political corruption in the country is uncontrolled expenditure by candidates in elections.

Bharatiya Janata Party wants the influence of money and muscle power in politics to end and political sanctity to be established. To end corruption, the present election law should be amended and a feasible plan of action must be worked out. We believe that this issue transcends political ideologies and is in national interest. Therefore, all parties should come forward with a consensus and show the way to making elections a healthy political contest.

Youth determine India's destiny

The youth of India will determine its destiny and will control the fate of this ancient nation. Today India is the country having the largest youth population in the world. The youth are engaged in establishing supremacy of their talent all over the world in spheres of science, technology, information technology and medicine. They will undoubtedly transform the current century into India's century and take India to the pinnacle of glory. The country's progress will be empowered by the keenness, prowess and strength of the youth. I call upon them to join us and build a new India.

Organisation

It should be crystal clear to us that in Indian politics today, the falling credibility of politicians, economic imbalance, secessionist forces raising their heads, *Swadeshi* economy straining under globalisation and the foreign influence on social structure are testing our mettle. Simultaneously, Communist control of the Government and the utterly negative behaviour of Congress have created a complicated, difficult situation. We should think over as to how best the country can be brought out of this vicious circle. Only that party can save the country from this complex situation which has the following three qualities:

1. Indubitable ideology of nationalism
2. Effective nationwide organisation
3. Popular and honest leadership

In Indian politics, only Bharatiya Janata Party has all the three qualities. It alone is purely Indian in origin, philosophy and conduct, and is undoubtedly the only symbol of nationalism in Indian politics.

Our organization has expanded and its acceptability increased in numerous parts of the country. We have reached out to many sections of the society. Our acceptability amongst political parties has also increased. Our alliances with parties having ideologies a different from us has been continuing for a long time in many States, such as Bihar and Orissa. Thus, today we have acquired the shape of a huge organisation.

But we will have to admit honestly that due to expansion and being in power in the past few years, we are faced with the challenge of maintaining a balance with the high ideals and expectations for us in people's minds. We will have to reawaken people's faith in us.

We should remember that the process of BJP's political ascent which began 16-17 years ago, was due to our ideological uniqueness and clean image. We will have to accept that in the test of uniqueness and clean image we have not got the desired success in fulfilling public expectations.

We need to be more vigilant in future because a small slip in this direction can destroy our uniqueness and image and create an existential crisis.

The foundation of our distinctiveness must be clear in our minds. Cultural nationalism from political point of view, *Swadeshi* from economic point of view, and *Su-Raj* from the administrative point of view and for all this, we need a clean image coupled with principled conduct.

Expectation from activists

All of us need to go in for introspection to preserve the phenomenon of expansion and strength we earned through sacrifices and privation after being face to face with complexities in all circumstances. Since intoxication of power blunts our capacity for struggle, our objective should always remain to keep alive that zeal in us. Capturing power is not the ultimate goal with us. Our objective is to change the future of India through political power. Today the complexity of situation in the country, many questions regarding national security, negative politics of the present ruling coalition, shadow of foreign influence, declining social values and new low depths in politics – all emit a clear signal that a tough struggle awaits us in future.

At this hour we should exercise full control over our personal ambitions and the competition within our organisation. The qualities we should imbibe as an activist can be divided into four levels as given below:

1. Restraint (*Sanyam*) required at an individual's level
2. Coordination (*Samanvaya*) necessary at the organizational level
3. Struggle (*Sangharsh*) required at the political level
4. Service (*Seva*) imperative at a social level

Thus, restraint (*Sanyam*), coordination (*Samanvaya*), struggle (*Sangharsh*) and service (*Seva*) are our ideals.

The humblest of work done by us as an activist should reflect our ideological uniqueness and clean image. This will lay the lasting foundation for our success. All our political parties and organisations speak of principles but public is not taken in by their professions of principles. Why is it so? It is so only because public is not impressed either by mere speeches of any party's leader, or by propaganda machinery of a party or government, but only by the conduct of top leaders of the party. A striking example is the decline of Congress in Indian politics. The Congress which led the freedom struggle, had a nationwide organisation and talked loftily of principles. But the fall in the standards of conduct of Congress leaders is solely responsible for the present dismal position of this large political party. Therefore, it is clear that the conduct, morality and personal image of leaders should always be above suspicion. We are trying to provide leadership to the society as representatives of Bharatiya Janata Party. Hence, our image is the primary source of strength of our political power.

Today terrible vices like criminalisation, corruption and casteism have overwhelmed our politics. Of these, casteism is the most serious and lethal problem because it goes beyond criminalisation and corruption in polluting not only the work culture but also contaminating our ideological base.

Hence, all of us activists should keep ourselves free from narrow, selfish feelings and strive as devoted workers with a honest, clean image to establish the ideological distinctiveness of BJP among the people and vow not to rest till the work of emancipation of the person standing at lowest rung of the social ladder is complete.

Acceptability of BJP has increased

Electoral victory and defeat are parameters of success or failure of a political party. Beyond election results, the ideological commitment to national concerns is the real measure of success or failure of a political party. The effort to bring about positive fundamental changes in a nation's life is a barometer of success for a party. Implementing anti-national policies for a vote bank is indicative of the failure of political parties. BJP has always remained true to its ideological commitment.

After the last General Elections, we were successful in forming a government in Jharkhand again. Regarding Bihar, people often said that the political sun of Lalu's rule would never set. However, in November 2005 democracy pushed that sun to set and the people handed over power to BJP-JD (U) alliance for Bihar's progress. BJP has created an ideological space for itself in the country. The results of recently concluded local body elections in Gujarat are indicative of BJP's growing popularity and public acceptance. Congress has not only shrunk, it has also been rejected by the people. Earlier BJP had secured overwhelming majority in the local body and *zila panchayat* elections in Madhya Pradesh, Chhattisgarh and Rajasthan. We got resounding success in Punjab too. The mass base of BJP is increasing in all the States. In the southern States of Andhra Pradesh and Kerala, BJP registered an impressive presence in municipal body elections.

Forthcoming Assembly Elections

Assembly elections are due in several States of the country within a few months. The States where elections will be held are Assam, West Bengal, Kerala, Tamil Nadu and Pondicherry. We believe that we shall also succeed in these States.

Pledge for the Future

The 20th century was the century of India's independence and there is no doubt that the 21st century will be that of India's greatness. If in 20th century, the credit for India's independence went to Congress, in 21st century, the credit for India's greatness is destined to be given to us.

We will take the message of *Swaraj* and *Shuchita* (clean politics) given to us by respected Atalji and Advaniji, to realise the dream of *Suraj* along with *Swaraj* in the times to come.

In the end I would like to clarify that organisation alone cannot be the be-all and end-all of everything. No matter how good or great the organisation is but without life, without the readiness to take risks, without the will to face dangers, it cannot provide solutions to the problems or challenges we face at present. That is why I believe that struggle should form the basis of our organisation.

We will struggle, strive and through peaceful and constitutional means mobilise public opinion. There is no place amongst us for people with lust for power, pelf and position. BJP shall have to pursue grassroot politics to restore people's faith lost to politics, political parties and political leaders. Manipulative politics of convenience does not last for long. We will have to jump into the fray carrying the Constitution in one hand and symbol of equality in the other. We will draw inspiration from life and struggles of *Chhatrapati Maharaj* Shivaji who sounded the bugle of national pride and from Mahatma Jyotiba Phule, the icon of social equality.

At the end, I would like to conclude by reciting two lines:

सेनानी तुम प्रयाण करो
भावी इतिहास तुम्हारा है
ये नखत अमा के बुझते हैं
सारा आकाश तुम्हारा है ।

–दिनकर

Bharat Mata ki Jai!

□

A Vow for a new Responsibilty

29-30 May, 2006 (New Delhi)

We have again assembled in the meeting of the National Executive. After the meeting of the National Executive on the conclusion of the *Rajat Jayanti* celebrations of Bharatiya Janata Party in Mumbai, this was the first meeting of the National Executive being held under my presidentship. The Mumbai session flashes to our mind the presence of Pramodji, as if he were standing right before us. But that is not so. National Executive was held without him. It was a great shock for the Bharatiya Janata Party. In the pursuit of social service we do come across such unbearable tragedies. We have to bear with Pramodji's loss and make our organisation to continue to move ahead.

Bharatiya Janata Party is an organisation with enormous capabilities and possibilities. As compared to other political parties, our *karyakartas* are more honest, more capable and have greater capacity to struggle. Among all the political organisations in the country, it is the Bharatiya Janata Party alone that stands apart in following democratic principles. We are rich in capable leadership. In addition to BJP governments in Madhya Pradesh, Gujarat, Rajasthan and Chhattisgarh, we have a BJP-led government in Jharkhand and BJP-supported governments in Bihar, Orissa, Karnataka and Nagaland. We have established ourselves as a great political force in the country.

In spite of that, we have to effectively extend the sphere of our influence in other States of the country too. It is the BJP alone that has not only challenged the Congress but also dethroned from power this well-entrenched Party in various States and at the Centre while ushering in a great change in the basic structure of politics. We are sure, God will smoothen our path in future also. People have started realizing that their future is safe only in the hands of BJP. It is the only party that rising above the vote-bank politics struggles for the welfare of the people all over the country right from Kashmir to Kerala.

Just concluded Vidhan Sabha elections

BJP has successfully established its political prowess in the Indian politics during the party's long, tortuous political journey starting from the days of Jana Sangh, despite numerous ups and downs.

In the just concluded elections to State assemblies, BJP contested on its own strength in all the States. The success of our strategy cannot, alone, be gauged from the number of seats we won. We have certainly taken great strides in expanding our organisation and spreading our ideology far and wide. Faced with the trend of election results in Tamil Nadu, Kerala, Pondicherry and West Bengal, we have to think afresh to chalk out our strategy in these States to achieve greater acceptability there. We are sure, we shall be crowned with better results in future. In Assam, our efforts have borne fruit with satisfactory results.

We have succeeded in both increasing the seats and vote percentage in Assam despite the fact that in the last elections we fought in alliance and this time all alone. In this perspective, the increase in the number of our seats becomes all the more encouraging. In Assam, we have also succeeded in extending geographical boundaries of our influence. For the first time, we have been successful in establishing our noteworthy presence in Brahmputra Valley. These elections established BJP as a political force to reckon with in Assam.

Bharat *Suraksha Yatra*

On April 6, BJP launched a countrywide public awareness campaign through the medium of Bharat Suraksha Yatra. Both of us, Hon'ble Advaniji from Dwarika in Gujarat and I myself from Jagannath Puri in Orissa, reached out to the countrymen through this yatra. Besides the issue of increasing threat of terrorism and of appeasement because of wrong policies of the UPA Government, the masses were educated about the issue of skyrocketing prices.

We got into a direct contact with the people during the yatra. We witnessed a great display of enthusiasm among our workers and the general public on these issues. The way massive crowds thronged to welcome the yatra in the far-flung areas of Naxal-affected States of Orissa, Chhattisgarh, Jharkhand, and Bihar where people did not dare come out of their homes after sunset, instilled in us a sense of confidence that the matters on which BJP is feeling worried, are equally a matter of concern for the people living in the interiors of these regions.

Because of soft approach and wrong policies of UPA, the morale of terrorists and Naxalites is on the increase. Violent attacks are taking place all over the country. In these circumstances, through the medium of Bharat Suraksha Yatra we have been successful in bringing home to the UPA Government the great anger and resentment prevailing among the masses.

During the Yatra we tried to bind the countrymen with our ideology and principles. This Yatra was to conclude on May 10 at Delhi but because of the unfortunate demise of Pramodji, it had to be terminated on May 3 itself.

Challenges before the country

It is two years since NDA demit office and UPA took over the reigns of government. Because of an incapable and ineffective leadership numerous problems have raised their head in the last two years. The country suffered a lot in economic, political and social spheres. The kind of damage inflicted on national security, dignity of the Constitution and international standing during UPA rule is unprecedented in the history of independent India.

The nation is faced with numerous dangers before it. It was during Congress rule that a historical blunder was committed on the issue of Tibet and the same is now being repeated today in the case of Nepal.

India shares with Nepal an open and unprotected border extending to 1751 kilometres. India is also a home to 22 lakh Nepalese who enjoy every right available to Indians. Gorkhas have a sizeable representation in the Indian Army. In these circumstances, if an administration not favourably disposed towards India comes into power in that country, it will certainly have an adverse impact on our security environment. We are receiving reports of a dangerous collusion between Maoists of Nepal, terrorists of Bangladesh and Pakistan's ISI. It is not clear with whose agenda did the Leftists visit Nepal - of Manmohan Singh government or of Maoists. I hold UPA Government responsible for the present complicated situation in Nepal because this Government failed to take any meaningful and constructive initiative on the issue in time.

Foreign policy

The Foreign Minister of this Government fell a victim to Volcker Committee report. Since then we have no independent Foreign Minister in this Government. CPM is managing the foreign policy of this Government by proxy, that is, on CPM directions. After interfering in Nepal, the Leftists have directed their attention to targetting Sri Lanka. Perhaps the Prime Minister is gambling with a new and strange experiment of allowing a political party from outside the Government to run the Ministry of Foreign Affairs. Before this, the Left parties tried to incite communal feelings among minorities on international issues, like Iran and Iraq, and India's relations with USA. I wish to warn the Prime Minister that the country will have to pay heavily for these follies.

Where does this Government wish to take the country? The Leftists and the Congress join hands to pass a resolution in Kerala assembly demanding release, on parole, of the main accused in the Coimbatore bomb blast case. They presented a new example in the history of the country of a State legislature supporting a person accused of treason.

The apprehensions which had been aired by the former Prime Minister Shri Atal Bihari Vajpayee about the nuclear deal signed with USA seem to be coming out true. In the name of developing nuclear energy, a question mark is being put on India's nuclear defence capability. The details of the agreement disclosed to Parliament about the agreement with USA do not tally with the details presented before the US Congress. It appears the UPA Government has misled the Parliament on this sensitive issue.

By withholding Agni-III tests the UPA government has generated apprehensions in the nation. It is not clear whether it is inspired by the Defence Minister's claim to nation's self-assessment of the situation or prompted by need to cater to the strategic requirements of powerful nations of the world. Every alert citizen of the country wants to know the reason for this because it certainly is a setback to our indigenous missile development programme, particularly in view of the fact that Atalji's government in 1999 had undertaken Agni-II test even in the face of strong economic and military sanctions against India. It, therefore, clearly establishes that the defence power that was strengthened during our regime has now been weakened under UPA Government.

Our neighbours

All our neighbouring countries are emerging into centres of anti-India conspiracies. Since long such anti-India activities had already been going on from Pakistan's territory. Now disruptive activities are also being directed from Bangladesh. We have already expressed concern over the situation in Nepal. On the one hand, LTTE is getting proactive again in Sri Lanka and, on the other, Taliban is again raising its head in Afghanistan. All this is a story of failure of the UPA Government's foreign policy.

Blackmarketing of nuclear and strategic technology from Pakistan is a matter of record and of special concern for India. From Doda to Delhi and from Varanasi to Bangalore terrorists strike, at will, with impunity anytime, anywhere and anyway they like. Not only this, Government of India permits Hurriyat leaders to travel up to Pakistan-occupied Kashmir but Pakistan escorts them up to Islamabad. Government of India fails to register a meaningful protest on the issue.

The Vajpayee government had put great pressure on Pakistan and made General Musharraf give an undertaking that he would not allow Pakistan territory to be used for breeding terror against India. But this Government made all these gains of Vajpayee government to go waste. The notorious terrorist organisation Lashkar-e-Toiba continues to spread its wings of terror in India by changing its nomenclature to Jamat-ud-Dava. UPA can, if it likes, bring in a resolution under 1373 in Security Council to get it declared as a terrorist organisation.

Not only the people of India, even the Indian army is stunned by the reports of UPA government's intention to withdraw forces from strategically important Siachen glacier. For the first time in the history of India, in just two months the Chief of Army Staff had to come out twice in public opposing the move of the government, first against Muslim head-count in the Indian Army and then, on withdrawal of forces from Siachen. BJP will not, under any circumstances, tolerate withdrawal of forces from a strategic point like Siachen glacier on the pretext of improving relations with Pakistan.

Internal Security

During this month itself, 32 Hindus were butchered in Doda and Udhampur in Jammu & Kashmir. Even after that, the security arrangements proved so lopsided that terrorists were able to mount an attack on peaceful BJP demonstrators. After that, government failed to prevent a terrorist attack on its own Congress party rally. It is a glaring example of government's failure on matters of internal security.

The situation in Kashmir looks very explosive. After Kashmir Valley, there seems to be a sustained campaign to completely push Hindus and Sikhs even out of the Jammu region. Terrorists from Pakistan have in the past, many a time, openly declared this intention of theirs. Two BJP workers got martyrdom in a grenade attack while demanding security for the people. The problem in Kashmir is already a threat to the sovereignty of India.

In view of a pre-planned conspiracy to push out minority community of Hindus, it has now taken the form of an outright challenge to the very secular character of India. The attacks on political rallies have put a question mark in Kashmir over the very nature of India's democratic setup. Therefore, Jammu & Kashmir has now become a challenge to our sovereign, secular and democratic country and, in other words, to the very national character of India.

At the same time, the condition of Hindu refugee camps in the country continues to be pathetic. In the light of these circumstances I wish to appeal to all the political parties in the country to understand the delicacy of the situation and review their stand on Article 370. I feel that the need to seriously think over Article 370 was never greater than it is today.

Not only in Kashmir, be it the attack on Sankat Mochan temple in Varanasi, or communal violence in Lucknow because of controversy over cartoons of Prophet Mohammad and, later in Aligarh or the carnage at Mau in Uttar Pradesh - all these are the living examples of the outcome of communal passions incited by wily politicians.

Common Civil Code

Common Civil Code is not an issue of politics but is an important requirement of the integral face of the nation. Not only once, but two-three times the Supreme Court has issued directions in this behalf. In addition to Constitutional experts, persons who have adorned highest offices in the country have also supported this issue. This issue draws its inspiration from the basic spirit of the Constitution. In the situation that has developed of late, the issue of common civil code has become all the more relevant. There should be a national debate on the issue.

Naxalite terrorism

Naxalite terrorism is fast spreading its tentacles all over the country. It is a new threat to the internal security of india. After assuming power at the Centre, UPA Government adopted a soft policy towards Naxalites and consequently Naxalism spread further and gained strength. According to figures presented by the Union Home Minister in Parliament, the casualty figure in Naxalite violence went up by 53 percent in 2004-2005. Because of the amalgamation of another 1000 cadres the Naxalites have further got strengthened. A big chunk of geographical area and about 20 percent population of the country has got itself under the sway of Naxalite and terrorist influence. Because of anti-people policies of the UPA Government, both prices and unemployment are on the increase. Exploiting this situation to their advantage, Naxalites are misleading the people, youth in particular, and arming them. Naxalites are bent upon destroying the social, political and economic structure of the country and the Government has failed to take effective steps to counter this menace.

Uncontrolled price rise

The uncontrolled price rise of essential commodities of everyday use has left the common man high and dry. From atta, daal, rice, fruit, vegetables, oil, sugar to petrol, diesel, cooking gas, and kerosene oil, everything is getting abnormally costlier. There is an indication of further rise in the prices of petrol and diesel. On the other hand, the common man is aghast at the disappearance of these commodities from the open market and their free availability in black-market. Under NDA's rule, inflation and black-marketing were kept under check. It is intriguing that every time Congress comes in power, price rise and black-marketing follow it closely and thrive. People wish to know the reason for this. During the reign of our government, we had helped the common man realise his dream to have his own home by lowering the rate of interest on housing loans. But with the advent of UPA Government the rate of interest on loans has started increasing constantly and the common man's dream is now getting shattered.

In spite of this increasing financial burden on the common man, supporters of Government are trying to project the spurt in Sensex as a proof of its success on the economic front. On the second anniversary of UPA, this myth too got shattered. The share prices crash on May 22 not only put the industry to a great loss, it also ruined about 2 crore small investors. It is the third time that business had to be stopped because of depression in the market. Finance Minister has termed it as a "manufactured crisis". Reaffirming its commitment to protect the interests of small investors, BJP wants to know from the Finance Minister as to who are the persons who "manufactured" this crisis? What action did the SEBI take against them? In the light of the Sensex falling 2000 points in five days, was this comment of the Finance Minister justified?

Employment Guarantee Yojna

Employment Guarantee Yojna is another fraud played by UPA on the crores of unemployed in the country. The recently enacted Employment Guarantee Act provides for an employment only for 100 days at the rate of Rs. 60 per day in a year in only 200 out of 400 districts of the country. Four crore unemployed living in urban areas have been kept out of the benefit of the Yojna. Can a family subsist on just Rs. 6000 a year as guaranteed by the Act?

Problems of Kisan

The increasing financial burden on the Kisans because of unstable policies of UPA Government is pushing them to despair. The incidents of Kisan suicides are on the increase in many States. All the farmer-friendly programmes and policies of NDA Government have been put in the cold storage. During our time, the food grains stores in the country were full to the brim and we were exporting food grains. But in two years the situation has so much deteriorated that we have to import food grains. Above all, the imported wheat is being purchased at a rate higher rate than that at which the Indian wheat has been purchased.

In this also, government has got wheat imported through an Australian firm AWB Limited whose name adversely figures in the Volcker Committee report. In the midst the pitiable condition of kisans and problem of food shortages, the spectacle of corruption is the most unfortunate. There is no indication of any serious attempt by the Government towards rejuvenation of co-operative banks in the country. BJP Kisan Morcha organized a dharna to draw the attention of Government towards the pitiable condition of farmers and presented a Memorandum to the Union Agriculture Minister.

Telangana people cheated

At the time of assembly elections two years back, the Congress and Telangana Rashtra Samiti had promised to the people that if they won, they would carve out a separate State of Telangana out of the present Andhra Pradesh. Both the parties won but Congress threw the Telangana issue in the cold storage. The other day I had been to Andhra Pradesh. The leading workers of our party briefed me on the Telangana issue. It was after consultation with them that I announced the party's support to the creation of a new Telangana State.

From the very beginning we have stood for smaller States. In accordance with the pre-poll promises the NDA government of Shri Atal Bihari Vajpayee had created three new States of Chhattisgarh, Jharkhand and Uttaranchal. We wish Telangana State to be a reality. During Bharat Suraksha Yatra, Shri Advani had highlighted the Party's stand on Telangana. If a motion for creation of Telangana is brought out in the Lok Sabha, we will support it. Party workers in Andhra Pradesh, particularly those belonging to Telangana region, have welcomed this stand.

Erosion of Constitutional institutions

During its regime UPA eroded the sanctity of numerous institutions of the Constitution. The list of such instances is unending.

It was for the first time in the history of the country that this Government gave a place of honour in the Union Cabinet to persons facing charges of heinous crimes in courts.

For the first time Governors were removed before completion of their tenure and a black chapter in history was written with the blatant misuse of the Constitutional Office of Governor in the States of Goa, Jharkhand and Bihar.

After the Supreme Court verdict declaring the IMDT Act and reservation to Muslims on the basis of religion against the spirit of the Constitution, the UPA Government reaction does not amount to respect to the court.

The Congress and the Communist parties publicly criticized the Constitutional institution of Election Commission. A Cabinet Minister in UPA not only charged Election Commission with partiality, but even went to the extent of charging it of being casteist. Never had the position of the Election Commission been targetted in such a manner during any other Government.

On the Office of Profit issue, without framing any criteria, a mention was made directly of a list of offices. The fact of first abruptly adjourning the Parliament on this issue and then reconvening Parliament on its own as per its convenience only shows that this Government is making Parliament an instrument of convenience.

On the basis of these instances, it is no exaggeration to say that during its tenure the UPA Government has severely eroded the power, prestige and authority of many institutions of the Constitution.

Divide the Society

Conversion

It appears the UPA Government has launched upon a well-planned campaign to destroy the very social fabric of the country. Religious conversion promoted with allurements or force by exploiting illiteracy and poverty is altogether unjustified. The Constitution does not permit it. The Supreme Court too has held such an attempts wrong. This is a serious matter of great social concern and it should not be given a political colour.

Appeasement

Instead of putting under restraint organisations like Jamait-e-Islami Hind demanding reservation to Muslims, Congress itself went ahead, against the provisions in the Constitution, with providing reservation in government jobs to Muslims on religious basis in Andhra Pradesh and reservation to Muslims in post-graduate courses in Aligarh Muslim University. Not only that. It went further to widen the communal divide by asking for a Muslim head-count in the Army.

Reservation

The manner in which the reservation issue has been handled by the UPA Government, leaves no one in doubt that its object is not social justice but to create social tensions. The Bharatiya Janata Party had supported the Constitution amendment to provide reservations in higher educational institutions. However, while doing so, any attempt at divisiveness must be avoided. Social fabric of the society must not be damaged. Consensus building is a must for such initiatives. The UPA Government has failed on that score. The government must ensure that while implementing reservations, the space for merit is not squeezed and excellence of institutions is not compromised. Efforts must be taken to ensure that the benefits of reservation must reach the most deprived amongst the socially deprived sections. The Government must ensure that the Economically weaker sections of the upper caste are included in the benefits of the reservation. The BJP is opposed to the exclusion of minor minority institution from the obligation of reservation. There must be no reservation on religious basis.

BJP - its past, present and future

As a political organisation, BJP is proud of its past glory. In every era of politics and under every circumstances, BJP has established itself as a powerful political entity.

As Bharatiya Jana Sangh we established ourselves as a political party with a sound ideology from 1951 to 1977. Re-emerging on the political scene in a new avatar as Bharatiya Janata Party in 1980, we reached the pinnacle of power on the strength of a vibrant and effective organisation with a definite ideology. We left an indelible mark on the political life of the country by giving a stable and a good coalition government to the people from 1998 to 2004, at the same time strengthening our organisation and spreading our ideology. Simultaneously, we created new milestones of running a smooth and efficient coalition government. In other words, we excelled ourselves in the three fields of ideology, organisation and coalition as a leading political organisation.

Our party has always maintained its distinct identity. There has been a distinct image of the party in the minds of the people and they have entertained a special type of expectations from us. But we have to admit that today that some questions have been raised on this special identity. We have to address ourselves to these questions collectively in a united manner.

Discipline is one of the main strengths of our identity. We have to make our views known by keeping ourselves within the limits of discipline. Even while admitting that decorum has been violated during the past some years, no one can say that what happened was right. Indiscipline at every level has to be dealt with a firm hand at all costs. Otherwise, we too are destined to meet the fate of other parties.

Thinking of our party has always been centered around the karyakartas. Along with the programmes of the party we are also involving the individual karyakartas in the promotion of public welfare. While being active in public life we must keep in mind that while being in opposition it is our duty to continue to struggle for promoting public welfare and while being in power to concentrate on finding solution to people's problems and not our own personal publicity. Rising above the considerations of personal benefit, our commitment should be to the nation's interests.

It is two years since we came out of power at the Centre. A review of the reasons that contributed to our failure in Lok Sabha elections in 2004 has already been undertaken. I consider the failure of more than 50 percent of our MPs to win again as one of the main reasons responsible for our defeat. It appears that there was something lacking in our efforts to create a place for ourselves in the hearts of the people. We have to ponder over this fact. This example is both a challenge and a lesson for our elected representatives, office-bearers of the party and, particularly, in the States where we are in power. Constant contact and communication between people, people's representatives and workers is the lifeline of an organisation. It is very necessary to keep it alive and continuous.

A great responsibility befalls on the governments where we are in power. We have to instil in the minds of the people a feeling that BJP-run or BJP-supported governments are their own. The work and conduct of our chief ministers, ministers, as also public representatives should be oriented towards the people and the karyakartas.

Organisational elections

BJP believes in internal democracy. To enrol members, active members and conduct elections down from Mandal up to the national level has been our distinct identity. Accordingly, the work of enrolment of primary members has already been launched all over the country. The outline for initial arrangements for conducting organisational elections was presented before the office-bearers at the national level by the National Election Officer.

Before taking any political decision, we should always keep in mind the feelings of our karyakartas. Before taking a decision, there should be a free, frank and open discussion. But once a decision has been arrived at, there should be no room for discussion or comment on it. Instead, we should devote ourselves to the implementation of that decision.

Neglect of development

The rapid pace of development that was set in motion during NDA regime has been made to continuously and rapidly slow down under UPA regine, Prestigious developmental projects have been put on the back burner. On the contrary, commendable projects of development are continuing at great speed in BJP-ruled and BJP-coalition States even without the necessary help of the Centre. These State governments deserve to be congratulated on this score.

Despite efforts being made by various quarters to hinder development, the exemplary grit and determination displayed by Gujarat and Madhya

Pradesh governments in the matter of construction of Sardar Sarovar Dam Project in the interest of public is all the more commendable.

Exhortation

After taking over as President I undertook an extensive tour of many States. I had the opportunity of interacting with the State leadership and the karyakartas. I am confident that our karyakartas are fully prepared to face any situation that may develop in the country. Next year is an year of challenge for the party. While in the earlier part of 2007, there will be elections in the States of Punjab, Uttaranchal, Uttar Pradesh, Goa and Manipur, in the latter part, elections are due in another important State of Gujarat. We have to gird up our loins for meeting the challenge of elections in these States. People of the country are fed up with the Congress and the Left Parties and they entertain no hope from these parties. Therefore, it is but natural that people nurture great hopes from BJP.

Fate has thrown on our shoulders the responsibility of making the country tread the path of progress and prosperity by taking it out of the present abyss of despair and dejection. We have to discharge this onerous and moral duty with diligence, commitment and honesty. If we fail to come up to the expectations of the people, history will never pardon us. I do not only hope, but I am confident also that the future belongs to us and we are destined to play our role in ushering in a prosperous India.

It is a time to struggle and we have to make good use of every moment available with us to stand up to play our role and play it well. Our victory is assured.

□

Exposing Educational Conspiracy

7-9 September, 2006 (Dehradun)

Uttaranchal, the land from where the holy Ganga and Yamuna emerge and is home to the holy shrines of Badrinath and Kedarnath, is the eternal abode of Gods. It is a pleasant coincidence that we have gathered here.

Last National Executive meet was held in Delhi. During this interregnum of three months several important events have taken place on the political scene, which are a cause of worry. The Mumbai bomb-blasts were a big challenge to the national security. The separatist mentality is continually expanding its sphere of influence. It has, therefore, become imperative to strengthen national unity both in principle and practice. During the year, the country is celebrating 150th year of the first war of independence and centenary of the National Song *Vande Matram*. The birth centenary of martyr Chandreshekhar Azad also falls during the year.

For any country such an occasion should be an opportunity for re-instilling and spreading the feelings of nationalism. But it is a regret to note that the UPA Government, instead of using this historic occasion to strengthen the feelings of nationalism, seems to be feeling more concerned in strengthening its own vote bank. Not only this, the Government does not have the courage to ensure that the National Song *Vande Matram* is recited by one and all in free India. *Vande Matram* – the song which was on the lips of many a freedom fighters while going to the gallows, the song, reciting which, independent India came into existence, the song which was the last word on the lips of every martyr, has now been sacrificed at the altar of vote bank politics by this UPA Government.

Through NCERT and IGNOU books, the UPA Government has done further damage to our rich and hoary past, which have kept our culture eternally alive. It is a gross injustice to deprive the young generations of the knowledge of the core elements of India's nationalism and culture.

Just to ensure the continuance of this coalition, the UPA Government is playing with the past, present and future of the Indian nation. It is a new phenomenon of political decline that has set in today's environment. The country is now witnessing the climax of ugly spectre of the minority appeasement policies of the Congress and bullying by the Left forces.

We strongly condemn such acts of the UPA Government. And we will not allow this government to tinker with our National Song *Vande Matram* and the sense of pride of our glorious past. We will not allow the UPA Government to succeed in its nefarious designs.

The nation is thus destined to meet this fate under the UPA rule. We have to mentally prepare ourselves to face this reality. We will have to pass through an acid test of the people in the days to come. The UPA is in the process of continually getting weak and ineffective. The coalition partners are diametrically opposed to each other and there are symptoms of their drifting apart. The internal squabbles are deepening. The Left parties have clearly declared that if they find a better alternative, they will withdraw their support to the Congress-led government. At the same time, a senior Congress minister has challenged the Left parties to withdraw their support instead of threatening the government every now and then. This is enough to unravel the internal contradictions within the UPA allies. We have been telling right from the beginning that the UPA coalition is an unnatural alliance. This coalition was born with the negative objective of preventing BJP from coming to power. It is evident that from the present indications it is more than clear that the UPA Government may fall any time and the country will have to go through the ordeal of a mid-term poll.

For the last two years, the pervading environment of lack of political direction, is a cause of worry for the nation. The alliance partners as also the ministers have become despotic. There is not one but numerous power centres operating in the government today. In such a scenario the pace of development and efficiency of both the government and administration have been taking a hit. The Central Government has not dealt with any issue with the honesty of purpose it deserves, be it the price rise, unemployment, terrorism, farmers' suicides, Indo-US nuclear deal, Pathak Inquiry Authority Report, management of natural disasters, Centre-State relations, foreign policy, or appeasement of minorities. These are numerous examples of incompetence and ineffectiveness of this Government.

Programmes during the last Three Months

During the last three months, we have fought for the cause of the people afflicted with high prices and carried our struggle from Parliament to the streets. Former Prime Minister Atal Behari Vajpayee, Hon'ble Advaniji, alongwith several senior leaders of every state led the party workers in courting arrest to awaken the Central Government out of its slumber. But the government has failed to rise to the occasion. Further, we undertook a sit-in Dharna and demonstrations against terrorism in J&K and elsewhere. We launched a programme to educate the people throughout the country on the issues involved. On the issue of farmers suicide, a long-drawn out plan of agitation was chalked out. Women's wing of BJP launched a signature campaign against price-rise throughout the country and submitted memoranda to the Governors in the states. Likewise, the youth wing registered its protest throughout the country by organising a human-chain against terror. During the monsoon session of Parliament, our members forcefully raised national issues and made UPA Government realise their acts of omission and commission. Along with this, the UPA Government's attention was drawn towards problems faced by the common man in the country today.

During the last eight to nine months, I have continuously been visiting different states to take part in demonstrations, executive committee meetings, Kisan Sammelans and workers meetings. I feel pleasure to see that the common worker of the BJP is spirited and enthusiastic. Workers are unitedly opposing the wrong policies of the Government at their own level. We, at our own level, should also take care of the problems facing our workers.

Uncontrolable Prices

The present UPA Government is decidedly anti-people. Everyone is a victim of price rise. Our Prime Minister, the economic expert that he is, is presenting strange economic theories and practices resulting in the rich becoming richer and the poor forced to lead a life of misery. It is unfortunate that, on the one hand, the air-fare, prices of luxury cars and airconditioners are becoming cheaper by the day but, on the other, essential commodities of daily use by the common man are becoming costlier. The unchecked prices of essential commodities of everyday use, like rice, pulses, vegetable oil continue to play havoc with the budget of most of the households. Under the UPA Government it is impossible for the common man to progress.

This incompetent government has made the life of the people difficult. Prices of gas, diesel, petrol, cement, bricks, sand and bamboo, as also the increasing interest rates on housing loans have shattered the dreams of people to build a roof over their head. Their dreams had started becoming a reality during the NDA rule. Meanwhile rising prices of seeds and fertilizers have dealt a blow to the farmers. The policies of UPA government are such that they can damage the thousand year old traditional agriculture. The most shameful thing to happen is that the self-proclaimed godfathers of the proletariat, the Left is enjoying power without responsibility. In the eyes of the people, the UPA Government stands exposed. It is a matter of shame for a government under whose rule the poor persons fail to manage two square meals a day. People of the country have begun to realise that whenever the Congress comes to power, it brings with it the gift of soaring prices. They now recall how during the six years of NDA rule the prices throughout remained most stable as compared to this and any of the previous governments.

Farmer's Suicide

It is a sad commentory on the state of affairs that the producer of food-grains, the farmer is today feeling compelled to commit suicide. As a consequence of anti-farmers policies of the UPA Government, the condition of Kisans in the country has gone from bad to worse. Farmers in Maharashtra, Andhra Pradesh, Karnataka, Tamil Nadu, Punjab, and Kerala are committing suicide. On the one hand, interest burden on the farmers is increasing and, on the other, shortage of power supply is leading to non-availability of irrigation to the farmers.

On the eve of Assembly elections, Congress had promised to give free power to the farmers in Maharashtra. On this hope, the Kisans gave their support to the Congress. But true to its real character and culture Congress ditched the farmers the moment it came to power with their support. The Kisans are finding themselves engulfed with manifold problems. Recently, Prime Minister announced a package for Vidharbha farmers and in spite of that the chain of farmer's suicides has not been broken in the region and their woes continue unabated . Does the responsibility of the government and the Prime Minister end with the announcement of a package?

The government will have to make far-reaching efforts to remove the problems of Kisans. Farmers constitute the very basic structure of

India's social life. India cannot be prosperous without ensuring prosperity of the farming community. While introducing new avenues of economic development into our metropolitan life, UPA's development agenda has failed to prevent the Kisans from taking the extreme step of committing suicide. Perhaps the economists in Prime Minister and Finance Minister have failed to understand this paradox.

Increasing Unemployment

The rapidly increasing unemployment is sounding an alarm to the nation. In spite of initiating liberalisation and globalization the number of rural and urban unemployed continues to grow fast. The statistics of unemployment are frightening. 17% of the unemployed are young graduates, meaning thereby that even literate youth are unable to find employment. Unemployment generates many ills in the country. The pangs of hunger are dangerous and devastating. As a consequence unemployed young men are being lured into anti-social and anti-national activities by forces inimical to the country.

The UPA Government launched a National Rural Employment Guarantee Scheme with a great fanfare. But it is afflicted with many shortcomings. For example, what will happen to the problem of unemployment in urban areas? What will people do in the remaining 265 days if they get employment for 100 days only in a year? Many doubts still persist about the proper implementation of this scheme. In several states, reports of misuse of this scheme have come to light. I feel proud to state that despite shortcomings, the BJP-ruled States have led the rest of the country in providing real benefits of the scheme.

On the organisation front, Bharatiya Janata Yuva Morcha has conducted a survey at the national level on a serious subject like unemployment. The statistics of the survey are startling. We will have to concentrate on ensuring creation of employment in every sector to banish the curse of unemployment. Further, special attention needs to be given to generate more employment opportunities in the country's core-sector of agriculture.

Economic State of the Country

The country's economy has gone in reverse gear and the reform-mode has converted itself into anti-reform. Disinvestment has almost been grounded. The Government is trying to role back the status of disinvested companies. And in this, the Government is not ready to fulfill those commitments, which it had made while selling them earlier. Price control has been enforced in the pharmaceutical sector. Energy sector has suffered a big jolt as a consequence of Government policies. There is a total freeze-frame status in this regard. Government has not rationalized Customs and Excise duties and instead resorted to revision of petro-prices seven times. By rejecting the 2003 Electricity Act by the regulator, the energy sector will suffer in its growth, expansion, competition and investment.

The UPA Government is reverting to Inspector Raj. By enforcing a ban on the movement of food-grains in the name of controlling prices, it is encouraging corruption and hoarding. It appears that the Government quickly decides favorably on measures that go against economic reform but lack the will to takes tips which augment growth. Consequently there is a negative impact on sectors like infrastructure, energy, agriculture and food processing.

Growing Terrorism

Terrorism is spreading its tentacles throughout the country as a consequence of the misplaced policies of the UPA Government. During the last two years, there has been a steep rise in the terrorist acts. Jaish-e-Mohammed, Lashkar-e-Toiba, and Hizbul Mujahideen type terrorist organizations are targeting national symbols, e.g. attack on the Ramjanma Bhumi- Ayodhya, an abortive attempt at RSS headquarters in Nagpur, attacks in Delhi on the eve of Dipawali, place of reverence like Kashi, and the symbols of modern India like Mumbai and Bangalore. Recent bomb blasts in local trains in Mumbai along with blasts in Srinagar have shocked the country. In Mumbai incidents more than 200 were killed and hundreds of others injured. The terrorists have dared the misadventure of bleeding innocents and created an atmosphere of fear and terror.

Growing terrorism is the biggest challenge to our country. It is unfortunate that the Congress-led UPA Government has adopted a soft approach towards terrorists. It is also a matter of concern that terrorism is being sponsored and promoted from the soil of our neighbouring country. Just last month, Government of India had stated on record that 52 terrorist training centres were operative in Pakistan and POK. Even US has accepted this fact. In such a scenario, the statement of Pakistani President that terrorist activities are not being conducted from Pakistan is a deceit played on India. BJP-led NDA Government made every possible effort to crush terrorism. To ensure proper punishment to terrorists, POTA was enacted but the UPA Government's first task was to abolish POTA and project this as a great achievement. UPA Government's approach to terrorism has not only been soft but in a way compromising too. First, this government granted legal concession to terrorists by revoking POTA. Then, Congress and Leftists passed a resolution in Kerala Assembly seeking parole to prime accused in Coimbtore blast Abdul Nasir Madani, and granted Constitutional concession to terrorism. Now this government is betraying moral and ethical bankruptcy by surrendering before communal bigotry on the issue of National Song. It is far serious consideration whether such acts can ensure the unity and integrity of the country. Is it appropriate for the Central Government to sacrifice national interests for achieving its selfish political agnda? This is unpardonable. BJP is of the view that Naxalism and terrorism are the legacy of Congress rule. The soft approach of Congress towards Naxalism has posed a big challenge to the internal security of the country. Outcome of the Congress taking help of Naxals in last Andhra Assembly polls poses dangerous consequences. Today 17% of the country's population is in the grip of Naxalism. It is also a matter of concern that Naxalism, Jihadi Terrorism and Nepal's Maosim have forged a nexus with the ISI. I wish to warn the Naxalites that there is no place for violence in India. Violence ultimately pushes the country into anarchy.

Because of these soft policies, this year, Independence Day was celebrated under the threat of terrorist attacks and such a frightening shadow of terror was never witnessed earlier on any Independence Day.

BJP is of the opinion that things have gone beyond control and comprehension. Therefore, there is need for tough anti-terror laws. BJP demands that POTA should be revived to contain terrorism. This is not only view of an opposition party like us but also reflects the feelings of the common man from all sections of society.

UPA's Failure to come to grips with Natural Calamities

We are aware that excessive rains during the recent past in several states and resultant floods have caused havoc with the lives of people and thousands have lost there lives. Property worth crores of rupees was lost. Gujarat, Rajasthan, Madhya Pradesh, Chhattisgarh, Maharashtra, Andhra Pradesh, Karnataka and Orissa suffered terrible floods destroying crops and dislodging lakhs from their homes. States ruled by BJP and its allies carried out relief works on their own and sought relief from the Centre. I am pained to state that the UPA Government acted in a partial manner while granting relief. They should not have acted like this. At the same time many States are in the grip of drought. There too the Centre totally failed in giving adequate relief. BJP state units and BJP CM's apprised the Centre fully of the natural calamities faced by the respective states. Our MPs also raised this issue in the Parliament and drew the attention of the Government to the prevailing state of affairs. In spite of all this, the UPA Government held out only assurances and in the name of relief all that the Centre gave was a pittance. We strongly condemn this discriminatory attitude of the Centre and demand that in the States facing natural calamities, the suffering of the people should be alleviated without any partial approach.

Pathak Authority Report / Attempts to Conceal the Truth in the Guise of Enquiry

There was a question mark on the credibility and intentions of the UPA Government when the enquiry report of Justice R.S. Pathak in connection with Volcker Report was leaked while the Parliament was in session. This has put the Central Government into the ambit of suspicion as to how some portions of the Justice Pathak Authority Report, submitted to Prime Minister were leaked out to the media within minutes of the submission. It is apparent, that it was deliberately done to create confusion in the minds of the people of the country and to equip the Congress to claim its innocence. Still the whole truth of this episode has to come out in the open. Who used the vouchers issued in the name of Congress for lifting oil and who received the payments?

On this issue, there has been a conspiracy to conceal the truth. The BJP has been demanding right from the beginning as to why the statement of Congress President Smt. Sonia Gandhi was not recorded? At the same time why Smt. Sonia Gandhi has not broken her silence on this issue so far? The Pathak Authority Report on this issue has raised not one but many questions.

Nuclear Deal

Indo-US nuclear deal is a cause of serious concern to every patriotic Indian today. The NDA Government also, had taken steps for strategic cooperation with USA. We had talked of cooperation for civilian use in the field of space technology, atomic energy and in the hi-tech areas. But we had refused to negotiate when the kind of conditions which have been placed before the UPA Government today, were brought to our notice then. I would like to ask the Government to explain the conditionalities on civil nuclear energy and answer the fundamental question, whether there was need at all to have this nuclear deal for India under these circumstances?

Till date we have conducted our nuclear programme on indigenous technology. We never sought to limit our development and potential of our own nuclear deterrent capacity. India has a reserve of sufficient Uranium and has the largest reserves of Thorium. In spite of all this, was it appropriate to agree to put almost two-thirds of our reactors on the inspection list and was it necessary to agree to inappropriate conditionalities which in many ways tantamount to accepting NPT and CTBT? What serious energy crisis the country was facing, that such a deal was considered inevitable?

Last year in July, former Prime Minister Shri Atal Behari Vajpayee had voiced his reservations to this deal. Consequent upon BJP pressure, the Government has changed its approach on many conditionalities. We however, feel that even this is not adequate. The BJP demands that this deal should not be concluded until the international community grants recognition to India as a Nuclear weapon state.

Our Neighbours

Amongst our neighbouring countries, Pakistan has been the centre of disruptive activities against us since long. And now the growing clout of Maoists in Nepal, coupled with sympathetic approach of the Left parties is posing greater challenge to the internal security of the country. The Taliban is becoming active once again in Afghanistan. In Bangladesh, new centres of Jihadi terrorism are emerging. In Sri Lanka clashes between LTTE and the Government have intensified.

Recently, Pakistan army killed the Baloch Leader Nawab Akbar Khan Bugti aggravating the struggle in Balochistan. This struggle might aggravate further and destabilize the entire region.

In this backdrop the UPA Government has failed to devise an appropriate policy which would protect India's interests. It will not be an exaggeration if it is stated that the entire Indian subcontinent is moving towards instability and the UPA Government has proved itself incompetent in protecting the geo-political interests of India.

Women's Reservation

The issue of granting reservation to women in Parliament and State assemblies was initiated during Hon'ble Atalji's government. For various technical reasons, it could not take a definite shape. In this, the biggest technical problem is deciding about the electoral constituencies. BJP is of the opinion that women's reservation bill should be brought before Parliament at once and if need be, adding one-third additional seats in the Parliament can also be considered. The increased additional seats can be reserved for women. In a fast developing nation, representation in the Parliament and growth in numbers is a natural process. We should consider this with an open mind. If the UPA Government is serious about the issue, it should introduce this Bill in the Parliament. We are ready to support it.

Minority Appeasement

The politics of Congress is very much centered on minority appeasement. It does not worry about national interests. It has crossed all limits during the last two years. Ignoring the Constitution, the Congress Government of Andhra Pradesh gave reservation to minorities in government jobs and the Congress-led UPA Government attempted to give reservations to Muslim students on religious basis in Aligarh Muslim University. Attempts were made for a head-count of Muslims in the Armed forces. In Kerala's Assembly, a unanimous resolution was passed to release the main accused of the Coimbatore bomb-blast, Abdul Madani from the prison. These are some of the most deplorable acts in the history of independent India. In the same manner, the anti-Dalit face of the Congress was exposed when it deprived the SC's, ST's and OBC's of their right to reservation in getting admission into minority educational institutions.

Conspiracy in Education

During NDA's regime a serious attempt was made by Dr. M. M. Joshi, the then HRD Minister, to purge the books of distortion in consultation with learned educationists and intellectuals. The Leftists and the so-called educationists raised a hue and cry and dubbed it the saffronization of education. Later, the Supreme Court upheld the changes made in educational curriculum during the NDA regime. And now, when Congress and Leftists are sharing power in the Centre they have included highly objectionable material in the NCERT curriculum. Insulting material has been written against National heroes like Guru Tegh Bahadur,

Chatrapathi Shivaji and Maharana Pratap. Every nation teaches its future generation its glorious history. It is nation's misfortune that power is in the hands of those who negate the very idea of Indianhood and it is because of this that the spirit of nationalism is on the wane.

Our revered Gods and Goddesses—Shiva, Krishna, Parvati, Kali, and Durga have also been portrayed in a distorted manner. Such things are taught about our revered objects of worship that I am ashamed even to refer to them. While, the Prime Minister refers to Naxalism is a big problem from ramparts of Red Fort, the poems of Naxalite poets are being taught to the students. Does it not amount to playing with the future of the nascent generation? Should there be a vote-bank politics in education? It is a matter of satisfaction that BJP Parliamentarians attacked the government on this issue forcefully. There is a country-wide echo that NCERT curriculum must be changed. Government will have to concede, otherwise BJP will be compelled to intensify this movement throughout the country. On this occasion I want to compliment the *Shiksha Bachao Aandolan* which has exposed through people's awareness through the seminars, demonstrations and the courts UPA Government's conspiracy in the field of education.

Telangana

The Congress had sought votes in last Andhra Assembly elections in the name of carving out a new Telangana State. People believed them and voted for them. But the Congress betrayed the people's confidence the moment it came to power. Make promises on the eve of elections and abandon them after acquiring power. This is essence of Congress culture and strategy. BJP has been an advocate of Telangana State right from the beginning. We are in favour of small States. If a Bill to create Telangana State is brought before Parliament, we will definitely support it.

Organizational Elections

In the coming months organizational elections will be completed. In the last executive meeting, we had discussed about the dates of organizational elections and had chalked an election schedule. My only request is that there should be transparency in organizational elections. The workers, who through their hard labour carried the party forward, should be given their due place and honour. It is also necessary that democratic traditions of the party should always be vibrant. I am of the opinion that organizational elections should be held on a regular basis and completed from the Mandal unit up to all India level in accordance with the Constitution of the party. It has also to be ensured that all sections of society should be given proper representation on the party executive. BJP is a disciplined and value-based political party. We should endeavour to ensure that BJP's special identity should remain in tact as ever.

Forthcoming Assembly Elections

Immediately after the organizational elections are concluded, the Party has to face Assembly elections in four important States of UP, Uttaranchal, Punjab and Manipur. All of us must be aware that we have been in government in the States of UP, Uttaranchal and Punjab in the past. If our endeavours succeed in these States and if we intensify our efforts in this, the outcome will definitely be a pleasant one for all of us. At the organizational level, preparations for elections have started in right earnest in these states. Yet we have to make preparations at many other levels. I am confident that if we engage ourselves without leaving any stone unturned, the electoral results will definitely be in accordance with our wishes.

The UPA Government is continually facing erosion of public credibility. It is not our political aim to seek consequential change of regime and be a beneficiary by default. We have home grown positive and constructive agenda. We have taken a vow to create a prosperous and mighty nation. We will have to expand the reach of our political ideology to enable us to achieve our target. I want to make it clear that this is not an ordinary task. This cannot be achieved by merely putting it in writing. This is however possible if we work collectively as a team towards this objective. Only then we will definitely succeed in our mission. We will have to pay special attention to expand our party's plan of action. We will have to reach those places where we have not reached as yet through our programmes and through our work and through the medium of our workers. We will have to increase the strength both of our supporters and voters. We have always been the votary of positive politics. This is not to suggest that we opt to remain deprived of the due advantages of being in opposition. But it is needless to say that all this is essential not only for the political future of the party but also for ensuring the secure future for our Great Nation. But the uppermost necessity of today is that we push full-throated to expand our political ideology and political base.

□

Reaffirming Faith in Coalition

22-24 December, 2006 (Lucknow)

I have emotional relationship with Uttar Pradesh. It is my work place and I have deep affection with it as the former Chief Minister of the State. Lucknow from political and cultural angle has historical significance as well as cultural importance. We all know that Lucknow is the parliamentary constituency of Atal ji. I believe that this National executive shall prove to be the illuminator for India and BJP. Three months ago, we all met at Dehradun. From the party's organizational view point, this is the final meeting of the present executive. But after this, again, the new National Executive has to be reconstituted. I also heartily felicitate, all the democratically elected State Presidents attending this meeting.

On 23rd and 24th December, the two-day National Council meeting of the party shall be held. On the culmination of this meeting, a massive rally and a public meeting shall be organized. In the National Council, I shall extensively deliberate on the current political scenario and topics of concurrent national interests. But , I propose to touch a few important subjects.

I am equally concerned along with my fellow citizens of India on our current explosive national scenario. Today, India is passing through a bad phase. The whole country is aflame with the fire of terrorism. In our agriculture centric country, the poor farmers are hanging themselves to death or are forced to consume poison. There is an all round atmosphere of dissatisfaction and anarchy. UPA is trying to split the country on the basis of religion and is on the verge of another partition. Instead of eradicating poverty, there is a conspiracy to finish the poor.

All over the country today, the agitation by the underprivileged, tribal, poor, labour and farmer slogan are brutally crushed. The problems are endless. But all this is happening during the reign of those who assumed power on the slogan "Congress Ka Haath, Aam Aadmi ke Saath" and promised to work for the benefit of the common man. The UPA led by Congress and subsisting on the crutches of Communists, stand totally exposed. The Govt. under whose regime, the countrymen are finding hard even to earn two meals a day, does not deserve to rule the country. The citizens of the country are regrouping against the Government. It is against "anti-people policies" of the Central goverment that BJP recently organized an agitation from road to Parliament.

Programmes organized in the previous three months:

During the last three months, at the national level we organized three major programmes. We had decided at Dehradun, that on the issue of "Vande Matram" we shall organize dharnas, protest demonstrations and seminars. This programme was successfully organized all over the country. The national office bearers visited major places in various cities on the issue.

On the issue of "phenomenal price rise", a national agitation was launched. BJP workers courted arrest all over India. Protest demonstrations along with *chakka jam* programmes took place at various vantage points. The main culprit for the terrorist attack at Parliament on 13th December 2001, Mohammd Afzal was handed a death sentence by the Supreme Court. But on the issue of granting clemency to Mohammd Afzal, the vote bank politics as pursued by Congress and Leftists was "shameful and disgusting". BJP demanded hanging of Afzal. On the issue of national security and its grave implications, BJP organized vociferous protests, effigy burnings and massive public protest marches all over India. Recently, on the opening day of winter session of Parliament on 22nd November, BJP organized a massive demonstration and thousands of citizens courted arrest outside Parliament. At the historic protest public meeting on the issue, the unanimously echoed demand was – "either the UPA Government. should change its policies otherwise the countrymen shall uproot it.

On the issue of Prime Minister's unconstitutional and divisive speech at the national development council, BJP organized nationwide protests from 15th to 20th December. BJP while remaining in Opposition has always played the role of a catalyst guard.

The Current National Scenario

After 59 years of freedom, today the country still encounters poverty, illiteracy, unemployment and terrorism. Today 28% of our population is forced to live below the poverty line. The issue of unemployment is assuming alarming proportions. Today unemployment is rising at the annual rate of 10%. During the Congress regime, epidemic of corruption has spread. The Volker report indicted the Congress as the prominent beneficiary in the oil scam, the foreign money channeled into the Congress and Leftists coffers as per the revelations in Mitrokhin Archives–II episode compiled by a former KGB archivist, Vasili Mitrokhin, and Bofors corruption accused Ottavio Quattrocchi bank accounts de-freezed by UPA Government are glaring examples of corruption. The Indian democracy was aghast and ashamed, when in the democratic history of India, a cabinet Minister was awarded life imprisonment in a case of murder. Today, many tainted ministers occupy cabinet berths in the Union Government.

UPA Govt. due to vote bank politics has adopted a soft approach on the issue of terrorism. During the past 2 ½ years, terrorists targeted Ayodhya, Kashi, Bangalore, Delhi and Maharashtra states with lethal bomb blasts. The whole nation panicked with fear and scare. On the Afzal issue, the UPA Govt. stands exposed. The attack on Parliament was an attack on Indian democracy, sovereignty and its leadership. Our security personnel gave away their lives while fighting the terrorists and defending the parliamentarians. On the issue of clemency for Mohd. Afzal, Congress and Leftists betrayed the nation. Naxalites are increasing their tentacles due to the ham headed policies of Central Government. The innocent poor, farmers and women are brutally killed and an atmosphere of terror has spread over various parts of India.

The Congress led UPA Government is inflaming passions on the issue of appeasement and its fire is damaging the fabric of the nation. The spirit of Indian Independence struggle and hundred years of singing of Vande Matram and the controversy generated by the UPA Government is deplorable. The UPA partners have humiliated the nation on this unsavory controversy. We rebuke the mentality of those who despise the nationalist insignia and our historical events.

The Supreme Court declared the I.M.D.T. Act, as passed by Congress Government as invalid. The Court equated the Bangladeshi infiltrators to an attack by a hostile nation. A few days ago, the Central Government was given a judicial slap on the face by a decision of Gujarat High Court, wherein it was stated that, with an eye on Muslim vote bank, the Central Government had notified and constituted Justice Banerjee Committee on the Godhra incident, just before the Bihar elections. This notification was set aside and was termed as vindictive. On the same lines the Government constituted Justice Sacchar Committee to deliberate on the status of Muslims in the country. The report as submitted by the committee is divisionary and loaded with myths. The Congress is solely responsible for the poor plight of Muslims, as it has always treated the Muslims as a vote bank ploy only.

The UPA Government has also transformed the national development council into a cheap political platform. Appeasement reached its peak when the Prime Minister stated that the muslim community has the first claim to natural resources. The communal psyche of the Central Government is a lethal weapon. But if the first right on natural resources is to be considered, then it should be in favour of scheduled castes, scheduled tribes and tribals.

During the NDA Government rule, the country rapidly progressed on the economic front. The NDA initiated development schemes for highways, communications and rural infrastructure were given prominence but the same are being neglected by the UPA Government just because these were initially associated with the name of Vajpayee Government. This is not a good omen for India's economic growth. The Government has no financial scheme to sanction small loans in agriculture and small scale industrial sectors. Due to this, the farm and agriculture sectors are the worst sufferers.

The ever increasing price rise has put a question mark on the life of the common man. The increase in income is offset by enormous increase in prices. During the past two and half years, there has been 30 to 35 percent increase in the prices of essential commodities of common use, including food grains.

But after increasing the price of petrol and diesel seven times, the Congress government has engaged in political gimmickry by announcing a one-time symbolic price reduction. It is nothing but trying to befool the people.

Under the present regime, the common man is sweating hard even to earn the basics for its livelihood. The home loans which were available at 7 to 8 percent during the NDA regime were increased to 12.75 percent during the UPA rule.

Due to the faulty fiscal and agricultural policies, the poor farmers are forced to jump in the death wells and the scenario is worst in Andhra Pradesh, Kerala, Uttar Pradesh, Haryana and Punjab etc. It is a strange fact that the farmer who is the curator of daily life of the common man is forced to hang himself today. The main factor for farmer deaths is the agri-loans from the money lenders. The State and Central Government should provide soft loans to the farmers.

The Communist led West Bengal Government is crushing the farmers with police atrocities. As the BJP President, I recently visited **Singur** to express solidarity with the farmers' agitation. But the West Bengal led Leftist government panicked and arrested me along with thousand of BJP workers. We believe that the agitation started by Ms Mamta Banerjee in support of the aggrieved farmers shall expose the tainted leftist face in the country. BJP is not against the Special Economic Zone concept but we believe that the fertile agricultural land should not be acquired by the government for this purpose.

Under dynamic leadership of Atal ji during the NDA Government India won global accolades. But under UPA's rule, the government has reversed its gears and kneeled backwards. Just before the visit of Chinese President Hu Jintao, the Chinese Ambassador proclaimed Arunachal Pradesh to be a territory of China. Indian Government should have lodged its strong protest on the issue. The Government failed to build strong bilateral relations with China. Also the current situation in Nepal is a matter of concern for us.

The world knows that Pakistan has sponsored terrorism in India and is its main fountain head. After lethal bomb attacks in Mumbai and Malegaon, the Mumbai Police Commissioner in a press conference had accused ISI, the secret service of Pakistan as the originator of these dastardly bomb attacks. But at the Havana Non –Aligned Summit, the Indian Prime Minister stated that Pakistan is suffering from the malice of terrorism. National interests received a rude setback due to this mis-statement of the Prime Minister.

The unfolding of facts in the recently concluded and ratified India-US Nuclear Deal by the U.S. Senate has made the country seriously concerned. The leading scientists have also expressed their deep concern on the nuclear agreement. We disagree with this deal because India is not accepted in the category of nuclear capped states. This nuclear agreement is against our national interests.

The issue of Ram *Janmabhoomi* is linked with our national sentiments. It is also a matter of concern that the UPA Government is not sincere in finding an amicable solution to the Ayodhya dispute. Lord Ram Lalla is our National Hero. BJP firmly believes that a grand Ram Temple be built at the Ram *Janmabhoomi* at Ayodhya.

Prime Responsibility in BJP ruled States

The states where we are in power on our own strength and where we share power in the coalitions, we need to spread the areas of our political influence. Public opinion should be mobilized in favour of our ideology. In BJP ruled states, the quantum of our responsibilities is manifold. We have to measure up to peoples expectations. Promises made in the election manifestos and providing essential services to the common man should be our main concern. While being a part of the coalition Government in a few states, we have to increase our area of influence while respecting the grand rules of coalition era politics. Whereever we are in power, we should periodically review our programmes and progress. Besides it, we should also get a proper political feedback and an assessment report on our public image among the common masses. This is essential for our political health and growth.

Empowerment of Women

We have to focus our attention to empower the women. BJP should have significant influence among the women folks who constitute half of our population. BJP has always supported 33 percent reservation for women in panchayats, municipal corporations, state legislatures and parliament. It is not a question of 33 percent reservation but how to increase their participation in the Indian political scenario. We have to plan and create powerful schemes for the upliftment of women and create mass awakening through public programmes among them.

Invitation to Youth Power

We should formulate schemes for harnessing youth energy for positive growth. Youth have the power to transform adverse circumstances into favorable. We should aim to organise and consolidate the youth of the country and plan our programmes accordingly. We should not ignore their capabilities. I am sure that all the state BJP units shall give them their due importance. I call upon the youth of our country to rise, face and confront the challenges faced by India. They should harness their youth energies for nation building. I firmly believe that upon the resurgence of youth power, the anti-people and anarchic UPA govt. shall be uprooted from absolute power.

Over Activated state of Morchas & Cells

BJP in order to increase its area of influence among various segments of our domain, constitutes various *Morchas* and *Cells* at the *Mandal*, state and national levels. A few *Morcha* and *Cells* have progressed in this direction. The office bearers with responsibility of Morcha and Cells should do justice with their entrusted assignments. How we should increase our influence ? We should organize programmes among various hues of our society so that people align with our ideological school of thought. All the *Morcha* and *Cells* should be constituted up to the lowest levels and regular meetings should be held at the district, state and national level. I am fully convinced that we shall provide strength and power to all the activities of our morcha and cells so as to provide inputs to our parent organization.

Over Expectations from Public Representatives

The party's image is synonymous with the public image of its elected representatives. Their behavioral patterns influence the common man. Their awareness strengthens BJP's areas of influence. The elected public representatives should always remember the prestige of their party. They should realize the level of people's expectations. BJP should be visible and audible not in words but in the deeds of our public representatives. But it is unfortunate that the image of a politician among the common man is at its lowest ebb. Our public representatives have to transform this bad image among the countrymen. The common man has many expectations from us. We should always try to measure up to their expectation levels.

When an elected representative is appreciated, it is not only an individual but BJP and its ideology is also widely acknowledged. So the responsibility of the elected members is far greater in dimensions. I firmly believe that all our elected representatives shall focus their attention accordingly.

Political Sanctity

The society does not want to see us following the Congress culture. The minimum it expects of us is to observe political sanctity in our political life. The political purity makes a deep impact on the society. Today it is a generally accepted fact that political sanctity is impossible. But we have to remain firm with our ideology. The results can be delayed but shall eventually be significant. We shall have to concentrate on political purity. When politics based on purity is practised then social problems start diminishing. It keeps us glued to national development and concept of nationalism. We shall overcome the cultural distress and emerge victorious. Today the nation is passing through a cultural distress. The main culprit for the same is the mentality of alienation with the concept of Nationalism. "Sanctity" has a direct correlation with determination and consciousness. Thus when political purity is achieved we automatically get free from various problems.

Tour Programmes, Contact & Communication

To increase organizational base and connect with the influential individuals, we shall have to keep pace and speed. We shall have to expand our ideological base. So all the senior functionaries undertaking tour programmes should ensure contact and communication programmes at the grass root levels. Tour programmes, from mandal to state levels, by party functionaries strengthen the organizational structure. During such tours, we come to meet, establish direct contacts and communicate with political workers for a first hand information of the ground realities. This enables us to judge the events conveniently. So the office-bearers should always undertake tour programmes. In the coming days, with impending state elections, we shall have to accelerate the pace and speed of our tour programmes. If we can do so, then that day is not far away when we shall reach where we are not in existence and shall become stronger where we are omnipresent.

Organizational Elections

We had deliberated on organizational elections in the previous working committee meeting. At the national level, the Election Officer Shri O.P. Kohli ji determined and decided the time framework. During the past two months, 22 out of 35 state BJP units conducted democratic unanimous organizational elections. With a eye on impending state assembly elections, it was decided to defer organizational elections in five states only. Our endeavor is to organize immediate elections in the remaining states, where due to various reasons, elections could not be conducted.

Politics of Coalition

In the coming days we strive to increase our political strength. We shall progress in the direction of fighting elections on our own resources. Despite this we shall keep a focus on political coalitions. There are still many states where we do not wield enough political presence. We shall try to strengthen there on the basis of coalition realities. I had previously stated that we should endeavor to have alliances with smaller political outfits so that we can reap rich political dividends. On this issue with political consultations, you all should take affective steps. It is a well accepted fact that BJP during its six years of coalition politics, successfully pushed the nation on the path of progress.

Hard Work for the Forthcoming Assembly Elections

The local election results in U.P., vividly exhibited the ground realities to the Samajwadi Party along with BSP and Congress. The success achieved by BJP drives home the message that BJP shall get phenomenal success in the forthcoming assembly elections. But we shall have to work hard. The organizational unity has to be strengthened further. During the recent elections to Lok Sabha and Vidhan Sabha in various states, we did not lose any seats. I on behalf of BJP, profusely thank the voters and workers in these states.

Next Elections

The next few months hold challenge for us. State assembly elections are soon to be held in U.P., Uttranchal, Punjab and Manipur. All eyes are concentrated there. The main reason is that previously we were in power in U.P., Uttranchal and Punjab. The people of these states have lost faith and confidence in the present ruling party's regime there. People are clamouring for change. Strong winds are blowing for radical changes. The environment is favorable. But this shall be achieved only when do and die spirit exists among the workers. I am sure the results will be positive. At the organizational level in these states, preparations are already in full swing. We all recently witnessed the local elections in U.P. The opponents were wiped out. The elements who used to term BJP a party with having lost its ground suddenly found themselves without any ground under their feet. We shall have to respond to signals from the public. We shall have to work with self-confidence but, at the same time, we need to avoid over confidence. I firmly believe that we shall gain tremendous success in these elections.

Organizational Expansion – Our Priority

While facing the challenges, we shall have to free the country from the bonds of various problems. It is not an easy job in the present situation. We shall have to work hard. Organization shall have to be strengthened. We all know that on our strength we reached the figure of 182 members in Parliament. But it is far away from majority. We on the basis of organization and ideology shall have to increase the domain of our polity. We still have to expand in Southern states, West Bengal, Jammu & Kashmir and in North Eastern states of India.

In democracy the political influence is measured by the yardstick of election results. The political party which wins the maximum seats in state legislature and parliament, is considered the strongest political outfit. We have not only to be the party of the masses, at the tehsil level in these states, but also have to highlight the problems of the common man and prove to be an active organization. This is possible only when we shall keep it in our mind. For immediate gains we have not to abandon our policies, principles, aims, objectives and programmes. We shall struggle to win over the confidence of the common man. People of India always admire and respect the struggling leaders for its common causes. We shall have to launch public crusade against social evils. We shall have to make people's movement result oriented.

It has been observed that during the past few years, the political leaders have developed a tendency to organize convenient struggles. This they do only for publicity. But we cannot win public confidence with such givnmicks. We shall have to be loyal in all our agitations. We shall have to work on the twin objectives of our agitations. Public agitations are organized with public awareness and public participation.

But during the past two years, people's participation in political struggles has decreased. This is a matter of concern for us. Agitations should highlight people's woes. And this is possible only with the active participation of the common man. For the *Bhagidari* of the common man, it is necessary for us to undertake frequent tours, establish contacts and communicate with the society.

Constructive Aspects

BJP is a massive organization. But we all have to make it well-knit, charming and organizationally constructive. On issues of public interest, we need to organize periodic public agitations. The political workers need to be sensitive. We have entered politics for social change. But this shall only crystallize, when BJP gets connected with the people of all hues. For this we shall have to induct fresh blood in the party. It is unfortunate that the Indian society is besieged with numerous maladies. We have to weed them out.

To eradicate untouchability on the basis of caste, adequate respect to women, awakening against female foeticides and for the upliftment of the downtrodden, we shall have to exhibit over activation. Today in various parts of the country, the factory workers, farmers and tribals are on the war path against the UPA Government. policies. We shall have to be sensitive to these public agitations.

BJP is the only political outfit, which can challenge the problems confronting the nation on the political, social and cultural fronts. Our able leadership has proved it. After independence many opposition parties remained in existence but BJP ruled the country with ability and stability. The whole country knows that we have always considered the nation above the party. A time came, when in national interest, we merged Jan Sangh with Janata Party. We gave up our election symbol of Deepak and adopted the Janata Party symbol of farmer with plough as per the nationalist demands. But when on the issue of dual membership of Rashtriya Sewyam Sewak Sangh (RSS), the leaders of Janata Party showed there true colours, we explicitly stated that there can be no compromise on our parental – paternity links with patriotic RSS. On this issue the Janata Party split and the erstwhile leaders of Jan Sangh were arbitrarily removed. Our leadership charted a new course of action.

On 6th April 1980, Bhartiya Janata Party was formed and by the end of 1996, it emerged as the largest political party in India. This could not have been achieved without the hard work of our workers.

The dedicated workers of BJP cannot be found in any other political party in India. It was the strong resolve of BJP workers that forced the Congress Government out and installed the NDA Government at the Centre. We have a great responsibility towards the nation on our shoulders. When I say these words, it means that this is the prime responsibility of each BJP member. We have to again reiterate that we are different from other political parties. These words are to be turned into a reality by our deeds. We shall have to observe internal discipline and prove our mettle as a seasoned and experienced political worker of the party.

It is Bharatiya Janata Party, the major political party alone in the country, which has a strong national will to take the nation forward. Today BJP as an all India party is expanding in all corners of the country. BJP is the originator of Indian Nationalism. Under the leadership of respected Atalji led NDA Government the nation surged forward in all spheres. After independence, BJP leadership provided stability, best rule and able governance. The country has many expectations from us. We shall have to stand firmly in support of people's problems. BJP's resurgence has taken place due to the worker's irrepressible enthusiasm as a Godly figure. With confidence at heart, rubbing shoulder with shoulder, we all have to be ever -ready to assume prominent roles in governance. Our struggle shall bear fruits and dividends. On the basis of this confidence, we all have to surge forward.

□

A Weak Government

25-26 June, 2007 (New Delhi)

Today's Occasion

It is noteworthy that the month of June is remembered for many reasons in Indian politics. We observe 23rd June as Martyrs Day. On this day, lodged in a temporary jail in Srinagar, Dr. Shyama Prasad Mookerjee sacrificed his life fighting for the integration of Kashmir. Dr. Shyama Prasad Mookerjee was the founder of the Bharatiya Jan Sangh. Post independence, he was one such leader who unequivocally said that Kashmir is an inseparable part of India and no one can stop us from visiting it. When he visited Kashmir without a permit, the then government had him arrested and jailed, where he eventually lost his life. The Jan Sangh was in its infancy. One can clearly imagine how our leadership must have felt at that time. Despite this, the Jan Sangh's development did not pause and it kept on marching ahead. Dr. Mookerjee was the country's first post independence leader who sacrificed his life for a national cause. Let us reverentially remember him and offer our tributes on behalf of the entire nation.

In the month of June, in 1975, on this very day i.e. on 25th June, the Prime Minister of the then Congress Government imposed emergency and attempted to murder democracy and the Constitution. We can never forget that black day of independent India. For 19 months the atrocities of emergency continued unabated and the majority of social and political workers were sent to jail. Censorship was imposed on the press. Personal independence was severely restricted. The nation had never witnessed such a horrific misuse of power. Friends, even in such insurmountable circumstances, our workers firmly continued working. They launched a people's awareness programme. They preferred going to jail rather than offer an apology. The situation changed and in 1977 for the first time the Congress Party, which believed itself to be invincible, lost power at the

Centre. On the 32nd anniversary of the struggle against emergency, let us offer tributes to the late Jai Prakash Narain and all those political and social leaders who are no more among us.

After this, a time came when on the issue of dual membership, the erstwhile Janata Party left us with no option but to leave the party. We were told to either snap our ties with the Rashtriya Swayamsewak Sangh or else leave the Janata Party. At this delicate time, our leadership clearly said that our relationship with the Rashtriya Swayamsewak Sangh is from the time of inception. Our relationship with the Janata Party has developed only recently. Left with no option, on 6th April 1980, our erstwhile leadership of the Jan Sangh came together and founded the BJP. After the formation of the BJP, the 1984 Lok Sabha elections were the first general elections of the country. The BJP won a mere two seats. We can well imagine that as a new entity what must have been our situation? Despite this, the BJP did not stop and kept on marching ahead. We had to face numerous difficulties. But whenever we faced challenges, we tried our best to convert them into opportunities. And on many occasions we were also successful.

Our Political Objective

Why are we in politics? Why did Dr. Shyama Prasad Mookerjee create the Bharatiya Jan Sangh? On such occasions, it is important to reflect on these questions. We should carefully read the speech delivered by Dr. Shyama Prasad Mookerjee on 21st October 1951 after founding the Jan Sangh. I would like to quote an excerpt from his speech.

"At the outset I would like to make it clear that the Bharatiya Jan Sangh is not being formed only for contesting the forthcoming elections. Undoubtedly, elections are important, and wherever possible, we will make our candidates contest. Elections enable us in taking our ideology to the people and will also assist us in giving our organization a pan Indian identity and strong foundation. No matter what the outcome of the elections, our organization even thereafter will remain ceaselessly progressive and will carry the message of hope and amity to all sections of society. Simultaneously it will attempt to make independent India's reconstruction both pleasant and prosperous." Therefore, we should not be adversely affected by circumstances and need to ceaselessly move in the direction of our core objective.

The Recently Concluded Assembly Elections

After the conclusion of the last national executive meeting and in the midst of the current national executive, assembly elections have been held in Uttarakhand, Punjab, Manipur, Uttar Pradesh and Goa. We won the elections in two states, namely, Uttarakhand and Punjab. Thereafter, we won the prestigious Delhi Municipal Corporation election. Then came the Uttar Pradesh elections. The election results there were both unexpected and shocking. In Goa also we did not get the expected success. The cycle of victory and defeat is continuous. No matter what the circumstances, we have to constantly keep working. With honesty, we must attempt to eliminate our weaknesses. Each one of us is well aware of their organizational and political realities. We need to reflect on how we can strengthen our inner weak links. By devoting ourselves to self restraint, extreme hardwork, the urge for struggle, full faith in the organization, together we need to move ahead with coordination. We have to protect the organization from ego, being self-centric, indisciplined, and all those factors because of which politics is losing its respect in society. We have lost the election but not our determination. When in a span of 15 years, we have displayed the capability of coming to power at the centre from just two seats in the Lok Sabha, currently in five states we have our own BJP governments. And in five states we have coalition governments. For the first time in history, in 10 states either we or our coalition is in power. We are bestowed with respected leadership and an extremely rare team of workers. On policy and principles, we are staunch nationalists.

Instead of disappointment, we should treat the Uttar Pradesh results as an opportunity to make us more alert and stable. While saying all this I am not trying to say that we should not evaluate the results. We have in fact honestly analysed the results. Numerous factors have been identified. And all of us have to jointly work in eliminating them.

It is worth noting that in Uttar Pradesh merely 15 days later, the BJP won the Khaga (District Fatehpur) Assembly seat by-election by over 8,000 votes while the BSP came third. It is also worth highlighting that the BJP had never won this seat earlier. Political analysts are also expressing surprise over the result. In my opinion, this clearly indicates that our support base does exist in every village; we need to ignite it and expand it further.

After the defeats in Uttar Pradesh and Goa, our adversaries have started saying that the BJP is shrinking. We should not be affected by such remarks. It is natural that when people congratulate us for winning, then they will also criticize us for defeats. I believe that this is the time for introspection, unity and returning to our task with self confidence. At this time we need to carry everyone along, and after removing our weaknesses once again march towards victory.

The Uniqueness of Our Organization

I accept that over the last six months, on account of the constant elections and by-elections, we could not lay the requisite emphasis on organizational matters. Over the next few months, our priority will be on organizational issues. Our organization has always been viewed for having a distinct and unique identity. I will not hesitate in saying that over the last few years our image as a party with a difference has been affected. This is a subject of concern for all of us. The expansion of the organization and our influence, irrespective of whether we are in power or in opposition, cannot take place at the cost of compromising with the ideology for which Dr. Shyama Prasad Mookerjee and Pt. Deendayal Upadhaya founded the party. In politics, we also need to protect ourselves from the overall decline in moral values.

It is imperative to enhance the feeling of mutual faith, collectiveness, credibility, principles, spirit of accommodation and coordination within the organization. Over the last few years, politics in India has witnessed a decline in all these areas. At our own level, it is important that we all work in this direction. One finds that what should be shared internally with the leadership is instead reaching the party through the media. We will always need the required exposure in the media, but we would certainly not like our party, leaders and workers to become victims of unnecessary controversy. The problems of the public can be solved only with sensitivity and effort and not through propaganda. We need not become instruments of the competitive struggle of the media. We need to follow the established do's and don't's of public life, both in letter and spirit.

Self Discipline

We have to be conscious of self discipline. At our individual level, we need to adhere to established ideals and maintain dignity. We have to sacrifice our personal egos. It is imperative that we should be willing to bear personal displeasure in the larger interest of the organization. I can clearly recall that Advaniji used to often say that no party has the capability of defeating the BJP; if we are defeated it is only because of our own shortcomings. We have to appreciate the agony behind Advaniji's statement. His agony not only symbolises our own organizational view but also reflects the feelings of millions of committed workers.

Our constant goal has been to ensure that globally India gets its due recognition and is respected in consonance with its rich cultural heritage. Our cherished aim has been to raise the standards of living of the common people by taking development to newer heights. We have to live up to the people's expectations and win their confidence and support. Given the constant decline of values in public life, this is an extremely difficult task and we have to work hard in this direction. I am fully confident that we will succeed in this endeavor.

BJP's Governance

We have witnessed how India achieved international recognition in the six years of NDA governance under the leadership of Shri Atalji. Under his able leadership, India could achieve a new political, economic and global prominence. Atalji set the vision of establishing India as a developed nation by 2020 and during his regime India made giant strides in this direction. India's national pride enhanced.

The world acknowledged our strength; one small example we can recall is after the Pokhran test, when the developed nations said that they would not help us in any way, then Atalji as Prime Minister clearly stated that we are not dependent on anyone. We are capable of standing on our own feet. And in those six years we were able to become self reliant. Under Atalji's able leadership, India started emerging as a capable and powerful nation and one felt that our commitment of making India a developed country by 2020 would definitely materialize into reality.

The BJP has returned to power in many states. Our party has enjoyed repeat terms in Rajasthan and Jharkhand. In Orissa we were re-elected alongwith with our coalition partner. In Gujarat, we have won successive elections and our government has already completed a decade in power. Recently, Shri Narendra Modi achieved the distinction of becoming the longest serving Chief Minister of the state. This is a major achievement for us. During this period, the Gujarat Government has established new records of development in the state. Our governments in Rajasthan, Madhya Pradesh and Chhattisgarh are also performing well and are acknowledged for their good administration and for undertaking fast paced developmental activities. Our recently formed government in Uttarakhand is also marching ahead in the same direction.

Three Years of the UPA Government

The UPA Government has completed three years in office. In these three years, the UPA Government has not taken any steps by which one can say that India would become a developed nation by 2020. And this is because an alliance formed by opportunistic and leftist parties has only made the UPA Government at the centre fail on every front and prove to be completely directionless.

Today there are serious questions on critical issues such as India's global standing, strategic security, internal security, nuclear sovereignty, economic growth, food security, energy security, and several other issues including suicide by farmers, increasing inflation and terrorism. The national scene today has been so drastically affected that our vision of establishing India as a developed nation by 2020 appears to have shattered and is withering away.

Even more disconcerting is how the UPA Government has devised a dangerous policy where the authority of the Prime Minister and other important positions have in reality been vested elsewhere. The most dangerous outcome of this policy is that the accountability of governance is not vested in that person who is the real power centre. The use of power without accountability has serious future ramifications.

Price Rise

Under this Government, price rise has made the life of the common man extremely difficult. The situation has deteriorated to such an extent that a senior minister of the government had to publicly state that the UPA Government is not a government for the common man. There is no coordination between the coalition partners. The UPA Government's short sightedness is seriously impairing development. The UPA government has completed three years. The wrong decisions of the Government have only led to a massive piling up of problems all over the country. Chaos is prevalent everywhere. The two basic national problems that have become a matter of serious concern for the people are uncontrollable price rise and increasing terrorism. On the one hand, income levels are not increasing and, on the other hand, prices of all essential commodities have increased by 25 to 30 percent. Instead of providing relief to the common man, the hand of the Congress is only causing misery. In stark contrast to the overflowing food stocks under the NDA, for the first time, after eight years, the country is forced to import wheat, foodgrains, pulses and other food items.

In addition to price rise, rampant corruption is weakening the country. Over the past three years, the Food for Oil scandal in Iraq, Scorpien Submarine scandal, War Room Leak scandal, Quattrochhi and many other deals have exposed the real face of the UPA Government.

Economic Policy

Apart from price rise, the UPA Government has also created numerous problems in the area of economic policy. The rate of interest of housing and other loans for the middle class and urban poor are constantly increasing. Even farmers have not got any relief on interest rates for agricultural loans.

What to speak about relief on interest rates for agricultural loans, the Finance Ministry is in fact now imposing new rules on the farmers which will only add to their cup of woes. The Finance Ministry has passed a special act called the Securitisation and Reconstruction of Financial Assets and Enforcement of Security Interest (SARFAESI) Act under which the bank can attach the assets of those business establishments that take loans, but instead of repaying them, seek to tangle the repayment process in court cases. Under the act, in case of any dispute between the bank and the borrower, the bank has the power to first attach their assets and thereafter the issue can be resolved between the parties.

The NDA Government had kept farmers outside the purview of this act. However, the UPA Government has made efforts to include even farmers under this act. In Parliament, in response to a question, the Agriculture Minister had stated that he had no information on this issue. However, after only a few days, on 17th May 2007, the Finance Ministry issued a notification and brought regional rural banks under the scope of the SARFAESI Act. This clearly demonstrates the insensitive attitude of the government's economic policies towards farmers. Such policies can lead to an increase in the number of cases of farmer suicides. Therefore, we urge the government to immediately consider excluding farmers from the purview of this act of the Finance Ministry.

Even today, 90 percent of the workers in the country work in the unorganized sector. Banks do not have any substantive loaning facilities for such a large section of people.

India's stock exchange has today emerged as one of the important exchanges of the world. In the recent past, the share market has witnessed several sharp rise and falls. In this context, many economic experts, the Reserve Bank and regulatory authorities like SEBI have expressed concern over the adverse effect of funds coming into the market via the "Participatory Note" or PN route. Between January 2006 and January 2007, there has been an increase of 70% in the quantum of funds coming through the PN route. Even the National Security Advisor has expressed apprehensions about terrorist funds getting diverted to the Indian stock market through this route. Despite such serious implications, the Central Government has so far not taken any steps in this direction.

We demand that the Central Government regulates the flow of funds coming into the stock market through the PN route.

Farmers

Today the country's farmers are highly burdened. The problems of helpless farmers are forcing them towards suicide. The cycle of suicides has not abated. I charge the UPA Government that where on the one hand they have completely failed in finding solutions to the problems of the farmers, on the other hand they cannot escape their responsibility for farmers suicides. Agriculture has greater connotations beyond farming; it represents our culture. Farmer suicides denote a clear threat towards our cultural ethos. We need to strengthen the voice of the farmers and launch a crusade for their betterment.

According to one estimate, about 58 percent of the farmers in the country own either one or just over one hectare of land. They survive close to the poverty line. Some of the government policies have only exacerbated the problem further. For example, this year the government has announced a Minimum Support Price for cotton in the Vidharba region at Rs. 1760 per quintal whereas the Maharashtra government in its report has said that the cost of production is around Rs. 2250 per quintal. Various media reports have also highlighted that wheat has been purchased from local farmers at just over Rs. 900 per quintal whereas the government is importing wheat from foreign companies at Rs. 1200 per quintal.

In this national executive we are not only introducing a resolution on agriculture but also plan to initiate detailed discussions with subject experts on the problems confronting the agricultural sector.

Youth

How is it possible for India to progress if the youth of the country remains uneducated and unemployed? 40 percent of the country's population is between the ages of 13 and 35. Two thirds of this population lives in the villages. The government does not have a policy for this large and energetic segment of our population. We need to better utilize their energy. We need to creatively make them use their abilities. We need to identify new job opportunities for them. We need to halt the migration of youth from the rural areas. Even though the various programmes of the Central Government for the unemployed youth are inadequate, it is worth noting that the BJP ruled states are leading in their proper implementation. This clearly exemplifies the BJP's commitment about providing proper opportunities for the youth.

We are deeply concerned about the nation's biggest reservoir of energy. Both at the political and social level, we need to effectively make use of them. Youth is the base of our organization. They learn about democracy at this level. They learn about the party's ideology. They actively participate in various programmmes. In fact, many of our party programmes are successfully moving ahead on account of our young leadership. It is our priority to ensure that we motivate the youth towards our ideology and programmes.

Minority Appeasement

The UPA Government is compromising national unity over the politics of minority appeasement. The creation of the Sacchar Committee, reservation on the basis of religion, the agitation against the singing of *Vande Mataram* and the Prime Minister's statement that Muslims should have the first claim over resources are among the numerous instances by which the Government has already started harming national unity. Now the Government is devising new ways for appeasement that one has never seen before.

The Government is also trying to paint poverty in communal tones. The policy of banks prioritizing disbursal of loans for the poor belonging to the minority community, is not only socially dangerous, but is also without economic foundation. Analysis of the data of the National Council for Applied Economic Research (NCAER) does not reflect any noteworthy disparity in the 2004 and 2005 average annual family incomes of both Hindu and Muslim families. The BJP believes that the poor should not be differentiated on communal lines.

Even beyond this, the Finance Ministry has recently decided to give scholarships only to minority students in premier higher educational institutions like the IITs, IIMs and AIIMS. And for this, the Government has already made a provision of Rs 761 crores in the 11th Five Year Plan. The Government's decision to grant scholarships in these prestigious higher education institutions in not based on the financial or economic condition of the students but instead on their religious identity. These new and astounding experiments of minority appeasement by the UPA Government can lead to future social unrest.

North-East India

Under the NDA, we began to reverse the traditional sense of alienation that was prevalent in parts of northeast India. A comprehensive developmental plan and financial package coupled with a tough approach on insurgency helped the region to rejoin the national mainstream. Unfortunately, today virtually the entire northeast is in the grip of insurgency and illegal immigration from Bangladesh. This needs to be reversed. Insurgency has to be firmly dealt with, developmental activities enhanced and the ethnic identity of the local population and rich bio-diversity of the region has to be preserved.

All Sections of Society

We must try to bring each and every section of society, be it the forwards, backwards, scheduled castes, scheduled tribes, minorities or women, closer to the party.

In order to attract the scheduled castes and scheduled tribes towards the party in larger numbers, we need to understand their specific problems. The party is committed to provide reservation for the SCs STs, and OBCs in minority institutions, which is currently denied.

Our opposition parties are conspiring to keep the minorities at a distance from us by spreading misconceptions. It is unfortunate that some political parties indulge in the politics of minority appeasement for the sake of vote bank politics. The BJP views the minorities as citizens and not as mere vote banks. To ensure that over a period of time, the minority community is able to appreciate this aspect and to bring them closer to the party, the BJP Minority Morcha needs actively work in this direction.

The party enjoys a vast support base among women. We are of the opinion that their proper representation in the legislature should be enhanced. For this, proper representation of women in the party needs to be enhanced. By raising issues that concern women, we improve our image. I believe that women deserve 33 percent reservation within the party organization. I am requesting the national executive to consider this issue in detail so that we can bring about the required change in our party's constitution for reserving 33 percent representation for women.

Future Programmes

Over the next three months we need to focus on strengthening and expanding the organizational base of the party. We have decided that from now on, we will treat the polling booth as our base and expand the organizational work accordingly. We are of the opinion that a team of workers should be formed at each booth. Without this, we will not be able to make the organization effective or fast moving.

Simultaneously, we need to launch a programme across the country. As part of a special membership drive, we need to increase our membership to 5 crore people. This must also include one crore youth and one crore women who should be made members of the party.

We should make efforts to explain why only the BJP. We are in the process of printing a small booklet on this subject and during the mass contact programme, we will distribute this booklet to every household. We need to move in the direction of the villages. We need to prevent migration from the villages. We need to understand the problems of the villages and then find solutions to them.

Neighbouring Countries

In recent years, in virtually every country neighbouring India, extremist and terrorist forces have increased their presence. This includes the influence of the armed Maoists in Nepal, the activities of ULFA and other ISI supported groups in Bangladesh, the resurgence of the LTTE in Sri Lanka once again, the revival of the Taliban in Afghanistan and the long standing anti-India activities of Pakistan and also the resultant political turmoil in these countries. Undoubtedly, these activities that are taking place in our neighbourhood have an adverse impact on our own internal security and development. We are amazed that despite the existence of such a situation, one does not find the central government displaying the required diplomatic dexterity.

With our other neighbour China, India's diplomatic failure is becoming a matter of serious concern. Just prior to the visit of China's President to India, the Chinese ambassador made objectionable statements about Arunachal Pradesh. We immediately criticized that statement and requested the government to give an appropriate reaction. However, the central government turned a deaf ear. Now the situation has reached such a point that recently an officer from Arunachal Pradesh, who was part of a delegation of central government officials visiting China, was not issued a visa by the Chinese embassy on the ground that Arunachal is a part of China. Under such circumstances the Prime Minister proclaiming that China is one of our great neighbours is far from convincing.

All these instances prove that India's foreign policy in our own neighbourhood is not only ineffective but also a complete failure. We strongly criticize Government of India for not comprehensively addressing these issues that raise questions on our sovereignty.

Foreign Policy

Since the UPA Government has come to power, there has been a complete reversal of our diplomatic successes that had been initiated by Shri Atalji. On numerous occasions, the party has clarified its position on the Indo-US Nuclear Deal. However, the Central government is yet to take either the people or the Parliament into confidence about the details of this deal. Recently, two former Chairmen of the Atomic Commission had raised their apprehensions on the deal. According to experts, there are major differences between the statement of the Prime Minister to Parliament and the provisions of the Hyde Act as passed by the US Senate on the Indo-US Nuclear Deal. In context of the Indo-US Nuclear Deal, it is also worth highlighting the statement of Anil Kakodkar, Chairman of the Department of Atomic Energy, that within the next five years India has the capacity to increase its Uranium reserves and through Thorium refinement we can become self reliant to large extent in the area of nuclear energy. Therefore, it is imperative that this deal should not compromise India's nuclear sovereignty at any cost.

In the near future, the US Secretary of State is expected to visit India. I demand that the Central Government before arriving at any conclusive decision with the US Secretary of State on the nuclear deal, should take both the Parliament and opposition parties into confidence.

Quattrocchi Issue

The Central Government had already facilitated the Italian middleman Quattrocchi, the main accused in the Bofors case, to withdraw his payoff money. However, the Government crossed all limits of decency when despite his arrest in Argentina, it not only failed in its attempt to repatriate him to India but also allowed the CBI to be demeaned by the local court there.

On such legal matters, the CBI has a limited role to play. On such matters, the Government is the final authority. A former director of the CBI has clearly mentioned in an article that prior to Quattrocchi's arrest on 6th February in Argentina, the high level legal officials of the government had already given him a clean chit. Quattrocchi used this very clean chit to get such a strong decision in his favour by the court in El Dorado (Argentina). If this charge is true, then it reflects the shameful attempts of the Government to help criminals.

Election Process

The Election Commission is a prestigious institution of the country. The Election Commission's capability has been clearly demonstrated in the recently concluded elections of state assemblies and in particular the elections in Uttar Pradesh. However, an important aspect that is worth noting is the issue of low voter turnout, which is contrary to the core values of democracy. In my opinion, one reason for this is that despite holding valid voter identity cards, at many places people could not exercise their franchise. According to one estimate, about 80 lakh people belong to this category in Uttar Pradesh.

I would suggest that the Election Commission should at least ensure that every person's name is included in the voter list. To prevent a repeat of this in the future, the Election Commission should not only treat this as a serious issue but also clearly fix responsibility in those cases where people's names are missing from the voter's list despite having valid voter identity cards.

All over the county, one regularly witnesses some kind of election activity at short intervals in some state or the other. In some senses, India experiences almost a continuous process of electioneering. As a result of this, political parties are constantly focused on elections. Parties barely get the time to think about constructive social programmes and given the constant electioneering, electoral activities inadvertently shift the focus away from constructive political programmes. I request the Election Commission to invite all political parties for a discussion about whether we can devise a system whereby we can simultaneously hold elections for both the Lok Sabha and state assemblies. Such a system will help improve the environment for creating a healthy political structure and the country's long terms developmental strategies.

Ram *Setu*

Over the last few months, a number of issues close to the hearts of the common people have come to the forefront. One such issue is the Ram *Setu*.

The UPA government is seeking to destroy the ancient Ram *Setu* built by Lord Ram.

In this context, one thing that I would definitely like to state is that it is unfortunate the UPA Government has rejected the views of various environmental experts, tsunami experts and other socio-economic experts and is going ahead with a project that will destroy an ancient symbol of our religion and culture. Ram *Setu* is not merely a structure that has been built in the sea and over which one can debate whether it is natural or man made.

In reality, Ram *Setu* is a symbol of India's ancient cultural heritage. Ram Setu is in fact a bridge between India's glorious past and great future. This bridge built by Lord Ram of Ayodhya at Rameshwaram is in fact a bridge between the north and south of our country. Ram *Setu* symbolizes the transcendence of human spirit from the depths of demonic evils towards the heights of divine inspiration.

Therefore, from every aspect, the protection of Ram Setu is a national responsibility and the BJP is committed towards this.

The 150th Anniversary of India's First War of Independence

Today the country is observing the 150th anniversary of the first war of Independence of 1857. We offer our tributes to the main protagonist of this war Nanasahib Peshwa, Mangal Pandey the first person who laid down his life, Tantiya Tope, Rani Laxmi Bai, Veer Kunwar Singh, Begum Harjat Mahal, Bahadur Shah Zafar and all those countless known and unknown persons who willingly sacrificed their lives for independence. On this occasion, let us commit ourselves for defeating all those forces that are damaging the elements of nationalism.

In the history of independent India, the BJP is a unique political party. It is unique not because of one or two factors; our uniqueness is on account of multiple factors. We are the only political party in independent India that has achieved maximum growth as a single entity. In terms of ideology, we too have achieved the maximum growth. We have given coalition politics the most effective and meaningful definition. We have led the most memorable and successful Central government of the country. And we are fortunate to have Atalji, the most popular and greatest leader of the country.

This year is memorable for another reason. This year, respected Atalji completes 50 years in Parliament. We are inspired by Atalji's phenomenal political journey between 1957 and 2007, during which he won the confidence of millions of people and enabled the party to achieve such heights. He is the only political personality of the country who has been continually respected by the people throughout the last 50 years, irrespective of whether he has been in power or not.

I am trying to highlight that whatever is required by a political party, we are indeed fortunate to possess all those capabilities. All we have to do is move ahead with full commitment. It is being said that for the next elections, we only need to prepare ourselves to benefit from the anti-incumbancy feelings prevalent against the UPA Government. While I accept that we will undoubtedly benefit from the wrong policies of the UPA Government, I would not like us to grow only on the basis of a negative vote but rather grow on positive foundations. Prior to this, in 1998 and 1999, people elected us on a positive mandate. I am confident that in the future also we will get a positive mandate and we will succeed in our vision of establishing India as a developed nation.

□

Indo-US Nuclear Deal

21-23 September, 2007 (Bhopal)

We all are aware of the historical role played by Madhya Pradesh in the political journey of the Bharatiya Jan Sangh to Bharatiya Janata Party. Madhya Pradesh has been the *Karmastali* of Rajmata Vijayraje Scindia. In the context of Madhya Pradesh, how can we ever forget the late Kushabhau Thakre who, through continuous travel and ceaseless hard work created a massive organizational structure right upto the grassroots level. From the organizational perspective, Madhya Pradesh has been always strong and vibrant. That is why on numerous occasions the people of Madhya Pradesh have supported us to form the government.

Three months ago we had met at the National Executive Meeting in Delhi. The last three months have witnessed many important changes in the political scenario and are also indicative about some future changes. During the past three months, India completed 60 years of independence. The new President and Vice President of the country have assumed office and the Congress led and Left Front supported UPA Government at the Centre, formed only on the negative basis of opposing the BJP, is evidently on its decline because of its own inherent contradictions.

Given the manner in which the relationship between the Congress and Left Front is increasingly getting strained, clearly indicates that Lok Sabha elections are not far away . However, two additional conclusions are also very clear. Firstly, governments formed on the sole basis of negative opposition can never create a positive environment in the nation. The entire scenario over the past three years from international diplomacy to increasing terrorism and increasing inflation clearly prove this. The second conclusion is that if coalition governments are indispensable in the national political scenario, then only and only the Bharatiya Janata Party is capable of following the *dharma* of coalition politics for taking the country forward in a positive direction. The difference between the performance of

Vajpayeeji's government and the Manmohan Singh government running in the shadow of Sonia Gandhi is clear proof in itself.

Even after three years of being in power, the abysmal track record of the Congress led UPA coalition clearly reflects their complete lack of understanding the basic dharma of coalition politics, an indispensable requirement of the national political scenario. Political maturity is a must for running coalition governments. Both the NDA and BJP displayed this political maturity and also shattered the myth that only the Congress is capable of providing stability. The NDA under the able leadership of Atalji established a new era in Indian politics. Today it is imperative that we firmly strengthen and further expand this process.

Therefore, it is clear that whether the subject is development or stability; in controlling terrorism or controlling inflation; the one and only alternative before the people of the country is a BJP led NDA government. Therefore we stand committed towards further strengthening the NDA so that we can jointly march ahead and once again win the confidence of the people.

The country's changing political situation today offers us an opportunity to once again establish ourselves at the centre of India's politics. However, for this we have to ensure that we successfully convert every challenge into an opportunity.

60 Years of Independence

Recently the country observed the 60th anniversary of independence. After 60 years of independence, we need to examine the extent to which we have established a new India, a dream that was seen by our immortal freedom fighters while laying down their lives during the freedom struggle. The nation also celebrated the 150th anniversary of 1857, the first battle of independence. On this occasion, the BJP has planned nationwide programmes. Today it is important to analyze how after such a long struggle we achieved our independence.

Today's India is an emerging global economic superpower, an emerging global intellectual centre, and an established global military superpower. The genesis of all these three achievements lie in the six years of NDA tenure. Today with pride we hold our heads high when Indian industrialists take over big companies in Europe like Arcelor and Corus, because this is happening for the first time in the history of modern India. However, the other side of the picture is also true as for the first time in India's history, farmers in such large numbers have committed suicide over the last three years. The gap of the difference between the two faces of India's economic picture is so wide and ugly that it needs to be the subject of a national debate. This subject is not merely theoretical but also has real political implications. In recent times, many good governments who undertook numerous praiseworthy developmental activities could not achieve electoral success. Some analysts believe that this happened on account of neglecting the common man, the poor, labourers and farmers.

The BJP's ideological core is cultural nationalism. Over the last one decade, the pace with which the western model of economic development is taking place, equally fast it is also damaging our eternal cultural values, social ideals and family structure. While other political parties may not be according due seriousness on this matter, but from the BJP's perspective, which is dedicated towards India and Indianness, I consider this a serious challenge.

If I have to summarize in one sentence the achievements and challenges of 60 years of independence, then I would say that India's biggest ray of hope for the future is its increasing economic prosperity and intellectual capital. And India 's biggest challenge for the future is poverty associated with agriculture and the villages and the degradation of values in society.

Out of these 60 years, for 54 years the Congress and so called secular parties have led the country. And for 6 years the BJP led NDA government was in power. Today the people of the country can make a clear comparison between 60 years on the one hand and 6 years on the other hand. The picture of 60 years versus 6 years is enough to tell the difference between the capacity and capability of the BJP and the other parties.

The Last Three Months

During the last three months, the Presidential and Vice Presidential elections took place. Both these posts are the highest constitutional posts of the country. While it is important that people with dignity shouls hold these offices, it is also desirable that the selection process should be based on consensus and completed with dignity. During the tenure of the NDA, as the ruling party we attempted an initiative for building a consensus for the posts of both the President and Vice President. However, this time what to speak about building consensus on the subject, the ruling party did not even indirectly speak with the important opposition parties. As our tallest and respected leader Atalji has already suggested in the past, the BJP believes that selection for such high posts as the President should be based on consensus and unopposed.

During this very period, Municipal Corporation elections were held in Punjab where the BJP-Akali Dal coalition succeeded impressively and our coalition captured all the municipal corporations. For this I would like to congratulate the Punjab unit and hope that our organization and coalition both become strong and continuously march ahead.

Many parts of Bihar were seriously impacted by floods. In Bihar there is a BJP-JD(U) coalition government. Our coalition government initiated numerous important steps to deal with this natural calamity. We convey our heartfelt sympathies for the loss of life and property in this calamity.

During this period, in Assam terrorists killed Hindi speaking labourers. To study the situation there, our party sent a Fact Finding Committee under the leadership of Shri Kalraj Mishra. Such activities are despicable attempts to weaken our national unity. We sympathize with all those families and people who lost their lives in this incident.

Failures of the UPA Government

The central government's Common Minimum Programme has been reduced to a Common Minimum Priority where the much touted "aam aadmi" has all but vanished from the consciousness of the Government. High interest rates, high price hike, and high taxation rates are this Government's only achievements.

While everyone can today clearly see the reality of rising prices and farmers suicides, the segment that has been most disappointed by the Congress led government formed in the name of the common man is the youth and women. So far not even a draft of the proposed Women's Reservation Bill has been prepared. Under Sushmaji's Chairmanship, the committee which was constituted in the last national executive for determining the representation of women in the party, will submit its report and then we can all discuss this issue in detail.

For the youth, while our government had created various new opportunities for employment, this government has in the name of Employment Guarantee merely repackaged old programmes.

I am unable to understand how the same Prime Minister who is soft towards terrorism can speak about zero tolerance. However, the Prime Minister should make it clear what is the limit of his tolerance towards the common man who is reeling under the killing impact of inflation and the farmers who are committing suicide under the crushing burden of debts.

Terrorism

The Congress led and Left supported UPA government at the centre has been disappointing at all levels right from the common man to India's international image. Recently, in Hyderabad , bomb blasts by terrorists claimed the lives of numerous people. We all convey our sympathies to the families of those persons who were killed in these terrorist strikes. However, this is nothing new in the tenure of the UPA Government. Prior to this, Bangalore , Mumbai, Aurangabad , Delhi , Kashi, Ayodhya and Nagpur have already been targeted. All these cities are in some way or the other symbols of India 's unique identity. What is surprising is that these incidents continued unabated despite the public statements made by the government's intelligence agencies, foreign intelligence agencies and even the National Security Advisor.

It is unfortunate that our citizens are being forced to live in an environment of heightened insecurity. The government's general soft approach in dealing with the perpetrators of terror and extremism has only emboldened their resolve in striking at will and causing higher levels of loss of life and collateral damage.

What is extremely disturbing is that when one carefully analyses the internal and external security situation of the country, the tell tale signs of politicization of national security and strategic interests at the altar of blatant vote bank politics is starkly evident by a government whose only claim to success is a sordid story of lack of political will to find solutions that solve the challenges before the nation.

At the external level, the recent Al Qaeda statement of attacking the US and India coupled with an explosive and internally imploding security situation in Pakistan, demand for further strengthening our efforts in ruthlessly countering terrorist designs with resolve and farsightedness and also enhancing our security presence on the borders and in all sensitive and violence prone areas.

According to news reports published in the newspapers, the northern commander-in-chief of the Indian Army, while opposing any move by the government to consider a ceasefire in the month of Ramzan had said that about 4 to 5 thousand militants are ready to infiltrate into Kashmir from the Pakistani side. 52 camps are operating within Pakistan for training the terrorists. To deal with this situation, in Jammu & Kashmir, the army requires a tenfold increase over the current number of troops there. It is ironical that in stark contrast to the requirements of the situation, in Jammu & Kashmir, the Government has taken a decision for withdrawal of troops from the terrorism affected regions of the state. Any such decision can prove extremely damaging.

Internally the unabated march of the naxalites and expansion of the red corridor, the continuing saga of violence against Hindi speaking people in Assam, the overall environment of insecurity in other parts of the northeast, and general drift in the national security situation indicate the complete failure of the Government in boosting the sense of security of the common man.

When someone is taken into police custody on the charge of being a terrorist, our Prime Minister is unable to sleep. I would like to ask why this Government does not feel the same concern when our brave soldiers become victims of terrorist attacks and also when despite being inflicted to torture by terrorists they still do not reveal our nation's security secrets. The government's discriminatory attitude towards those accused of terrorism and the soldiers who fight against terrorism is deplorable. On behalf of the BJP, I convey our support and solidarity to all the soldiers of our security forces who are involved in the fight against terrorism.

Instead of sending out a strong and unequivocal signal to the supporters and perpetrators of such heinous acts that we will not tolerate such anti-national designs, the Government as part of its blatant policy of appeasing the minorities, is busy painting everything in communal tones. On the serious subject of internal security, the BJP will not permit the constituents of the UPA to adopt narrow and competitive appeasement policies and dilute the required levels of national preparedness in dealing with terror. The nation has paid a very high price in dealing with terrorism. Mr Prime Minister, kindly rise above the politics of appeasement and let not the blood of innocent victims of terrorism tarnish the dignity of the highest executive office of the country.

As a nationalist party the Bharatiya Janata Party will not permit any compromise with our national security and will oppose any such policy of the government. Even today and in the national interest, we will fully support every honest move of the government to demolish terrorism.

The UPA Government claims that the withdrawal of POTA is one of its achievements. We have always opposed this move. Our demand is for an alternative law. Today India is the only big country in the world that despite being targeted by the Al Qaeda and other prominent terrorist organizations, continues to fight terrorism without any specific law against it. This is an unequal battle which reduces the morale of the security forces. If the BJP once again gets the opportunity to form the government in the Centre, we will reverse this policy of the current government and will firmly fight against terrorism and pass an effective anti-terrorism law.

Sachar Committee

As part of its blatant vote bank politics, the Sachhar Committee formed by the Congress led UPA Government has suggested many unwise recommendations. However, Central Government has decided to implement them both in letter and spirit. According to a recent directive of the Central government's Department of Personnel & Training (DOPT), all the State Governments and Union Territories have been asked to ensure that Muslim policemen be posted in police stations and posts with large Muslim population and there should be more Muslim teachers and health personnel in Muslim dominated areas. The UPA Government is embarking on a dangerous path of sowing the seeds of communal divisions that can seriously impact the country's social fabric and even its unity and integrity. Prior to this, the Government has undertaken many measures such as the headcount of Muslims in the armed forces and the Prime Minister accepting that Muslims should have the first right on national resources, all these can sow the deep seeds of communal discord.

The first right of any community on national resources, the communal segmentation of the army, prioritization of loaning facilities in the banks for a particular community and now a communal approach to security and policing. Are these being undertaken to protect the secular structure of our country? Will it strengthen India's current Constitutional framework? Will it promote communal harmony or hatred? On behalf of the party, I want to raise these questions before the people. Let the people of the country think about this and give an appropriate reply to the Government.

Disappearing *Gram Swarajya*

For us villages, the poor and farmers are not just a slogan. They are the primary foundation of India 's economy. Every leader who has understood India's real identity, understands this core substance. Be it Mahatma Gandhi, Vinobha Bhave or the source of our ideological inspiration Pandit Deendayal Upadhayaya. Gandhiji's "*Gramodaya*", Vinobhaji's "*Sarvodaya*" and Deendayalji's "*Antyodaya*" all primarily focused on village based socio-economic empowerment. Gandhiji had also announced *Gram Swarajya*. Today the self styled successors of Mahatma Gandhi are managing the affairs of the country. However, the village itself has disappeared from their *Swarajya*. It appears that villages have totally been removed from our imagination, our developmental vision and even all announcements. The BJP will not allow this to happen. Our unequivocal belief is that, be it the government or the organization, the village must be made the primary basis for the development of society. That is why the village, the poor and the farmers are not just a mere slogan but are an indispensable part our political ideology.

Farmers Plight

The BJP is fully committed for ensuring that in our nation's march towards economic development, the urban poor and the farmers in the villages must get their appropriate share. The government constantly disregarding farmers, the vicious cycle of debt forcing farmers towards suicides, the ever increasing prices of seeds and fertilizers, farmers not getting the appropriate Minimum Support Price, and the government's not only inappropriate but also suspicious policy for import of foodgrains have all collectively created such an environment that the current UPA government at the Centre has literally become a nightmare for the farmers. To effectively highlight these very problems of the farmers, on 20th August the BJP organized a massive Kisan Rally in Delhi and then while marching towards Parliament, respected Advaniji, myself, the party's complete senior leadership alongwith thousands of farmers courted arrest. The success of the Kisan Rally has silenced our all those opponents who used to raise doubts about our grassroot strength. I congratulate our complete organizational cadre and the Kisan Morcha for the success of the Kisan Rally. To highlight the plight of the farmers, the BJP is considering a widespread programme. The National Executive should also think about this.

Wheat Import Scam

The wheat import policy of this government is not only directionless and insensitive towards farmers but also is suspicious. Over the last three months, the government first rejected buying wheat at $263 per MT by stating that the price was too high. Suddenly, within only 10 days, the government approved the order for import of wheat at $325 per MT. Not only this, the government has further decided to order an additional 8 lakh tonnes at a price of $390 per MT. The entire process indicates towards the existence of a scam.

Indian farmers unable to get remunerative and timely support prices, are over-burdened in debt and are regularly committing suicide. On the one hand, the government is willing to only pay approximately Rs. 850/- per quintal to the Indian farmer despite their demands for Rs 1100/- per quintal. On the other hand they are purchasing foreign wheat at approximately Rs. 1600/- per quintal. This is clear proof of the government's intentions and their total insensitivity towards farmers. The BJP demands that the Minimum Support Price for wheat and other agricultural produce be immediately raised for farmers to get their appropriate rights.

The Suffering of the Middle Class

Given the developments and emergence of new economic opportunities over the last 15 years, both the number and influence of the middle class has increased in India. This includes the upper middle class, middle class and lower middle class. This is the very middle class that is emerging as the face of a new India. However, with the UPA Government coming to power, even this class is facing new problems. Owning a single house is both the primary dream and requirement of the middle class. During the tenure of the NDA government, interest rates on housing loans were at their lowest levels. Today they have increased by over one-and-a-half-times. Owning a single house is once again becoming a dream. All sorts of new levies, the slowing down of numerous infrastructural projects are already having an adverse impact on development. Given the tremendous rise in the cost of living and the resultant burden of new taxes on the middle class, the BJP demands that in the forthcoming budget the government should raise the income tax limit and the income tax rates should be made more rational and practical. In addition to this, also provide specific measures for our various income groups, the poor, and for people in the agricultural sector.

Discarding the Opposition

With the Congress government coming to power at the Centre, diametrically contrary to the established democratic norms and traditions, the manner in which the opposition parties are being treated is not only inappropriate but is also alarming. Over the past three years, the manner in which our governments in Goa and Jharkhand were dismissed; the misuse of the office of Governor in Jharkhand and Bihar to prevent the formation of our government; disregarding the demands made by our state governments; and above all, no dialogue or involvement even on the subject of foreign policy which requires consensus among all political parties. The opposition was not privy to any type of information on the Indo-US Nuclear Deal. And it was not deemed fit to even open a dialogue with the opposition prior to the President and Vice-President elections. All these instances clearly indicate that the attitude of the Central Government towards the opposition is not only discarding and disrespectful but also despotic. These are not righteous indications for democratic traditions. This despotic attitude is an integral part of the Congress' nature. The tradition of the Congress has also been similar. The imposition of Emergency in 1975 marked the high point of its complete arrogance.

Whether it is within or outside Parliament, the government has never made any attempt to take the opposition into confidence. That is why on numerous occasions the proceedings of Parliament got stalled and precious Parliamentary time was wasted. The BJP believes that Parliament is a forum for debate and discussion and that's why its time should be suitably utilized. However, on account of the discarding and despotic attitude of the government, numerous such situations arose that we never wanted.

Even more worrying and ludicrous is that the allies of the government themselves are creating barriers in the smooth functioning of Parliament, which results in wastage of precious national time. The Left Front opposes the government outside Parliament. Inside Parliament they stall the proceedings but always support the government to prevent it from falling. This height of duplicity is not only being witnessed in politics but is also being seen in Parliament. The Parliament is a forum to solve the problems of the country. However, given the conduct of the UPA and its allies, the dignity of this august forum for solving problems has also degenerated.

The manner in which the Left Front parties are continuously enjoying the benefits of power without accountability is a peculiar example in itself. Over the last one-and-a-half years probably the Left Front has not won even a single seat in the assembly elections of Goa , Uttar Pradesh , Uttarakhand, Punjab, and the municipal corporation elections of Punjab, Maharashtra, Delhi and Uttar Pradesh . However, given the manner in which the Left Front as a super national party is bulldozing its point of view on every national policy makes one wonder whether the Left Front in a complete anti-thesis has moved away from the concept of Marxism and emerged as the new "political bourgeois".

Nuclear Deal & Indo-US Relations

The BJP has already made its position clear on the recently concluded Indo-US Nuclear Deal. From time to time we have been reacting to the various steps taken by the government in context of this deal. However, over the past few days, the manner in which the Left Front has been raising the issue, appears to be guided less by national interests and more by prejudices. Our opposition to the deal is not opposition for the sake of opposition, nor it is the virulent anti-Americanism of the Left Front. Our opposition is for India's sovereignty and national pride. Our opposition is to prevent our strategic independence becoming strategic subservience.

The BJP will neither oppose nor support any country based on prejudices. It is worth recalling that the NDA under the visionary leadership of Shri Atal Bihari Vajpayeeji laid the foundations for the paradigm shift that ushered in the golden era of the relationship between the United States of America and India. But we initiated this tectonic shift in the existing level of strategic cooperation and understanding between both countries following the 1998 Pokhran tests - after we established the might of India 's national pride and sovereignty in the international community. In 1999, despite facing economic sanctions, we did not allow the passage of a resolution against India's economic interests at the World Trade Organization meeting in Seattle. This indicates that we initiated the new era of friendship with the United States on an equal footing and after protecting both our strategic and economic interests. Under the NDA, India's diplomatic relations substantially improved not only with the United States but also with other countries of the world. We will continue with this even in the future also.

Be it the Congress or the Left Front, in 1998 they all opposed the Pokhran Tests. The Left had even called these tests as unnecessary. In 1964 the Left supported China's nuclear tests and in 1998 opposed India 's nuclear tests. But today they have become supporters for the independence to conduct nuclear tests.

It is clear that both the Congress and Left have never been concerned about India's nuclear capability in the past or present. They are only playing politics on the nuclear issue.

The government has committed a mistake by compromising on India's long term strategic interests. Under no cost will we ever accept our atomic sovereignty to be controlled or our foreign policy to be influenced. That's why we want that before finally accepting the Indo-US Nuclear Deal a Joint Parliamentary Committee should study it. To prevent a repeat of this in the future, a mechanism needs to be evolved so that any international commitment is operationalized only after parliament endorses it. Parliament reflects the collective will and aspirations of our people. And Parliamentary approval will ensure that none of our present and future national interests can ever be mortgaged or compromised with on account of the myopic vision of a government and its negotiators.

Neighbouring Countries

With the UPA coming to power at the Centre, it is well known that our foreign policy has become unsuccessful and there seems to be only policy confusion regarding our neighborhood. By acknowledging in Havana that Pakistan is also a victim of terrorism, the government in one stroke diluted the strategic and psychological advantage that we had achieved after several years of efforts and through various agreements. Recently, General Musharraf in a Pakistani weekly television programme remarked that they have not abandoned their old issues and they have even made Government of India to agree in accepting Jammu & Kashmir as the core issue. General Musharraf termed this as a "sea change" in Indian diplomacy. One wonders into which sea of uncertainty will this "sea change" push Indian interests.

Under the NDA tenure this very General Musharraf had not only declared his commitment to prevent anti-India terrorist activities from his soil but had also said that we can keep the Kashmir issue aside and begin discussions on other issues. This changing attitude of Pakistan is a clear proof of the current UPA Government's utter diplomatic failure as compared to the NDA Government.

There appears to be confusion about where we stand on the Sri Lankan issue. The government's policy on Nepal under the influence of the Left has moved in such a direction that it is creating a threat even for our own internal security. Domestic turbulence in Pakistan already existed. Bangladesh is now witnessing a similar type of internal turbulence. Bangladesh is emerging as a new centre for anti-India activities. ULFA extremists are taking shelter in Bangladesh. They are running their terrorist camps there and cause bloodshed in Assam at will. The ISI has strengthened its stronghold in Bangladesh. Despite all this, the Government of India has not registered a protest with Bangladesh which would have at least sent a message that India is unhappy with the activities there.

In the meantime, the UPA Government is twiddling its fingers and burying its head in the sand like an ostrich while Pakistan and China are busy bolstering their presence all across the region. China has established a deep naval base at Gwadar in Pakistan. China has now emerged as the biggest arms supplier to Bangladesh. China has also set up monitoring centres in some islands of Myanmar and Sri Lanka to keep watch on the movements of the Indian Navy. Given India's slack diplomacy, China has once again raised its claim over Arunachal Pradesh. Pakistan is getting involved in the internal affairs of Sri Lanka. There are constant reports of an association between the ISI and the Maoists in Nepal.

This indicates that in all the activities that are taking place from the Himalayas to our coastal boundaries within our neighboring countries, we do not see any possibility of being able to protect our strategic and political interests, given the UPA Government being in power.

Ram *Setu*

Be it India's international image or the country's cultural identity, nothing is secure in the UPA's tenure. Hindu centres of reverence are being constantly damaged after the UPA-Left Front coalition government has come to power. Over the last few days, this reached the extreme when the Archaeological Survey of India, in an affidavit submitted to the Supreme Court on the Ram *Setu* issue, stated that there is no proof that Lord Ram and all the other characters of the Ramayana ever existed. The BJP's effective agitation forced the government to withdraw the affidavit and seek three months extension. However, the affidavit has established the government's anti-Hindu mindset.

On the questions of scientific and historical fact, I would like to ask the government whether it has undertaken any scientific effort to establish the historical reality of all those places in the country that are associated with the Ramayana? If not, then on what basis did it submit such a colossal statement? Subjects related to people's faith should not be linked with science and historical reality. Otherwise this will result in opening a pandora's box where the key elements of various religions will be interfered with and this will lead to serious communal tension.

We believe that Ram is integrally enmeshed in each and every grain of India 's physical, emotional and social fabric and he eternally inspires our people. If Ram did not exist, then I would like to ask the Congress Party which is running the Central Government, was Mahatma Gandhi's dream of *Ram Rajya* a delusion based on a hollow foundation? The self styled successors of Mahatma Gandhi may not have any respect for the common Hindu beliefs, but they should at the very least respect the Ram inscribed on Mahatma Gandhi 's memorial. By disrespecting Lord Ram, the Congress Party has taken vote bank politics to its lowest point. The Prime Minister should publicly apologize for the unpardonable crime of politically playing with people's beliefs.

My demand for an apology is not for political reasons but is based on our reverence towards India's eternal beliefs since not even the foreign rulers of the country under colonial rule had the courage to reject the existence of Lord Ram. Then why is this happening under this Congress led government? What are the reasons behind this, which power is guiding all this, and why is this power seeking to challenge the core foundations of India's eternal beliefs? The people of the country want an answer to these questions.

Ram *Setu* is not a mere structure made from rocks and stones that can be debated as to whether it is man-made or natural. On the contrary, Ram *Setu* is a bridge of India's eternal values, a bridge that symbolizes the foundations of *Dharma* through the obliteration of demonic tendencies. Not only from a religious or cultural point of view, from the perspective of scientific, strategic, prevention of tsunamis and nuclear energy, the destruction of Ram Setu will be detrimental for India. The BJP will oppose this at every level.

Minority Government

On account of its unsuccessful and insensitive policies, this government has already lost the confidence of the people. And now allies like the DMK who are within the Government, parties like the Left Front which are supporting it from outside, are all speaking against the government. This indicates that the government has lost the confidence of the people, lost the confidence of its allies and lost the confidence of the parties which are supporting it from outside. Therefore, today it can no longer be assumed that this government enjoys the adequate confidence of Parliament. In my opinion, this government has for all practical purposes become a minority government within Parliament. This is the fear which has led to the Parliament being adjourned sine die. On behalf of the people of the country and to prove its credibility in these circumstances, I urge the government to immediately call a session of Parliament and seek a vote of confidence.

And if this government does not have the courage to face Parliament, then it should quit office and approach the people. The BJP is prepared for this and challenges the government to approach the people.

BJP–Symbolizing Development

It is no secret that the model of development which was adopted by the NDA Government at the Centre during its tenure of 6 years, is responsible for laying the foundation of today's emerging new India . However, it is disheartening to learn that the extensive infrastructural projects which we had launched, their pace has either slowed down or they have been placed in cold storage. Considered the *"Dream Project"* of respected Atalji, the National Highway Development Programme according to the basic plan of action should almost have been completed by this time. However, this has not happened. The pace of the *Pradhan Mantri Gramin Sadak Yojana* is also unsatisfactory. The Agricultural Income Insurance Scheme was halted even before it was launched. This government has not even discussed the plan for opening new All India Institute of Medical Sciences in 6 states. The government did not deem it fit to even consider the various programmes started by the NDA for strengthening irrigation and the inter-linking of rivers project.

Even today, wherever our state governments are in power, there are many programmes that are worth highlighting. We do not consider the Centre's Employment Guarantee Scheme appropriate, yet even here, the BJP ruled states are leading in its implementation. Our governments have also been successful in effectively controlling jehadi terrorism and maintaining law and order. Given the pathetic condition in which we had inherited Madhya Pradesh, we have been successful in dramatically improving its condition.

Forthcoming Challenges

In the forthcoming months, very soon the Gujarat elections will be held. The government of Gujarat has established itself as a role model for development. Gujarat 's rate of development is one-and-a-half to one-and-three-fourth times higher than the country's rate of growth. The Gujarat government has been successful in implementing Special Economic Zones without any controversies and also in attracting the maximum foreign direct investment. Our government has been in office for the past 12 years. Shri Narendra Modi has set the record of being the longest serving Chief Minister of Gujarat. Even former President Dr. Abdul Kalam and the Rajiv Gandhi Foundation have praised the Gujarat government. In the forthcoming elections, all our leaders and workers will definitely collectively pave the way for victory. I am confident that all our leaders and workers will together ensure that the BJP emerges victorious in the elections.

The assembly elections in some states which are due next year are fast approaching us and we have to prepare ourselves for them right from now itself. The Lok Sabha elections appear to be fast approaching. We should not proceed on the basis that we will be the automatic beneficiaries of the anti-incumbency wave against the central government. To effectively capitalize on this anti-incumbency, our organization and Members of Parliament have to literally tighten their belts and immediately become active in their respective areas. Normally, many of our MPs are unable to get re-elected. If we are able to control this situation, then in the next Lok Sabha our numbers can be very effective.

Testing Times

In various states, the evolving current political situation clearly exemplifies that in the future we will have to prepare ourselves for new challenges in context of the political and social adjustments. Among the large states, in Maharashtra the atmosphere of confusion regarding the alliance has come to an end. In Karnataka, I expect both our organization and coalition will remain strong. In Uttar Pradesh, the largest state of the country, we need to make efforts to once again establish our old position. In Rajasthan, Madhya Pradesh, Gujarat and Chhattisgarh we will have to prove our capacity to hold onto our existing position. Among the northeastern states, the elections in Nagaland, Meghalaya and Tripura are not far away. Our coalition government is in power in Nagaland. I am hopeful that we will put up a good performance in the Nagaland elections. In addition to this, there can be numerous opportunities for us in Arunachal Pradesh, Manipur and in Assam, the biggest state of the north east.

Last time, I had charged the government for not according adequate attention towards the northeast. We had demanded that the government should make provisions for a special package for the northeast region keeping in mind its unique geographical, social and cultural realities. I once again urge the government to meet this demand of the BJP.

After the defeat in the 2004 Lok Sabha elections, in addition to being politically unsuccessful, even the media questioned our ideological commitment. Within the NDA, with some parties we witnessed a change of emotions as compared to our previously harmonious relations. To summarize, one can say that our opponents created an atmosphere of confusion about the BJP's organizational capability, coalition capability and ideological commitment. We have to end this atmosphere of confusion. That is why whenever the forthcoming elections are held, we will have to prove ourselves not on any one but on all three fronts.

BJP at Every Booth

Our organizational strength has always been our uniqueness. To further expand this very strength, the party took a decision that our organization should be expanded at every booth. I hope that the organizations of all states are fully involved in this programme. From time to time, I will also attempt to directly telephone and speak with the members of these booth committees. Only recently I directly spoke with Raghurai, a member of the booth committee in Gujarat's Rajkot district. We have to establish relations upto this level of society. Only in this lies the hidden reality of our organizational strength, the key to social justice and the dream of Deendayalji's *Antyadaya*.

Resolve

In conclusion, I would like to remind about last National Executive Meeting held in Bhopal. Last time, 11 years ago in 1996, on 21st, 22nd and 23rd June, our National Executive Meeting was held in Bhopal in this very Deendayal Upadhayaya Hall. The Bhopal National Executive Meeting was historical. In that meeting our respected leader Atalji had come after submitting his resignation as Prime Minister for thirteen days. The political situation in the country was taking a new shape. In Parliament we had emerged as the largest party. While the people of the country were unhappy to witness the resignation of their beloved leader Atalji, the intrigues of the Congress and Left had anguished the country. In 1996 all the so called secular parties were actively trying to stop the BJP, but in 1998 we moved ahead. Atalji as Prime Minster for 6 years enhanced India's global prestige; by taking along 24 other parties, crafted the history of coalition politics.

Even today the situation is similar. There are obviously some changes in the roles. The Congress led government is being supported by the Left Front from outside; in 1996 the only difference was that the Left was in government and the Congress was supporting it from outside. At that time also the ruling dispensation was in minority. Today also the UPA is a minority. At that time mid term elections took place, and today also there are similar indications. At that time the country was experiencing a frightening phase of uncertainty, misgovernance and instability. Even then the ruling party and the supporting allies were busy checkmating each other. By and large even today the situation is similar. Here we need to think about how to change this situation. The place is the same, the circumstances are the same, the party is the same, all we need to do is once again bring to the fore the same self-confidence and commitment. I am confident that like the last National Executive of Bhopal, we will once again create new history. And by winning the confidence of the people, we will convert the dream of *Mahan* Bharat into a reality.

□

Society Facing Severe Crisis

National Executive (New Delhi)

Since 1996 the Bharatiya Janata Party never looked back. BJP continuously kept marching ahead. The time arrived when NDA came to power and Atalji became the Prime Minister of the country. I once again want to remind that the pledge in Bhopal is once again appearing auspicious for us. The political situation that has emerged between the last executive and this one makes it clear that in the coming days NDA is again becoming extremely powerful. I fully believe that string of successes would further lead us to victory in Lok Sabha elections.

The year 2007 has become significant for the politics of BJP. This year, we have won in four state assembly elections. It is the first time in the history of BJP that we formed four governments in one year. The month of December of the year 2007 was also very important for us. In this month, we have decided the name of Mananiya Shri Lal Krishna Advani as the future Prime Minister of the country from the side of our party. In the last week of the same month we won the elections held for the assemblies of Gujarat and Himachal Pradesh. The victory of Gujarat has silenced all our opponents. This victory has sent a positive message with regard to our ideological commitment and our ability in the field of development. In Himachal Pradesh, by defeating the Congress we were able to snatch one more state from its fold. In the last ten months, the BJP and its allies won three states viz. Punjab, Uttarakhand and Himachal Pradesh where Congress was in power. At the same time in Gujarat we retained our government in a prestigious contest.

I extend heartiest congratulations to the common people of Gujarat and Himachal Pradesh, activists and organization along with our popular Chief Ministers Narendra Bhai Modi and Prof. Prem Kumar Dhumal for victories in these states.

NDA–Need of the Nation today

The people have completely rejected the Congress led UPA. In Bhopal, I had said that UPA lost the confidence of the Parliament for all practical purposes because many of its supporters have separated from it and the parties (Leftists) that are supporting are also continuously opposing it openly. If we look at the scenario today, the situation has gone too far. If we look at the elections and political developments then I can claim that UPA has also lost the confidence of the people.

In the last three and half years, Congress has lost its governments in six states. Its ally RJD has too lost power in Bihar. Telangana Rashtriya Samiti (TRS) has withdrawn the support. Shri Vaiko's party in Tamil Nadu has also left the UPA. Lok Dal has also distanced itself. Though technically Congress has BSP's support but the situation between them is such that both are engaged in publicly denigrating each other. The behaviour of the Left Front, which is extending support from outside, is known to all.

I had termed UPA an unnatural alliance right from the outset. The only aim of the UPA was to stop BJP from coming to power. I feel contended in saying that in comparison to *Mananiya* Atal Bihari Vajpayee led NDA government; the people must be definitely finding UPA not only a failed but also a worthless government. The more bitterly the leftists criticize the Central Government in media the more warmly they are hand in hand insidiously. In fact, Congress and Left are engaged in befooling the people through their shadow boxing. The people of the country are intelligent and now they have understood these tactics. In the United Progressive Alliance there is nothing that either appears 'united' or 'progressive'. UPA had never had the confidence of the people and the "artificial confidence" that they had gained by sheer manipulations, they have failed to respect that too. People are getting united against UPA government. An atmosphere against this alliance and government has been created in the country.

It is not easy to run an alliance by mutual trust and coordination. The manner in which the BJP has observed the responsibilities of alliance and continues to follow that responsibility in several states has become an ideal in the Indian politics. Along with Centre, in the states, our alliances with Shiv Sena in Maharashtra for more than two decades, with Akali Dal in Punjab and with JD (U) in Bihar for more than one decade and with Biju Janata Dal in Orissa for nine years have been continuing successfully. All these alliances are among the most stable alliances in the Indian politics.

Today, we can claim what millions of people also believe that under the leadership of Atal ji, the BJP led NDA government had opened the doors for all round development of the country. The prestige of India increased in the world. The new light of hope dawned on the people. The most important thing was that the leadership of Prime Minister Atal Bihari Vajpayee in the BJP led NDA government was recognized not only in the country but also in the entire world. Therefore, when the people are rejecting UPA, BJP led NDA would be their natural choice. NDA is the need of the hour and the demand of the nation. Therefore Bharatiya Janata Party has started to take successful and effective steps keeping in mind the need of the hour and demand of the nation.

When I am talking about the NDA as 'natural choice', I also want to clarify that in view of the coming Lok Sabha elections we have declared the 'natural choice' of our Party and the country, *Mananiya* Advaniji as the future Prime Minister of India. I feel elated in saying that by approving our decision of declaring *Mananiya* Advaniji as future Prime Minister all our friends in NDA have given a message of unity and collectivity. I believe that this collectivity would lead us to success. For this, I extend my thanks to all the constituents of NDA on behalf of national executive of Bharatiya Janata Party. The name of *Mananiya* Advaniji is well known in the Indian politics having a special place among all the political parties in the contemporary politics. Respected Advani ji has given memorable contribution along with Respected Atal ji for the political rise of BJP and I hope that Bharatiya Janata Party under his leadership would achieve memorable victory in the next election. *Mananiya* Atal Bihari Vajpayee has blessed *Mananiya* Advani ji while handing over responsibilities to him. Atal ji has always been source of our inspiration and guide and he will remain so in future too. We all are fortunate that we have been getting the guidance of *Mananiya* Atal ji and *Mananiya* Advani ji all these years.

Expansion of BJP

In our political journey numerous challenges came before us from time to time. We have continuously marched ahead by giving befitting response to all these challenges. We are the first political party in India that came to power after being in the opposition and raised our stature at par with Congress and even surpassed it in many aspects.

Bharatiya Janata Party is the only party in the country which has not only expanded itself through political struggle but continuously maintained strong and live internal democracy. In our party, organizational elections are always held on time. Regular meetings take place. Our commitment to the ideology remains intact. We view politics not from purely political angle but from social and national point of view. Therefore we consider BJP as a movement for cultural nationalism along with a political party. People are continuously accepting us due to our policies and principles. Our acceptability is continuously increasing. We will have to work day in and day out so that our acceptability increases more and more and we are accepted by every one.

On the organizational front we have taken the programme of organizing "BJP on every booth" to make its expansion practical and broader; it has to be achieved actively. I hope that in all the states this task must have been completed, if it is yet to be completed in some places, it must be in the process of completion.If we are able to implement the programme of "BJP on every booth", then I can bet that no one can stop BJP led NDA from coming to the power in the Centre. At the same time it will make a stable base of power on the ground which will carry forward the organization in the days to come.

Coming Elections

In the month of February 2008, elections are going to be held in Nagaland, Meghalaya and Tripura. I have complete faith that in these states people would be relieved of the incompetent administration and in Nagaland where Democratic Alliance of Nagaland was in power of which BJP is a constituent and which was wrongly removed before the completion of its tenure, the people of Nagaland will give a fitting reply to this injustice in the elections and our alliance will again get victory.

In May 2008, elections may take place in Karnataka. In Karnataka we fully abided by the dharma of alliance but the manner in which our alliance partner behaved has raised a big question mark on the credibility of the politics of alliance. I have complete faith that in the coming elections in Karnataka the BJP government would be formed.

Though elections in all the states are important for us, in the states where we are in power our responsibilities increase in the assembly elections particularly in Madhya Pradesh, Chhattisgarh and Rajasthan. Elections are also supposed to be held in Delhi but eyes are fixed on BJP ruled states. I urge the state leadership of these states to completely engage themselves with the preparations for the electoral battle from now itself. We have much more task ahead and time is limited. Our governments have worked very hard in their respective states and unfolded new dimensions of development. Our Chief Ministers should emphasize on the issues that bring the common people nearer to them and they are made aware of the government's work. The government and the organization will have to jointly organize a massive campaign for this.

We have shattered the myth in Gujarat that BJP government cannot return to power twice or thrice. Madhya Pradesh, Chhattisgarh and Rajasthan should also try to repeat this kind of success. The activists and leadership have agni-pariksha before them. In all these three states our organization is also very strong. We will have to keep ourselves free from the overconfidence owing to strong organization and being in power. We will have to engage ourselves in the work with collectivity and coordination keeping in minds the ground realities until we are able to reach our goal. I fully believe that we will together awaken the people and gain majority in these states and in the Centre.

The attempt to endanger National Unity and Integrity

Never before the governments at the Centre had taken the decisions that would have created so much problem for the national unity and integrity. Every decision of the government is supposed to strengthen unity and integrity of the nation. But it appears that the UPA on the line of the British government has started taking decisions on the basis of 'Divide and Rule' policy which might be in accordance with their political interests but its impact was dangerous for the country. Can opposing *Vande Mataram* and the Prime Minister stating that the Muslims have first claim over country's resources not become a danger to national unity? Had there been no brotherly relations in India and our secular sentiments not strong, the atmosphere would have deteriorated. UPA government did not stop there. It seems that it has decided to invoke reaction. How much is it fair to give communal colour to poverty? The notion of minority community is itself dangerous but it is also entirely baseless from the point of view of economy. In the fight against poverty and for development communal views should be entirely abandoned but we have information that UPA government has selected the districts where minority population is more. The central government will pay special attention for the development of these districts for which special provisions would be made in the budget.

Bharatiya Janata Party strongly condemns this kind of mentality of UPA government and warns the UPA not to put secularism, harmony and fraternity of India at stake for the sake of its vote bank politics.

Common Man: Basic needs and Crisis of Security

Today, neither the basic needs like bread and house are easily available to the common man nor his life is secure. Bread is becoming dearer and life is becoming cheap. It is an irony that in the midst of the talk of India becoming a developed country starvation deaths are taking place and food riots are occurring. Price rise has adversely affected the budget of the common man. The fierceness of situation may be understood from the fact that the godowns that were full with food grains in the time of NDA are today filled by the wheat imported from Australia. The short sightedness and incompetence of UPA has drifted the country far away.

The prices of pulses, vegetables, bread, fruit, milk, salt and cooking gas have been continuously increasing. It appears that peace and happiness of common man have been eclipsed. The farmers' suicide is on rise. The farmers of India have been pushed out of the agenda of UPA Government. In the last four years, UPA has not taken a single step to stop increasing suicides of the farmers. The leftists who talk a lot about poor farmers are maintaining studied silence to remain in the comforts of power. Leftists have not spoken a single word against rising prices even in Parliament. The real picture of Human Development has come to the fore in the Arjun Sen Gupta report. In this report Shri Gupta has said that 77% of the population is living in extremely miserable conditions. Most of these somehow manage to earn a paltry sum of Rs.20/- per day. The era of economic inequality is sending warning signals to us.

Unbalanced Development

There are extreme imbalances in economy under UPA Government. While 70% of the country's population is dependent on agriculture, according to economy survey 2006-07 agriculture has a share of only 18.5% in the GDP. It means that the contribution of majority of people in GDP is only 18.5 per cent. It makes it clear that the economic condition of the majority i.e. 70 percent people in the country is extremely miserable.

At present there is 39 crore labour force in the country. Among them, 22.5 crore are engaged in agriculture, 5 crore in industries and 10.5 crore are engaged in service sector. These data make it clear that the production by more than half of the labour force is meagre.

Starvation deaths have increased in our country. Official estimates suggest that the number of people living below the poverty-line has decreased on paper but on real ground the number has increased. At the same time there is evidence that in the last three-four years starvation deaths have increased.

Terrorism related incidents and need of POTA

After the UPA came to power certain decisions were taken which were beyond the comprehension of the people. POTA was one of them. We have also been continuously demanding the enactment of POTA. Our demand is legitimate but UPA government fails to understand it. We have been demanding the implementation of POTA from the time UPA came to power. If we ponder over as to why POTA is needed then we will find that after the enactment of POTA terrorism related incidents had decreased. After the repeal of POTA explosions took place in Ayodhya, in the precincts of Ram *Janama Bhoomi*, Shramjivi express near Jaunpur, Delhi, Banglore, Varanasi, RSS office, trains of Mumbai, ISCKON temple in Imphal, Malegaon, Train in West Bengal, Samjhauta Express, Mecca Masjid in Hyderabad, Gorakhpur, Lumbini Park in Hyderabad, Ajmer Sharif, court complex in Lucknow-Varanasi-Faizabad and in CRPF camp in Rampur. In this manner we see that after the repeal of POTA terrorism related incidents have increased manifold. UPA Government takes all decisions with an eye on the vote bank which is completely inappropriate.

Uttar Pradesh is becoming a new target of the terrorists. It appears that terrorism has been able to strike roots there. It is a matter of concern for all of us. There is no central policy for India infested with Naxal-secessionist forces. 165 districts of the 14 states of the country are affected. Even the Prime Minister has himself accepted this fact. But till now the UPA Government has made no concrete policy. None of the terrorism related incidents that took place during UPA rule has been conclusively solved. It points to the abject failure of the government.

The crisis of security is not unilinear but it is multi dimensional. The national security, food security, energy security, internal security, strategic security is in danger. Now a new dimension has been added. Today our cultural security is also in danger. The situation has become unfortunate to such an extent that the government files an affidavit in the Supreme Court shamelessly stating that *Bhagwan* Shri Ram had no existence at all. The government which has no faith in Bhagwan Shri Ram, there is no way that the people will have faith in such a government.

Farmers and Workers: Victims of Leftist Violence

Farmers and workers are oppressed by the undemocratic behaviour of the Leftists in the states ruled by them. The real face, character and functioning of the Leftists was exposed in Nandigram and Singur. The Leftists have no qualms in killing the farmers and workers of the same suppressed class of whose welfare they talk about to capture power. The fault of the farmers is only that they are demanding their rights from the Leftist government. Not only the police but according to the news reports, CPM cadres also resorted to unrestrained firing. All human values were trampled in Nandigram. The governor, Judges of the High Court and intellectuals in West Bengal have strongly condemned the Leftist government. This incident has sent a shock wave to the entire country. I clearly believe that the attack on farmers in Nandigram was the result of a well thought out plan by the CPM and West Bengal government. Immediately after the incident a delegation led by *Mananiya* Advani ji reached Nandigram. All the information related to incident were collected. The issue was raised in the parliament but the UPA Government hog washed the entire incident. Prior to this, I had also visited Singur to support the cause of agitating farmers there.

Chaos prevails everywhere in West Bengal. According to National Statistical Survey the families living in starvation for maximum number of days in a month is the highest (10.64%) in West Bengal. A large scale food scam took place in Public Distribution System (PDS) in West Bengal. It is to be noted that the committee authorized to distribute PDS license is constituted of one respectable person, one Panchayat Pramukh and a food officer. Here, *Panchayat Pramukh* and respactable person, both are leftists. CAG report cites a scam of more than 2000 crore in PDS. The people of West Bengal have started a food-agitation against it in the entire state. In place of providing ration on subsidized rates to the people the West Bengal government has started suppressing them with bullets and batons.

It is an irony that the reins of the UPA Government are in the hands of these leftists who oppress farmers and workers in this manner. Congress, setting aside the national and people's interests, is not taking any step against the Leftists; instead it is affirming all such actions to remain in power. In Kerala and Tripura also the common people are becoming victims of the Leftist oppression. The corruption of the ministers and CPM cadres are openly coming to the fore.

Elections every now and then: How long will it continue?

Some time back elections would not take place at such short intervals as they are taking place today. Even elections for Lok Sabha and Vidhan Sabhas used to take place simultaneously. The situation has taken such a turn that in every two to four months one or the other state goes for elections. In the year 2007, elections were held in six states. In February 2008, elections are supposed to be held in Tripura, Nagaland and Meghalaya. Assembly elections are also supposed to take place in Karnataka in April-May. The state assembly elections of Jammu and Kashmir are slated to be held in September this year. Elections will also take place in Rajsthan, Madhya Pradesh, Chhattisgarh, Delhi and Mizoram in the month of November. Soon after the elections in these states preparations for the elections to 15th Lok Sabha will start, In May 2009 Lok Sabha elections are supposed to take place. Immediately two months after the Lok Sabha elections, Maharashtra assembly elections are supposed to be held.

Repeated involvement in elections leaves no time for the national political parties to engage themselves in political-social and constructive work. Elections make it a compulsion for the political parties to participate in it. In such a situation while expenditure increases, much of the time is also spent in elections. Not only the time of the political parties is spent but all the sections making the electoral machine function have to spend time. An indirect impact of this is that continuous elections practically make electoral interests supreme and constructive approach gets de-prioritized. Today it is required to bring back the system on track. I appeal to the Election Commission and all the political parties to start thinking in this direction so that a way out is found. It may lead to solve many problems and set the national political parties free from the elections held in every two-three months.

Problems of North Eastern states

Entire region of Northeast not only presents unique beauty of nature but also represents a proud historical tradition. Great persons like Raja Bhaga Datt, Lachit Bare, Fukan, Chila Rai, Shriman Shankar Deva were born in the north-east. The region is today in the grip of violence, hatred and anti-national elements. It is extremely unfortunate that the Congress, which was in power for a long time in Centre and states, has paid no attention after the independence for development and internal and external security of the region. Today, crores of Bangaldeshis have infiltrated in the region. Anti-India forces have changed the social structure in many districts and activated terrorist outfits in this region.

The artisans and labourers from Jharkhand, Bihar, Rajsthan, Andhra Pradesh, Orissa and other states were brought here to work in the tea gardens. But today anti-national forces are planning to expel these people brought from other states to Assam. It is so because the Bangladeshi infiltrators would then find avenues of employment and control over the economic resources. It is unfortunate that the Bangladeshi infiltrators are living comfortably in Assam while the original inhabitants are leading a life of helplessness and insecurity. The Congress government in the centre and in Assam in stead of stopping them appears to be standing in their support.

Authoritarian approach of UPA Government

UPA Government continues to work in an authoritarian manner till date. On the issues of national importance it took neither the opposition nor its own allies into confidence. Whether the issue was of nuclear deal with US or Chinese incursions in Arunachal Pradesh, UPA failed to present its viewpoint on both. The Central Government failed to raise the issue of terrorism effectively in the international forums. UPA remained inactive even on the Supreme Court verdict on IMDT Act related to Bangladeshi infiltration. The crisis in Nepal worsened due to the weak policies of the UPA.

Elections in North-eastern states

Most recently the UPA Government imposed President's rule in Nagaland after dismissing the elected government there. The Nagas are extremely agitated by this undemocratic and unconstitutional step. In the 2003 elections Rio's party NPF got 18 seats alone in an assembly of 60 seats while constituents in its alliance BJP got 7, JD (U) got 3, Samata Party and Nagaland Democratic Party got 5 seats each. In this manner the Congress was ousted from power in 2003. After the imposition of President's rule, the Congress is indulging in misusing the administrative machinery in Nagaland. When NDA was in power, a special package was given to Nagaland, but when UPA has come to power it is imposing President's rule. We hope to defeat Congress here again. In Meghalaya, no single party is in majority now. In Meghalaya also, one who was made Chief Minister by the Congress has left it and joined UDP. Common people are in a miserable condition here under the UPA rule. We got two seats here in the last elections; we will try to increase our tally.

Tripura is the only state in the Northeast where Leftists are in power. The people here are also fed up with the corruption of the ministers and oppression by the Leftists. Law and order machinery has collapsed. The government is itself involved in financial scams. Leftists are divided into different factions. BJP will fight the elections with full force in Tripura.

Appeal

Our political journey had started in the form of Bharatiya Jan Sangh in 1951. We have seen many ups and downs as political activists and political party. In 1975, when a reign of terror was unleashed in the country by murdering democracy, then also we the activists bore the travails in jails but never yielded before the Centre. We never gave up courage and patience. Finally Indira ji had to lift emergency and leave power. The rule of Janata Party came. We merged Jan Sangh with Janata Party. We even gave up the election symbol of Jan Sangh. Situation became difficult. The dispute over dual membership started and Jan Sangh constituents were compelled to leave Janata Party. BJP was formed on 6th April 1980.

A situation emerged in 1984 when BJP was relegated to the margins in the Parliament. We never gave up. The constant and committed attempt to reach at the top from the margins continued and finally we played main role in changing the political scenario of the entire country. The main reason behind this is that we are a cadre based live political organization. We have taken the pledge of continuously dedicating ourselves in the service of Bharat Mata with or without power. Power is only a medium for us. Our politics is not for forming government only but also to reform society. The medium to form government should also act as tool aimed at reforming the society. In politics, gaining power is complete in itself. Our political journey continued with these ideas.

We also engaged ourselves in novel experiments by keeping national interests in mind and in accordance with the political situation. In 1998, NDA Government was formed under the leadership of BJP. *Mananiya* Atalji became the Prime Minister. The prestige of India increased in the world under the leadership of Atalji. The rays of development started to show itself from the farmland of villages to the high rising towers of the cities. We presented before the people a comprehensive form of development from agriculture to field of high technology. The attempt to build a magnificent and strong India started. In the Lok Sabha elections 2004, this dream remained unfulfilled owing to certain reasons. We have to move forward to realize this dream.

Once again time has come when we can again gain the reins of power by our labour and coordinated efforts. The responsibility of realizing the unfulfilled dreams of *Mananiya* Atalji has been given to *Mananiya* Advaniji. We have to convert this golden opportunity into victory. It will be possible only when we engage ourselves in our areas with commitment and dedication. I fully believe that we will move with full commitment. Victory will be ours. There are a number of issues yet to be discussed. All the issues will be deliberated at full length.

□

Growing Influence of BJP

28-29 January 2008 National Council (New Delhi)

The Sun God has already begun his transit from the south to the north. Winter's freezing ice is beginning to thaw; thus paving way for spring. Rituraj, (the king of seasons) symbolic of new enthusiasm and maturity, is about to grace us with his presence. I mention all of this because the manner in which the BJP is achieving important electoral successes one after the other, clearly indicates that the people's support for the UPA Government is melting in favour of the BJP. A new golden era beckons all of us. We are all aware that true devotion, hard work, mutual confidence, coordination and self-restraint alongwith meticulous planning are the prerequisites for success. If we all truly follow this path, then in the forthcoming year further glorious achievements await us. All of us need to pledge ourselves for victory. To attain this we will laboriously make constant attempts and in the process also meet our social and political responsibilities with maturity.

Events since our last Council

We had all met in Lucknow in December 2006 for the last meeting of our National Council. During these 13 months we have won four elections. First Punjab and Uttarakhand and only last month in Gujarat and Himachal we achieved glorious success. We snatched three states from the Congress and in the prestigious battle of Gujarat we again retained our government. However, during this period, the election results in Uttar Pradesh were not upto our expectations and in Goa we were not successful in wresting power from the Congress. However, this is a historic occasion where in a single year the BJP formed the government in four states. The victory in each of these four states has a separate significance. In Punjab where we have emerged as the main constituent and effective coalition partner of the government, in Uttarakhand the people of the state voted for the BJP for the first time since the creation of the state. The recently concluded election in Gujarat was unique in itself where the entire nation focused on that Gujarat where unprecedented development has taken place under the leadership of Shri Narendra Modi. The splendid success of Gujarat has given the twin message of ideology and development in favour of the Bharatiya Janata Party. For this splendid victory I congratulate both the people of Gujarat as well as the efforts of the dedicated workers of our organization. During the period of the Sri Ram Janambhoomi movement of 1990-91, we had rapidly grown in many states. Gujarat was also one of them. However, the current victory has established that over the last 16-17 years, Gujarat has emerged as an invincible bastion of the BJP.

The victory in Himachal Pradesh was also a grand achievement. The people of Himachal, the efforts of our committed workers as well as the collective efforts of Chief Minister Shri Prem Kumar Dhumal and former Chief Minister Shri Shanta Kumar needs to be lauded for this impressive victory. The Himachal victory has literally silenced our critics who made a hue and cry about our non existent internal strife.

Both Gujarat and Himachal have given a befitting reply to those who tried to paint the BJP as being communal and inflicted by internal strife.

Out of the four states which we won last year, in three states the BJP has its own chief ministers and in Punjab our trusted ally and the senior Akali leader Shri Parkash Singh Badal became the Chief Minister of the Akali-BJP coalition government. Shri Badal is among the country's seniormost chief ministers and has been the enduring pillar of Punjab politics for over half a century. On behalf of the entire National Council I congratulate and felicitate the four Chief Ministers, our NDA ally Shri Parkash Singh Badal of the Akali Dal and the three BJP Chief Ministers Shri Bhuvan Chand Khanduri, Shri Narendra Modi and Shri Prem Kumar Dhumal.

During this very period, we also experienced a glimpse of power in Karnataka. After much dithering on the terms of the coalition, the Janata Dal (S) finally supported the BJP. Shri Yediyurappa became the Chief Minister. However, prior to the vote of confidence, the action of the Janata Dal not only resulted in the demise of the BJP's first government in the south within its infancy itself, but has also further worsened the crisis of credibility that is increasingly impacting the country's political scenario.

We are however satisfied that the BJP had fulfilled its commitment towards the *dharma* of coalition. The BJP has been ditched but the BJP never took any step that may have led to a breach of trust. I am confident that in the forthcoming assembly elections in Karnataka we will win the confidence of the people to successfully form the government, and in this year we will also establish the BJP's first government in the south whose glimpse we had witnessed last year.

The situation of the governments in Goa and Jharkhand clearly stands before you. Nothing can be said about how long the governments in these two states will last. The current political instability is a consequence of misuse of power, trampling the spirit of the Constitution and making a mockery of democracy only to prevent the BJP from forming the government in both Goa and Jharkhand. I hold the Congress and the so-called secular parties directly responsible for today's instability in Goa and Jharkhand and also appeal to the people of the country to understand how undemocratic political machinations merely for opposing the BJP can create such instability, Goa and Jharkhand being examples of this.

Only recently, our coalition government in Nagaland was dislodged and President's rule inappropriately imposed despite elections being due in a few days. Prior to this, by misusing the constitutional authority, the Congress dislodged our governments in both Goa and Jharkhand. The Nagaland incident is the latest example of this very mindset. Despite all of this, I am confident that in the forthcoming assembly elections in Nagaland, our coalition will once again emerge victorious.

Today, across the country the BJP is expanding state by state and the influence of the Congress party which is ruling at the centre is constantly eroding. Today, the states which are being governed by the BJP on its own or alongwith coalition partners, in those states (including Karnataka) there are over 200 Lok Sabha seats. In contrast, the states which are being governed by the Congress alone or with coalition partners, in them there are less than 125 Lok Sabha seats. These figures are a clear indicator about the country's current political pulse as well as the prospects of the forthcoming Lok Sabha elections. If the democratic results of Goa and Jharkhand had not been hijacked, then this figure and the gap could have been even larger.

Another fact worth considering is that Congress Party has consistently declined over the last six consecutive Lok Sabha elections. The situation today has conclusively changed since twenty years ago, when in 1984, the Congress Party stood at 400 seats as compared to the two seats of the BJP. During this period, the people of the country have rejected the Congress in 225 seats, while the BJP has grown from 2 seats to 183 and in the present Lok Sabha we got 137 seats. Where 20 years ago we did not have a single government in any state, today in six states we have our own governments, in three states we are in power through coalitions and if we take into account both Karnataka and Nagaland at the time of the dissolution of the assemblies, then in total we would have been in power in eleven states. At the same time, the number of states where the Congress is in power is far less than us. These facts indicate towards the constantly changing face of India's political scenario over the last two decades. In the forthcoming Lok Sabha elections, we need to change this in a decisive manner and ensure that the BJP gets a stable change in its favour.

Whether the Lok Sabha elections take place this year or on the due date, for all practical purposes the country has already entered into an election year. After the defeat in Gujarat and Himachal, the Congress is in a state of shock. Even the Left which on virtually every matter threatens to topple the government, is keen to keep away from the very thought of elections. The so-called secular parties are still busy calculating the pros and cons of future political possibilities. The parties that have recently emerged as powerful regional centres and which are nurturing national political ambitions, have also faced setbacks in the recent elections. However, the BJP is way ahead of the other political parties and has already started tightening its belt in preparation for the elections.

The seniormost leader of the party after respected Atalji, respected Shri Lal Krishna Advaniji, has been declared as the party's Prime Ministerial candidate. During his long political life, while working with Atalji, the additional political strength that Advaniji has given to the BJP is indeed everlasting. Advaniji's personality, his far sightedness and staunch commitment towards values has always inspired party workers. The entire leadership of my generation has gradually matured under the guidance of Atalji and Advaniji. When I compare ourselves with other political parties, I am unable to find another pair of leaders as respected Atalji and Advaniji who have worked so closely together for such a long period of time. The close coordination between these two leaders during the entire journey from the Rashtriya Swayamsevak Sangh to Jan Sangh, from the Janata Party to Bharatiya Janata Party and from a numerically irrelevant party in the Lok Sabha to the ruling party, is nothing less than being God gifted in Indian politics. As I mention the name of Shri Lal Krishna Advaniji, I feel I am literally taking the name of the future Prime Minister of India. He is no longer only the leader of the BJP but now he is the leader of our entire nation. I am certain that with the cooperation of all our workers and the blessings of Atalji, the BJP will definitely be successful in the forthcoming Lok Sabha under the leadership of Advaniji.

The BJP is the first political party in the country to announce the formation of its Election Campaign Committee in which we formulated an initial framework for the forthcoming Lok Sabha as well as over ten assembly elections that are due this year. This means that in terms of both leadership and campaign we are already far ahead of other parties.

The BJP as a political party does not belong to a single personality or family. Rather, the party leadership is carefully nurtured through a natural evolution process. In the past, we have contested several parliamentary elections after clearly declaring our leader. From 1996 till 2004, we contested all elections by projecting Atalji as our leader. Today, in a unique situation, the Congress Party, known as a party under the influence of one person and family, is unable to take a decision about its leader for the elections. While we have already announced our prime ministerial candidate, on behalf of the entire country, I would like to ask the UPA, who will be their candidate for the post of Prime Minister in the forthcoming Lok Sabha elections? I don't think the Congress will be able to answer this question, because ironically while the Congress does have a Prime Minister yet it does not have a Prime Ministerial candidate.

Only a few months ago, the Congress had voiced its support for single party rule. While the Congress is talking about single party rule, it is not clear about a single centre of authority within the government of their party.

Required Direction for the Country

This is the fourth year of the UPA government. As a result of the wrong policies of the government, over the last four years, people have had to face numerous problems and hardship. The UPA government is entering the last phase of its tenure. Therefore, it is natural that it should be compared with the erstwhile Vajpayee government. During the tenure of the Vajpayee government, from control on prices to foodgrains, gas, milk, fruits, vegetables and even salt and other daily use items as well as the dream of owning a house were all within the reach of the common man. Today with increasing prices and increasing interest rates, everything is going out of the reach of the common man.

Our government, in contrast to earlier governments, undertook totally new initiatives such as the National Highway Programme, *Pradhan Mantri Gramin Sadak Yojana*, development of the IT sector, disinvestment, and nuclear tests among others. These novel initiatives laid the very foundation of a new India.

The BJP led NDA Government had a grand vision for a comprehensive development to make India a global superpower. We established a new epoch in Indian politics and international diplomacy.

I would like to remind the people of the country, that immediately after coming to power, we conducted the Pokhran test. Virtually all the superpowers of the world went against us. Economic sanctions were imposed on us. It was the farsightedness of the Vajpayee government that we became prosperous by issuing India Development Bonds for the purpose of investments in India, and through other diplomatic means we came to be recognized as a nuclear power. This repositioned India in the global scenario. In this process we not only established India as a strategic power but also practically enhanced the emotional bonds of our non-resident Indians with the country's development. Along with this, we achieved spectacular progress in the field of technology, became leaders in agriculture and food grain production, and thus, by overcoming all hurdles started emerging as a global economic superpower.

No country can become a strategic power only on the basis of military might. For this, diplomatic dexterity is also required. The biggest diplomatic achievement of the NDA was that we were able to finally end the era of comparison between India and Pakistan.

Through the Seattle (1999) and Doha (2001) WTO summits, we ended the hegemony of the western world and the United States on global trade. We further democratized the internal structure of the WTO. For the first time in history, India was triumphant in economic diplomacy.

Therefore, through the excellent diplomatic initiatives undertaken during the tenure of the NDA, we clearly established India as one of the military and economic powers of the world.

However, beyond this, I would like to draw your attention to another dimension of the evolution of India's power. For any nation to establish its influence in the world, it requires to become a military superpower.

This is not a new concept but has been in practice for centuries. In world history, the earth was shaken on several occasions by many, from Alexander who claimed to be the son of Apollo to Chengiz Khan who hoisted his flag from the Mediterranean Sea to the China Sea, by the massive army of Greece or the Roman Eagle to the might of the Spanish Armand or the slogan of Rule Britannia, or Hitler's Third Reich.

The indispensibility of military power cannot be negated. It makes a nation into a "Hard Power". Any big country in the world can acquire this power. Military might can establish one's awe but cannot ensure one's respect, affection and oneness. For this a nation has to possess "Soft Power or Gentle Power". Under the NDA, we were even able to establish India's inherent and eternal soft power in the world.

The concept of Soft Power was propounded in 1990 by Harvard University's eminent intellectual Joseph Nye. In 2004, in his book titled *Soft Power: the Means to Succeed in Global Politics* he explained how any country can influence global politics by combining cultural and emotional bonds with its social and economic power.

Our government at that time made meaningful efforts to establish a live contact with the over 2 crore people of Indian origin. Through the government, we started the process for observing the *Pravasi Bharatiya Divas* every year. For the first time, we appointed a special ambassador for non-resident Indians whom we called Ambassador at Large, so that the Indian community in different parts of the world could collectively spread our culture and contribute towards India's interests. During the tenure of our government, we also launched the Indian Entertainment Industry and Cinema on the international scene. I would like to remind you that in Afghanistan, after the defeat of the Taliban, when our Foreign Minister went there, he not only carried relief material and a package for economic assistance, but also took with him numerous CDs and cassettes of Hindi films, songs and Indian dance music. This also laid the foundation of a new and close relationship between the common people of India and Afghanistan. On account of such efforts, the global community slowly and indirectly gets deeply influenced and this becomes evident only after some time. An American journalist in Beijing, Jehangir Pochha, wrote that a Russian youth was so highly influenced on seeing the sacraments and process of an Indian wedding in a film, that he is believed to have said that Indian sacraments are so full of life and colorful enthusiasm that one's heart feels like becoming an Indian.

Soft Power and Gentle Power can also be understood from a famous example. Hu Shih, China's ambassador to America from 1938 to 1942, and later the Vice Chancellor of Peking University from 1946 to 1948 had said that India culturally conquered and dominated China for 2000 years without ever having to send a single soldier across her border.

I am only trying to say that during the tenure of the BJP led NDA Government and under the leadership of respected Atalji, India not only emerged as a Hard Power or Military-Economic Power but also emerged as a Soft Power or Gentle-Cultural Power in the world. Under us, India's real power evolved in a complete manner. In my opinion, this marked the real *Bharat Uday* or "India Rising". In politics, sometimes it takes many years to get the message across to the masses. I believe that after experiencing the mis-governance of the UPA Government, the people of the country will be able to better understand how the real rise of India was taking place during the tenure of the NDA. If the people give us another opportunity to govern, then we will effectively establish India's rise before the entire country and the rest of the world.

Challenges before the Nation

Today under the UPA, whatever little development is being seen, it is merely an expansion of the foundations that were laid by the erstwhile NDA Government. I would like to ask the UPA government to inform the nation about even a single novel developmental project that it has initiated during the last three and a half years of its tenure. The novel initiatives undertaken by the NDA Government in the country are clearly evident in the present circumstances of the country.

Pitiable Conditions of Farmers

Since the UPA Government has assumed power at the centre, the common man has been facing numerous hardships. However, if a single category of persons has to encounter misery literally falling from the skies, it is the agricultural sector. In addition to the farmers not getting electricity, water and fertilizers at the appropriate prices, they are increasingly getting trapped in a vicious cycle of debt to such an extent that after a point they have no other option but to commit suicide. Over the last few years, the huge increase in the number of cases of farmers, suicides is a shameful chapter in the history of India.

At one end, one sees new dimensions of industrial growth across

India. It is indeed a matter of pride for us that many Indian industrialists are taking over prestigious foreign companies and we laud their efforts. However, at the other end, it is indeed a matter of great shame for us that farmers in such large numbers are being forced to commit suicide and the government's incapability and insensitivity is truly deplorable.

On the one hand, the number of millionaires in the country is increasing and markets are sparkling with expensive luxury items, and on the other, according to the facts of the United Nations that were published recently in a leading national newspaper while making an economic comparison between India and China, the daily earning of 80% of India's population is less than US$ 2 i.e. approximately less than Rs 80 per day. The massive imbalance between these two aspects of progress is a clear proof of the UPA Government's shortsightedness, incapability and insensitivity.

I constantly reflect about a comprehensive vision for development, central to which are the villages, the poor and farmers. As the Union Agriculture Minister and with the blessings and support of our then Prime Minister respected Atalji, I could successfully bring down the interest rates on agricultural loans from an enviable 14 to 18% to 8 to 9%. At that time we also set up the National Commission on Farmers. Last year the National Commission on Farmers submitted its report to the Government in which it had expressed concern on the current condition of the agricultural sector. Our demand for bringing down the interest rate on agricultural loans to 4% has been included as one of the suggestions of the commission. I wrote a letter to the Prime Minister demanding that an all party meeting should be called for immediately implementing the recommendations of the National Commission on Farmers and all the political parties of the country should rise above political considerations to help farmers come out of this vicious cycle. But The Government did not pay any heed to this demand. Thereafter, to focus attention on the misery of farmers, the Bharatiya Janata Party resorted to political means and on 20th October 2007, at the Ramlila Ground in Delhi, we organized a meeting of farmers in huge numbers and then marched towards Parliament where respected Advaniji, myself, many BJP leaders and thousands of farmers courted arrest.

Farmers are not burdened only with debt, and in the different parts of the country, farmers have to face various types of severe hardship. In West Bengal's Singur and Nandigram, the manner in which farmers were suppressed in the land acquisition process is totally shameful and deplorable. Even beyond this, the CPM cadre went ahead and unlawfully used force to recapture land and spread terror amongst the inhabitants of Nandigram. This exposed the true character of the so-called champions of the proletariat. Last year, the BJP was the first to react on the Singur and Nandigram issue when I personally visited Singur and expressed our support to Ms Mamata Bannerjee, who was spearheading the movement. Recently in November, an NDA delegation led by respected Advaniji toured Nandigram to nationally highlight the atrocities being perpetrated on the farmers there.

Over the last few years, thousands of farmers have committed suicide in Andhra Pradesh and Maharashtra. For many years, the Vidarbha region of Maharashtra has become a graveyard for farmers. The maximum number of cases of farmers suicides are from this region. Both the state and Central governments are not being able to find a solution to deal with the problem. The Prime Minister's package for the Vidarbha has proved to be nothing more than an illusion. That is why the BJP once again took steps and I went on a two day Kisan Yatra in Vidarbha. During the yatra, the misery of the farmers that we witnessed was truly heart rending. I also realized that sitting in Delhi, we cannot even judge the amount of fury that the village and farmers feel towards the central government. This anger is natural and we will feel its true impact in the times to come.

It is indeed a sad irony to see the pitiable condition of our food providers that too at the hands of a government that has been elected by the people. The UPA Government today is an example of this irony. Those who claim to be with the common man stand fully exposed. The issue is no longer about ignoring or being insensitive towards the farmers but has reached the point of exploitation and suppression. Both Vidarbha and West Bengal are glaring examples of this.

Despite all of this, the Congress boasts of the magnificent 10% growth rate of the economy. Does the Congress believe that a great India can be founded on a heap of dead bodies of farmers? This is impossible. In these developments, I can clearly foresee even greater concerns for the future. Similar to the manner in which the Congress accepted the partition of India during the independence movement in the 20th century, which laid down the foundation of everlasting communal tensions within the country, if the Congress rule persists for a few more years, it will sow the deep rooted poisonous seeds of economic disparity in the country and this may create major chaos in the times to come.

The upliftment of farmers is not a political issue. Even more than a social issue it is a national priority. In the north, from the Sutlej to the Ganga, and in the south, from the Tungbhadra to the Cauvery, lies one of the largest fertile plains of the world. This is one of the most densely populated regions of the world. In this region, it is worth considering as to how practical is it to follow any developmental scheme that keeps agriculture and the human resource on the margins. The service sector based model of economic development of those countries which were not having a large and developed agrarian sector cannot as such be appropriate for India. The visions of Mahatma Gandhi and Pandit Deendayal Upadhyaya appear even more relevant today.

The pitiable conditions of villages is a matter of concern not only because the *Annadatta* farmer comes from the villages, but also because our brave soldiers of the security forces come from the same families. If the farmers continue to desert agriculture like this, then we may have to confront another complicated dimension of this problem. The pathetic condition of farmers will not only impact the social imbalance and food security, but beyond a point, will also have far reaching consequences where it may lead to a dearth of committed human resource for our security forces. Jai Jawan Jai Kisan was much more than a mere slogan. It reflects the inherent and natural corelation between the jawans and kisans.

I would like to clearly point out that no country can continue to ascend the path of progress by ignoring the interests of the villages, poor, farmers and the youth and soldiers. That is why we need to carry them along and reorient ourselves in the direction of the villages. A people awareness movement needs to be taken to every village.

The farmer is the country's largest working class. In terms of population, they comprise the largest group of producers and consumers. Economic progress cannot be material without enhancing the purchasing power of farmers. We need to inform our farmers that they are the architects of India's future. And who are eclipsing their progress will have to leave power. We will also tell the farmers which political party is their true sympathizer. They need to reflect upon this prior to casting their vote. The farmer should neither be dazzled by the hollow talk of development nor should they be misled by the fog of regionalism and casteism. In fact, they need to support the committed nationalist forces to bring to the forefront the real power of both the Kisan and Jawan.

I demand that the government should seriously apply itself to the problems of farmers and convene a special session of Parliament for an extensive discussion on this.

Directionless Economic Policy

The fast growing share market is considered to be symbolic of the country's prosperity, but this prosperity cannot be treated as all-inclusive until the interests of the small investors are clearly protected. The BJP is ever vigilant about protecting the interests of the small investors. A serious matter of concern is the volatility that is being witnessed in the share market particularly over the last six months, where the sensex dramatically rose from 15000 to 21000 points in a mere 190 days. In the recent crash, in only two and half days, the sensex crashed by about 3000 points and thereafter within a single day rose by 850 points. Such volatility impacts the small investor the most, and creates doubts in their minds. The BJP has already voiced its concern about the role of Foreign Institutional Investors (FII) and funds coming into the Stock Market through the PN route. Given all this, the BJP demands that the Government should immediately investigate about who are the people behind the upheaval in the share market, what are their objectives, who are the main beneficiaries and also how the government is planning to compensate the billions of rupees that small investors have lost in the process. And the government needs to ensure that a repeat of such an event does not take place and a few people are not able to manipulate the entire market in future.

The Central Government is stoutly claiming that the country is economically progressing at a fast pace. I am unable to comprehend what sort of economic progress is taking place wherein over the past three years and eight months, prices have consistently been increasing, interest rates for housing loans have increased to such levels that owning a house has once again becomee a dream for the middle class.

To provide relief to the common man who is burdened by increasing inflation as well as interest rates, the BJP demands that the government should increase the income tax standard exemption limit to Rs 1.5 lacs, bring down the interest rates for housing and education loans to the 2004 levels, and reduce interest rates for agricultural loans to 4%.

On account of the rising level of urbanization across the country, the demand for commercial and residential properties is increasing. However, the speed at which the prices of these properties are increasing, does not augur well for inclusive development. Housing is a basic human need. This sector cannot be left unregulated or uncontrolled. To bring about healthy competition in this sector and also to ensure that the common man is assured the availability of a house, the BJP demands the setting up of a "Real Estate Regulatory Authority."

Terrorist incidents have increased in the country. The National Security Advisor has expressed an apprehension that terrorist funds could be injected into the share markets. This makes it imperative to strictly monitor funds that are coming in through the overseas Foreign Institutional Investors (FII). The government's measures to monitor funds coming in through the PN route are not adequate and there is a need for even stricter vigil to be maintained on this front.

The theme of the Eleventh Five Year Plan is comprehensive development. 27 goals have been identified for achieving comprehensive development. Out of these, the states have been given the responsibility for achieving 13 goals. This indicates that the Planning Commission itself is not sure about achieving these goals. According to the Commission, poverty reduction is not taking place at the same pace at which the country is progressing. The scheduled castes, tribes and other weakes sections of society are not benefiting from this progress. Gender disparity continues to be a big problem. Undoubtedly, the Eleventh Five Year Plan will have to deal with huge challenges.

The biggest challenge before the Eleventh Five Year Plan is the fact that foreign trade and foreign investment comprises 40% of the Gross Domestic Product (GDP). This implies that the forecasted slowdown in America and the western countries can also impact India. According to the country's economists, it will not be possible to achieve the difficult and specific goals of the Eleventh Five Year Plan.

During the tenure of the NDA, our economic policy was not limited to making India only a leader in sectors such as the service sector, housing, IT and telecom, but was also to take the country to a commanding position for all items of the common man's daily use. Under the NDA, India became the number one producer of the world in the areas of milk production, fruit and vegetable production, tea production and jute production. In the areas of wheat and rice production, we achieved self reliance and also became the world's third largest producer. This was possible because we sought to link the economy with agriculture. Today, we need to import even basic food grains such as wheat and that too at high prices and of lower quality. This explains as to why the country is suffering from a sense of insecurity in the context of food grains. In terms of employment, agriculture is a highly labour intensive sector, which appropriately can utilize a large number of the human resource. Agriculture is India's largest employment sector. Without its development, neither unemployment nor inflation can be controlled.

In a single sentence if one is to sum up what the UPA Government has given India during the last three years and eight months, then we can say that the people of the country have got only two things – "Unequal Society" and "Sense of Insecurity".

Requirement for a National Policy for Infrastructural Projects

After the exit of the NDA Government at the centre, the present UPA government has either halted numerous developmental projects or neglected them only for political reasons. For example, the pace of the core infrastructure milestone programmes like the National Highway Development Programme has immensely slowed down. By now, work on the Golden Quadrilateral Programme linking the four metropolitan cities should have been completed. I mention all this because at the time of the launch of these programmes, I was the Shipping & Surface Transport Minister. Beneficial programmes for the country such as the Golden Quadrilateral, North-South & East-West Corridor and the *Pradhan Mantri Gramin Sadak Yojana* should not be affected with a change in government.

The NDA Government had sanctioned six hospitals on the lines of the All India Institute of Medical Sciences (AIIMS) in Delhi to ensure the availability of high quality medical facilities in all regions of the country. This programme has gone into cold storage.

The Agriculture Income Insurance Scheme that was started to provide farmers with an assured income on the basis of their land, has been stopped. Even the Kisan Credit Card Scheme has gone into cold storage. Even those farmers who have the credit cards, are no longer getting credit.

One can clearly foresee a major problem of water availability in India, in times to come. To deal with this potential water problem, the NDA Government had initiated a programme for efficiently utilizing rain water and also the massive inter-linking of rivers programme, something the UPA Government has not even applied any thought to after coming to power.

All these schemes were not meant for the benefit of any particular segment but instead are beneficial for the people of the entire country.

Their unexpected closure or slowdown will prove to be extremely problematic for India, which is emerging as a global power.

I believe as in the case of foreign policy and economic policy during the last 15 years, just as a change in the direction of the basic policy of the country is not considered correct with change in governments, similarly if India wants to become a developed country and a global superpower, then fundamental infrastructure projects and policies should remain unaffected with change in government.

Minority Appeasement

Minority appeasement is foremost among the most disturbing tasks that the UPA Government has undertaken over the last three and half years. After being rapped by the Supreme Court for attempting to introduce reservation on religious basis in government jobs and educational institutions, the Central Government tried to allocate a separate communal quota in bank loans and funds earmarked for development. The Prime Minister's statement that the Muslim community should have first right over national resources was truly shocking. The Government was keen to introduce communal budgeting in the meeting of the National Development Council which was called to discuss the forthcoming five year plan. However, a day before to the meeting of the National Development Council, I issued a statement opposing this and requested all BJP Chief Ministers in the meeting to oppose any such attempt in every possible manner. In the meeting, the BJP Chief Ministers raised this issue. I would also like to assure the entire country, that despite being in opposition, the Bharatiya Janata Party will go to any extent to thwart every such move. The BJP believes that every section of society must be developed. Any attempt to communally colour development is condemnable.

According to a report of the Government of India, the allocated funds earmarked for development of the minority community have been increased from Rs 400 crores to 1400 crores. On the other hand, the allocated funds for the development of Schedule Castes and other backward sections have been reduced by 2%. This is sheer injustice with the backward and reserved segments. If there is any requirement to ensure that benefits of the government programmes need to reach any particular segment, then actually this segment is of the Scheduled Castes and Scheduled Tribes. The government should do away with the reduction of allocated funds earmarked for the Scheduled Castes and Scheduled Tribes and if required a nodal agency should be created to monitor that the funds appropriately reach the needy persons in these sections.

Today many misconceptions are associated with the term minority. Various court judgements are also echoing questions such as who is a minority, on what basis and in which region, and this takes different connotations depending on the prevailing situation and geographical area in different parts of the country. On account of such reasons, there is a greater possibility of politically misusing this. I request the government to legally define the term minority and also appropriately determine in what spheres it would be applicable.

Terrorism

Terrorism is acquiring stability in India. Both Naxalite violence and Jehadi terrorism have increased since this Congress led and Left supported government has come to power at the Centre. Naxalite terrorism has become particularly problematic in Chhattisgarh, Jharkhand, Bihar and Andhra Pradesh. Since this government assuming office, Jehadi terrorism has literally spread its feet all over the country. Over the last three years, there have been terrorist attacks on virtually all prominent cities which are considered to be the country's political, economic, intellectual, cultural and nationalist centres. Now even religious centres and places of worship are being targeted in a ruthless manner.

We are also worried about how terrorism, over the last year or two, has been spreading in Uttar Pradesh, the largest state of the country. The terrorist attack on Sri *Ramjanambhoomi* two and a half years ago, then the attack on the Sankat Mochan Temple in Kashi, the blasts in the courts of Lucknow, Varanasi and Faizabad two months ago, as also the blast in the camp of the Central Reserve Police in Rampur, all indicate that terrorism is increasing its foothold in the inner parts and Hindi heartland of the country and specifically in Uttar Pradesh. The terrorist attacks that have taken place in Uttar Pradesh over the last two months are important from the point of view that for the first time, terrorists have tried to terrorize the judiciary. This is because the lawyers of Uttar Pradesh took a decision not to fight the cases of terrorists. In my opinion, if the Central Government had not kept pending for so long the decision of the Supreme Court to hang Mohammed Afzal, the main accused in the Parliament attack conspiracy, then terrorists would not have dared to even think about terrorizing the courts. I would like to ask the Central Government that at this point of time, where exactly is Afzal's clemency appeal lying between the Home Ministry and *Rashtrapati Bhawan*? This is because former president Dr Abdul Kalam has said that when he had referred the matter to the Home Ministry, then during his tenure, the Home Ministry did not return the file to him. What message does the Government want to give to the terrorists?

Secondly, for the first time an incident outside Kashmir and involving an attack on the camp of a security force has taken place. This situation in Uttar Pradesh has begun only after the tenure of the BJP governments ended there. For us, this is a matter of national worry because given the long and open border with Nepal, if the law and order situation in Uttar Pradesh weakens, then it can open a new gate of insecurity for entire northern India.

I would like to ask all those human rights activists who speak about human rights at the time when tough measures are used against terrorists, why are they silent when innocent civilians and brave soldiers of the security forces are killed in horrific incidents of terrorist attacks? The BJP expresses its sympathy for all those citizens who have lost their lives in terrorist attacks and is grateful to all those soldiers of the security forces who have laid down their lives as well as expresses its deep respect to their families.

I believe that from every aspect the time has finally come for the Central Government to correct its past mistakes, and for effectively controlling terrorism once again enact POTA. If they have a problem with POTA merely because it was enacted during the tenure of the BJP government, then let them by any other name introduce an anti-terror law in Parliament. Today India is the only big country in the world which is combating terrorism but does not have any anti-terror law. In the absence of an anti-terror law, asking security forces to fight terrorists is an unequal battle, a destructive battle in which the self-confidence of the terrorists increases and the self-confidence of the security forces reduces. We will never let this happen. On behalf of the BJP, I would like to reassure the people of the entire country that if the Central Government introduces an anti-terror law in Parliament, then we will support it, and if after the elections we form the government at the Centre, then we will restore POTA for the security of the country's masses.

Unstable Indian Subcontinent

Pakistan is progressing towards instability, given the conditions that have existed there for a long time. Internal dissatisfaction, revolt in Waziristan, news reports about differences within the army, the autonomy of the ISI, the developing extremism against the presence of American troops, and among all these the application and withdrawal of emergency, all indicate towards a dangerous and disturbing internal situation within Pakistan. In the midst of all this, the assassination of Pakistan's former Prime Minister Smt Benazir Bhutto has only added fuel to the fire. Pakistan appears to be moving in the direction of serious problems. In the past also, Pakistan has never enjoyed an image of being a responsible nation, and the creation of new complications only increases the possibilities of further irresponsible actions which in turn can become a serious problem for India. I am not stating all this merely on the basis of evaluation. Recently a report published in an international magazine (America's Newsweek) stated that Pakistan has become a safe haven for terrorists. As Afghanistan, even Pakistan offers a lot to al Qaeda's chief Osama bin Ladin. The report further stated that al Qaeda has spread its net across Pakistan and Taliban fighters are able to freely move across the border between Pakistan and Afghanistan. According to "The Economist" magazine, Pakistan has today become the most dangerous place in the world.

While the decades old American policy towards Pakistan has proved to be incorrect, at the same time their policy of seeking to control politics through the army has also not shown any positive results. It is difficult to believe that all the economic assistance that Pakistan has been receiving is only to control terrorism. One cannot accept that F-16 fighter jets with nuclear attachments are meant only for combating terrorism. This is definitely a matter of concern for India.

The growing belligerence of the Maoists in Nepal coupled with increasing anti-India propaganda is now reaching dangerous levels.Recently, Maoists from Nepal tried to cross the border in Uttarakhand which was foiled through the peaceful demonstrations by the youth workers of the BJP and other allied organizations. However, this points towards the possibility of a new type of future problem.

The Madheshi problem in Nepal is a matter of concern for us. Given the growing influence of the Maoist forces in Nepal, it appears unnatural that a democratic framework can be established through them. Inherently, Maoism does not believe in democracy. Therefore, under the influence of Maoism, the talk about democracy appears paradoxical. The impact of this is clearly visible. The Maoists by exerting pressure have, through an interim Parliament, brought about a fundamental change in the structure of Nepal. Whereas if a fundamental change in the structure is necessary, then this should be done by a parliament that has been elected by the people. For stability of Nepal, it is imperative that a democratically elected government which can administer the country in accordance with the wishes of the people is established. The Government of India should also apply its mind in this direction.

The manner in which the anger of the people against military rule is taking to the streets, reflects the diminishing control and support for the military rulers inside Myanmar. Buddhist monks took to the streets in large numbers to protest against the government there. We condemn the deplorable manner in which the government there acted against the Buddhist monks. The representative of any religion should not be mistreated.

In Sri Lanka, the ceasefire against the LTTE has ended and once again the LTTE has become aggressive and active. Bomb blasts are taking place in Colombo on almost daily basis. On account of the increasing impact of terrorism, the Government of India will have to keep a close watch to ensure that an occasion does not arise for another country to establish its influence in Sri Lanka. On several occasions a demand has emanated from within Sri Lanka that the Indian government should get involved in the peace talks there. However, the Government of India does not appear to be making any move in this direction. In my opinion, the solution for Sri Lanka's Tamil problem is possible only through dialogue. The Government of India should try to ensure that the war comes to an end in Sri Lanka and the peace process begins once again.

Like Pakistan, Bangladesh is also becoming a new hub for anti-India activities. The ULFA militants of Assam take refuge in Bangladesh. Many insurgent groups of the northeast organize themselves from across the borders in Bangladesh and Myanmar. Only recently, Bangladesh did not permit the gas pipeline coming from Myanmar to India to pass through its territory. Recently, certain facts have surfaced indicating that over the past few years China has been the largest supplier of arms to Bangladesh. However, the Indian Government continues to be a mute spectator.

The manner in which China has established a post in Myanmar to monitor the activities of the Indian Navy and set up their deep naval base at Gwadar in Pakistan, are also becoming matters of concern for us. One notices a sharp edge in the recent language being used by China. If one takes into account how active China is in Myanmar, Bangladesh, Sri Lanka and Pakistan and also combines this with the influence of the Maoists in Nepal, it appears that China is attempting to encircle India. The honourable Prime Minister should have raised this issue during his recent visit to China, but what to speak about effective protest, one did not see even a desire to protest. On the contrary, the Left which is supporting the government, accuses India of becoming a part of the design to encircle China. These accusations are not only ridiculous but also reflect the commitment of some political parties to countries across the border and casts doubts about their nationalistic commitment. The recent Chinese intrusions into Arunachal Pradesh and by declining to issue Visas to officers from Arunachal, in a sense amounts to China trying to create a legal claim over Arunachal before the government. Only recently, the Foreign Minister has publicly acknowledged that Chinese intrusions on the borders do happen from time to time. In this background, in the absence of seeking any clarifications, it is beyond my understanding how can the Prime Minister justify his China visit.

Therefore, across the entire Indian sub continent, democratic traditions are being impacted in all our neighbouring countries. Situations that promote dictatorship, terrorism and internal strife are getting created. In addition to instability, the Indian cub-continent is becoming a region of anti-India activities. However, given it's ostrich like approach, the Indian Government is probably not being able to see all of this, or despite seeing all this, does not want to see reality. As a result, the present government is not being able to draft any meaningful policy for the entire region. In my opinion, in addition to foreign policy, the time has now come for the government to formulate a Comprehensive and Integrated Vision for the entire region so that stability, peace and democracy are further strengthened. Our relationship with the Indian sub-continent is important not only from the aspect of security but also from the aspect of economic development and increase of trade. However, Government of India does not have a policy even for this. That is why the borders of the country have become easy targets for infiltration by militants.

Jammu & Kashmir

Despite the existence of Congress coalition governments in both the centre and Jammu & Kashmir, one is not being able to see any sort of improvement there. Instead of trying to bring Jammu & Kashmir into the national mainstream, the state government constantly keeps floating trial balloons that enhance separatist feelings. Sometimes they talk about the pre-1953 situation or make a completely ludicrous demand such as asking for a separate currency for the state of Jammu & Kashmir. Prior to 1953, when Kashmir had a separate parliament, prime minister and flag, at that time also they did not have a separate currency. This shows that the Congress is going even one step beyond that point in history.

In the midst of all this, the government is not paying any attention towards the plight of the Kashmiri Pandits who are leading a life of misery. There is no special provision for the Kashmiri Pandits in the government package announced for Jammu & Kashmir. We demand that the government should immediately announce a special package for the rehabilitation of Kashmiri Pandits. In my opinion, to bring Kashmir into the national mainstream and also to weaken separatist forces, the time has now come for all political parties, in the national interest, to once again consider removal of Article 370 and implementation of Union Civil Code.

Continuing Neglect of the North East Region

The northeast region of the country is not only unique geographically, but also has a unique economic, social and cultural situation. Unfortunately, the Congress has never properly understood the feelings of this region, and under the UPA Government, the entire northeast region continues to suffer from serious neglect. This beautiful part of our country has been virtually bypassed in terms of development under decades of Congress misrule. Over a period of time, the ever increasing influx of illegal immigrants from Bangladesh, started creating grave implications on both their identity and limited avenues of economic sustenance. Unfortunately, instead of adopting a remedial long term approach to permanently solve the problem, successive Congress governments both in Centre as well as in the northeastern states, treated these illegal immigrants as captive vote banks for narrow political gains and in the long run directly became responsible for socially and politically destabilizing virtually all parts of the north east region. This shortsighted approach, particularly of the Congress party, led to the emergence of various insurgent movements that sought to protect their unique identity as well as regional interests. Today, many areas bordering Bangladesh have been demographically altered by the illegal immigrants and reducing the indigenous population to a minority, in the process thereby creating social tensions coupled with serious security implications. This is in turn is proving to be highly detrimental to the long term national interests.

The BJP led NDA Government sought to permanently reverse this trend and substantially increased focus on development to ensure that economic prosperity percolated to all parts of the north east region, and they could conclusively join the national mainstream. However, under the UPA government, there is an evident slowdown in this process and once again violent incidents are on the rise. The northeastern states have encountered numerous problems on account of the infiltration of Bangladeshis. It appears the social structure of the region is being altered through a well thought out plan. Assam under the Congress is the most glaring example of this trend. The continuing massacre of Hindi speaking workers in Assam is a nefarious design to spark a feeling of separatism and also segregate the north east from rest of India. The BJP strongly condemns this. The involved militants are operating from the soil of Bangladesh.

Recently in Nagaland, the Central Government, in an unconstitutional manner, dismissed the government of the Democratic Alliance of Nagaland, of which the BJP was also a part. I would like to remind everyone that during the tenure of the Vajpayee government, a special package was gifted to Nagaland, whereas the government of today has gifted it President rule. I am confident that in the forthcoming assembly election on the 5th of March, the Congress will once again be defeated and the BJP alongwith its alliance partners will emerge victorious.

Tripura goes to the polls on 23rd February and Meghalaya on 3rd March. The Left Front has been ruling Tripura for a long time. Despite this, the poor condition of the state is a clear indicator that change of government is essential. In Meghalaya and Tripura too, in accordance with the aspirations of the people, new governments will be formed and the people will be freed of the misgovernance of the Congress and Left Front.

To increase our political strength in the northeastern states, we need to toil hard in sync with the unique situation there. For this, we must also endeavor to jointly work with other partners who subscribe to similar political beliefs. The BJP is committed towards bringing these states into the national mainstream in accordance with their potential and traditions.

Insult to Hindu Religion and Culture

Numerous and continuous assaults on the various symbols and core beliefs of Hindu religion and culture have been taking place since this government has come to power. The insulting and discarding attitude of this government towards *Hindutva* is well known. And now, some Congress party leaders have started using phrases such as Hindu terrorism. I would like to state that it is impossible to even imagine how can the *Hindutva*, which has from the vedic times given the message of *Vasudev Kutumbakam* (the entire world is one family) to the entire world, and from Lord Buddha to Mahatama Gandhi hoisted the flag of *Ahimsa* (non-violence) across the world, become a terrorist.

The height of this government's attack on Hindutva became evident when in an affidavit on Ram *Setu* that was submitted to the court, it dismissed the very existence of *Maryada Purushottam* Lord Ram. Even during the period of direct foreign rule, the British and the Mughal government even under Aurangzeb, could not dare to say what this democratically elected government of independent India has done. Despite three months passing by, the government is yet to file a new affidavit. Maybe the government is thinking of some other idea to further insult the Hindus.

Recently, the well known Bangladeshi author Taslima Nasreen was assaulted in Hyderabad. In a way she has been ousted from Kolkatta. Even beyond this, a Union Minister while expressing his views about extending the duration of her visa, said that the government should do so. However, he went to the extent of saying that since in her book she had hurt the sentiments of the Muslim community, therefore she should apologize to them. I would like to ask this government, when an artist paints the nude images of Hindu Goddesses, then no question was raised for an apology and instead this was termed as freedom of expression. I would like to ask if this government is so sensitive about hurting the religious sentiments of one community by any author, then on the other hand why are they not seeking an apology to the entire community that has faith in Lord Ram from their ally and the Chief Minister of Tamil Nadu when he used derogatory words for Lord Ram? To begin with, the government itself should apologize to all the believers of Lord Ram for denouncing his existence in the affidavit submitted to the court on the Ram Setu issue. This is because, denying the very existence of Lord Ram is not a personal opinion of an individual, any one leader, a writer or an artist. Hindu society is benevolent enough to ignore such issues. But the government's affidavit is the constitutional expression of its opinion in the Supreme Court. Therefore, if the constitutional expression of the government in the Supreme Court denounces the faith of the entire Hindu society, then it is totally unforgivable.

By extending the date for submitting a new affidavit, the doubts about the government's intentions have deepened further. I would like to ask the government that why are they so hesitant in submitting a new affidavit? How ironical it is that the government of another country, Sri Lanka, is acknowledging the entire Ramayan as a historical reality and has formally announced this in India and expresses respect for the religious sentiments of Hindu society. Whereas, our own government is insulting the believers of Lord Ram all over the world, by denying his very existence.

The Central Government that in the new affidavit, should express regret for hurting the sentiments of the Hindus in the previous affidavit and should pay attention to ensure that in the new affidavit there is nothing that directly or indirectly casts a shadow on the faith in Indian beliefs.

The BJP always tries to, in every possible manner, stop anything that could hurt the religious sentiments of any sect or community. When we were in power, at that time, the then Human Resource Development Minister Dr Murli Manohar Joshi had removed the objectionable references about the Sikh Gurus, Guru Teg Bahadur and Guru Govind Singh, as well as the Tirthankars of the Jain religion from the NCERT textbooks. However, this government's intention always appears doubtful. That is why, we demand from this government they should should make public the report of the *Setu Samundrum* Project that has been submitted to it.

The Ram *Setu* is not a mere structure in the sea that can be debated on the issue of being manmade or natural. Rather, it is a symbol of Indian identity and the first word of the ancient thought of *Aasetu* Himachal (describing India's expanse from *Setu* to the Himalayas) which highlights India's national unity and geographical expanse. This is the same mindset that considers the nation to be a mere piece of land and then carries on debating whether the inhabitants of this country originated from here or came from abroad. Thus, the pledge for the protection of Ram Setu, is a great pledge for the national identity, geographical unity and the cultural continuity of India. It is the duty of every nationalist Indian is to fulfill this pledge. Therefore, I declare that the Bharatiya Janata Party will give its complete moral support to the movement by the Sri Rameshwaram

Ram Setu Raksha Manch for the protection of Ram *Setu* and we are also committed to actively support this.

Given the enormous faith that I have in Indian culture, I firmly believe that the principles of *Dharma* are not confined to any belief, sect, or way of worship but beyond that they are the absolute, omnipresent and eternal principles of nature. I would like to remind all those who hurt the faith of *Dharma* about the principle of *Dharmo Rakshati Rakshita* which is applicable to everyone. This phrase means that if we will not protect *Dharma*, then our own protection is also not possible.

The New Experiments for the Organization

The BJP is a party with a distinct ideology and unique organizational structure. Our organizational structure is quite different from other political parties. On account of this, the BJP's character is also seen as being distinct to other political parties. After assuming the responsibility as the President of the party, I considered about undertaking two novel experiments within the BJP's unique organizational structure. Then, after having detailed discussions within the organization, last year we arrived at two important decisions, which in the years to come, will subsequently give a new shape to the BJP's organizational structure.

Women's Reservation

The manner in which our social structure is changing and acquiring a new look, the real development of society is not possible without the appropriate involvement of women. Be it society or the country, Dharma or morality, they all originate from *Shakti*. All political parties do make tall claims about this, but in reality, do not take any steps that can ensure the natural involvement of women in the political sphere. The UPA Government during its tenure has not yet presented even a draft of the Women's Reservation Bill. This clearly indicates the insensitivity of the Congress, Left and other so called secular parties towards the issue of women empowerment,

To give a practical shape to the women reservation issue, at the BJP National Executive Meeting in May 2007 in Delhi, I constituted a committee under the Chairmanship of Smt Sushma Swaraj to prepare a draft about how to give 33% reservation to women within the organization. This committee submitted its report at the Bhopal National Executive Meeting. The endorsement of the report is expected in forthcoming National Council.

After undertaking the required constitutional amendment in this regard, the BJP will become the first political party in the country to accord one third reservation to women within its organizational structure. Undoubtedly, this step will prove to be an epoch not only for the BJP but the entire nation, and its impact will be felt by the people in the years to come.

BJP at Every Booth: Constitution of Booth Committees

In terms of principles, the BJP is an ideology-based party and in terms of organization, the BJP is a cadre based party of the common masses. We consider ourselves to be a cadre-and ideology-based party. Keeping in mind the expansion of the party upto the lowest unit of society, and also keeping in view the continual electoral process within the country, we have decided to strengthen the party organization upto the booth level. The booth is the primary unit of the electoral process and during elections, the victory or defeat of the party is impacted by the booth level management. For this, it is imperative that the party's structure should be there at the booth level. Till date, about 65% of the booth committees have been constituted. Recently, prior to the elections in the two states of Gujarat and Himachal Pradesh, the booth committees had been constituted there. In Gujarat we also had a meeting of one lakh booth level workers. Even in Himachal Pradesh and Jammu & Kashmir, this experiment was undertaken. I hope that most of the states would have completed the formation of the booth committees and those who are in the process will complete it at the earliest. Given the manner in which the Lok Sabha elections are approaching, this task assumes greater importance. Therefore, all the State Presidents should take up this task on a war footing so that it can be completed within the stipulated time.

The Strength of the Organization and Goal for Winning the Forthcoming Elections

As I mentioned earlier, the BJP has a unique ideology and a distinct organizational structure. The inbuilt foundation of our distinctiveness lies in the nature and emotion of our worker.

The Lok Sabha elections are approaching. They can also take place before the scheduled time. This year, there will be the elections of many state assemblies. On 23rd February Tripura, 3rd March Meghalaya and 5th March the Nagaland elections will be held. The Karnataka assembly election can also take place by May. In the second half of this year, elections are scheduled in four important states - Delhi, Rajasthan, Madhya Pradesh and Chhattisgarh. Given the nature of the developments in Goa and Jharkhand, elections can also take place there at any time. It will not be an exaggeration if we say that this is a time for continuous electoral battles. For the first time in the last 20 years, we are encountering so many assembly elections alongwith the Lok Sabha election. What does a political party want for the elections? A clear ideology, a mature leadership, a strong organization and an enthusiastic worker. If any political party possesses all of these, it is only the Bharatiya Janata Party. From an ideological point of view, only our ideology of cultural nationalism is capable of providing answer for all the threats that loom over the nation. From the point of view of leadership, no other party has such a capable, mature and spotless leadership like respected Atalji and Advaniji. From the point of view of workers, we are indeed blessed with such true, honest and committed workers which is nothing less than a divine gift.

Today we are having all the required factors for wining the elections, be it ideology, leadership, organization or the committed workers. The vast expanse of our workers that I can see in front of me, almost appears as if a bird is about to take to the skies, with its destination clearly visible to it. I am fully confident that we will achieve our destination.

Another thing that we should keep in mind is that when the party marches towards victory, then in enthusiasm or sometimes due to competition, some minor problems can erupt.

On several occasions mutual difference of opinion may surface. To resolve this, we require self restraint.

The organization may at times witness divergent directions. To overcome this, we require coordination.

Our influence among the people may at times appear to be weakening. To overcome this, we require firm struggle.

Today is the era of communication. In this age of media, it is important to appropriately use the various channels of communication. However, our basic attention should be focused on making a live contact with the masses at the grassroots. Only then our actual influence on politics will be truly visible. And this influence will finally help us reach our destination.

Apart from the workers and sympathizers of the BJP, I want to appeal to all the voters of the country that in the forthcoming elections, they must definitely cast their votes. A negligent and lethargic attitude about casting one's vote, despite having the capacity and facility to do so, in principle not only weakens the democracy but in practice also paves the way for unhealthy elements getting into the polity which in turn is detrimental to the health of democracy. Voters should also bear in mind that they not only form the government by casting their vote but also indirectly pave the way for someone to form the government by not exercising their franchise. And such a government cannot truly reflect the will of the people. Therefore, I once again appeal to the people of the country, that they all must vote in the forthcoming elections to establish a government in the country and their respective states, which reflects the true will and aspirations of the masses.

□

Preparing for a new ground

1-2 June, 2008 (New Delhi)

Today's National Executive is witness to a historical moment not only for the BJP but also for the entire country as it is taking place immediately after a glorious achievement of the BJP. We are all aware about our achieving a grand success in Karnataka. For this, firstly I would like to express my gratitude to the people of Karnataka and also congratulate all the dedicated party workers and leaders in Karnataka for their tireless work and efforts. Along with them I would like to specially congratulate the newly elected Chief Minister of Karnataka Shri B. S. Yeodyurappa, State President Shri Sadanand Gowda, National General Secretary Shri Anantha Kumar, the State Prabhari for the past one year and National Vice President Shri Yashwant Sinha and Shri Arun Jaitley who as the Election *Prabhari* went there to efficiently manage the elections.

The victory of Karnataka will prove to be a milestone in Indian politics for both BJP and NDA. The victory of Karnataka symbolizes not only the political expansion of the BJP but also its social and geographical expansion. The blossoming of the 'Lotus' in Karnataka is a message of the blossoming of lotus in South India, the long term impact of which will be visible in the years to come.

In addition to being an expression of the people's lack of faith in the Congress and UPA Government at the Centre, the victory of Karnataka also is a message to all political parties that the lifespan of the politics of opportunism and betrayal is very short. The victory of Karnataka is a vote of confidence given by the people in answer to the politics of duplicity.

Our winning streak over the last two years in Punjab, Uttarakhand, Gujarat, Himachal and now in Karnataka will not halt. I am confident that in November 2008, with the support of the people, we will hoist the flag of victory in Madhya Pradesh, Rajasthan, Delhi and Chhattisgarh. Thereafter, in the elections that will take place in March-April 2009, the

NDA will form the government at the Centre and the people of the country will hand over the reins of the country to our beloved leader Shri Lal Krishna Advaniji by giving the responsibility of Prime Ministership to him.

I can clearly assert today that the BJP is the natural political party of this country. I feel elated in saying that we have been able to once again win the election to Betul Lok Sabha seat in Madhya Pradesh which had become extremely prestigious. At the same time we won Hamirpur Lok Sabha election in Himachal Pradesh with record votes. Our ally the Shiv Sena has won the Thane Lok Sabha seat. Alongwith Karnataka we have won three Lok Sabha by-elections while the Congress could not win a single seat.

After the victory in Karnataka if we visualize the expanse of the BJP in the national scenario, then in the north in Punjab and Himachal, in the west in Gujarat and Rajasthan, in the east in Orissa and Bihar, in the north-east in Meghalaya and Nagaland, in central India in Madhya Pradesh and Chhattisgarh and now in the south in Karnataka the governments of the BJP and our allies are giving a clear indication that the BJP has now become the largest political party of the country. More than 200 Lok Sabha seats fall in these states.

On the other hand, less than 125 Lok Sabha seats are in the states ruled by Congress and its allies. Not only this, over the last six months we have been able to expand our organization upto the booth level. More that 60% of the booth units have already been constituted, whereas, the organization of the Congress exists only upto the block level. Therefore, we can clearly say that the Congress Party's long standing claim of being the largest party of the country both politically and organizationally has weakened and the BJP has emerged as the largest party of the country both in political and organizational terms. Now we are the obvious frontrunners for the Lok Sabha elections.

We are passing through a historic phase. The eyes of the nation are set upon the BJP-led NDA. The role of each one of us has become important. The BJP's duty towards the nation has increased. We will have to be alert about our duties at our respective positions. People are not willing to accept even a minute mistake on our part. We need to pledge towards becoming a strong link of trust in politics through which we will create a wave of faith and exuberance in the minds of people and meet their expectations.

Our meeting was to take place in Jaipur. The meeting was supposed to last for three days. Now it is taking place over two days. We all know why we had to cancel the meeting in Jaipur and shift it the venue to Delhi. Rajasthan has been inflicted by a double setback. The soil of the pink city of Jaipur was bloodied simultaneously at several places by bombs of the terrorists. I pay my condolences to all the innocent citizens and their bereaved families who were killed in this dastardly act. On the other hand, the sad and unfortunate incidents of violence that have taken place on the issue of reservation have shocked not only the people of Rajasthan but also the entire country. I appeal to all the sections of society in Rajasthan as well as the neighbouring states to exercise restraint and offer my tributes to all the innocent people who have been killed in this reservation movement.

The Congress led UPA presented a report card on its four years rule. We believe that the real report card of the UPA has been presented through the mandate of the people in the form of the election results of Punjab, Uttarakhand, Himachal, Gujarat and Karnataka over the last one year. In democracy, only the report card presented by the people can be considered as the real one. In the people's report card, the Congress led UPA is already counting its last days in the last year of its tenure.

Price Rise

It appears that the current administrators of the nation are completely oblivious about the extent to which the common man has been burdened by the unending price rise. Today's price rise is multi-dimensional. I am calling it multi-dimensional because not only have prices risen but the availability of products has also been impacted. Items of daily use such as food and cooking gas that were easily available in the market in abundance during the NDA regime, today not only have their prices increased but their shortage is also being felt.

Simultaneously, the government comes out with statements that are not only peculiar but also painful. For example the Deputy Chairman of the Planning Commission Dr. Montek Singh Ahluwalia said that development cannot be sacrificed for the sake of inflation. I would like to ask not only the learned Deputy Chairman of the Planning Commission but also our leaned economist Finance Minister and Prime Minister: Is development possible only by crushing the common man under the burden of inflation? Can't these experts see an alternate model of development?

Did not development take place in the tenure of the NDA? Was not inflation under control? Is this the same hand of the Congress Party which came to power on the claim of being with the common man and today is willing to sacrifice all the requirements of the common man for the sake of building a so-called palace of development. And that too such development that is not being reflected anywhere. The BJP will never accept a policy that seeks to build a palace by sacrificing a hut.

I would like to remind the people of the country that during the tenure of the NDA Government the international situation was even more hostile. We conducted nuclear tests at Pokhran. I would like to remind everyone that on account of the Pokhran nuclear tests we were facing international sanctions. During the same period while we were facing sanctions we had to encounter foreign aggression in Kargil. Therefore, despite facing aggression and sanctions, we were able to control inflation and also undertake development. Does the government today have to face an international scenario that is worse than facing aggression and international sanctions? The government is merely making excuses to cover up their incapability in controlling inflation.

Food Crisis

In a country where from the Indus to Sutlej to the Brahmaputra, and from the Narmada to the Cauvery lies the world's most fertile and possibly largest alluvial plain, in that country a food crisis and that too getting created in absence of drought, floods or natural calamity, then besides the government's short-sightedness and incapability what else can it be called? One of the biggest factors for rising prices is lack of adequate food stocks with the government. These food stocks have not reduced overnight but the situation has built up over the last two years. The situation which began in April 2006 reached a point of shortage of 5 million tones by July 2007. Despite these circumstances, the government decided to permit wheat export by private companies. The government was aware that this food shortage is not because of lower foodgrain production but rather on account of lack of proper storage and adequate distribution facilities. Yet, by permitting export of wheat by private players, the government further aggravated the situation.

Farmer's Package

In the Budget the government had claimed that the loans of the farmers will be waived. By the end of June the work on waiving off the farmers loans was to be completed. It is 1st June today. I would like to know from the government what is the progress with respect to the farmer's loans being waived off? By now the loans of how many farmers have been waived off and these farmers belong to which category and how much relief has till date reached those farmers who are trapped in the vicious debt cycle of private moneylenders? Now that three months have passed since the Budget was presented, the country's farmers want to know at what pace is the much publicized loan waiver package meant for them progressing?

In my opinion and I have been repeatedly saying that until the farmer's purchasing power and capacity for investment is increased, till that time agriculture will continue to be a losing proposition. And farmers will continue to leave agriculture. In the decade of the 1990s, according to the figures presented in the census, around 80 lakh people felt compelled to leave agriculture between 1991 and 2001. These 80 lakh people left agriculture in the absence of any alternate employment opportunities. This means that unemployment is not rising only on account of increasing population but also on account of people leaving agriculture.

During the last National Council I highlighted that 77% of India's population still survives on an income of less than Rs 20 to 40 per day. This segment virtually comprises people in rural and agricultural areas. According to data of the 59th Round of the National Sample Survey, the average monthly per capita expenditure of an Indian farm household in India is only Rs 503 per month and this is very close to the poverty line. You can well imagine that out of an income of Rs 503 about 60% gets spent on food alone and what must be left for other expenses of a poor farmer. It is difficult to even imagine how much rise in prices of foodgrains would have impacted these people. It is worth thinking about what meaning independence holds for this huge segment of the country's population even after 61 years of independence.

The government declares an incomplete loan waiver package but mere loan waiver will not help those farmers who have already quit agriculture. For improving the agrarian system the government will have to undertake some concrete measures. In this budget the government has not made any provision regarding the farmer's purchasing power, assuring them income and securing their economic future. In this situation the farmers cannot get any substantive or permanent benefit.

I am not saying all this from a political point of view but on the basis of solid facts. The government announced a special package for the Vidarbha region. First the Chief Minister of Maharashtra and then the Prime Minister announced packages. However, according to the CAG report even after the announcement of both packages the number of farmers suicides kept increasing. The CAG report also states that farmers suicides went on increasing even after the announcement of the loan waiver package. The true picture of the much talked about loan waiver package for the Vidarbha region is clearly seen in the report of the Comptroller & Auditor General. That is why I say that the agrarian crisis has to be studied in great depth and on the basis of its extensive dimensions. No relief will be possible only through short term remedies.

The National Sample Survey and CAG report, the evidently visible pathetic condition of the farmers as well as the ever increasing farmers suicides which even the Agriculture Minister has accepted in Parliament that over the past few years one lakh fifty thousand farmers have committed suicide, are these not enough to force the government to think about convening a special session of Parliament to discuss only the problems of the farmers and the agrarian crisis? I had raised this issue in our last National Council Meeting. The government has not paid any attention to this. The subject with which 75% of the country's population is directly or indirectly connected; because of which the food crisis impacts every person, on that issue can't the Parliament take out seven days for a discussion? This is a sad irony.

In reality, in the policy of the government, agriculture is not treated as a primary subject but instead has become a second rated subject. The policy of treating farmers and agriculture as second rate started under the British and continues even today. This not only impacts India's economic and social reality but also negatively impacts our national existence.

This is not my personal view. The Chairman of the Farmers Commission and eminent agricultural expert Dr M S Swaminathan has also said that unlike other nations, in India agriculture cannot be treated as merely a food grain producing machine but rather it is the backbone for the livelihood of three-fourths of our population. Those who are advising people to move away from agriculture are ignoring a harsh reality that on doing so 50 crore people will get added to the list of landless labour and the unemployed.

The importance of agriculture has been understood not only by experts but also by great seers. The great visionary of modern age Maharishi Aurobindo in an article written by him in Vande Mataram in March 1908 said *"The life of a nation is always rooted in its villages but that of India is so deeply and persistently rooted there, that no change or revolution can ever substitute for this source of sap and life. The Western system makes the city centre and the village a mere feeder of the city. This has been perhaps an obstacle to national unity but it has also been an assurance of national persistence. It is an ascertained principle of national existence that only by keeping possession of the soil can a nation persist."*

If life is not possible without food then a nation without land is not possible either. The pledge of nation building is a farce without it encompassing agriculture and the villages, the perpetual symbol of our great nation's life and vibrancy. This is what the present UPA Government is doing with the villages, poor and farmers. If we get an opportunity to form a government at the centre then we will revive and re-establish both agriculture and the villages.

Sixth Pay Commission

The government had declared in the budget that by 31st March the Sixth Pay Commission report for the government employees will be made public. The report of the Sixth Pay Commission has come out but the kind of dissatisfaction its recommendations have generated among the various groups has never been witnessed before.

The officials, staff and personnel of the military and paramilitary forces have registered their objections. Probably for the first time in the history of India retired officials and military personnel belonging to the security forces were compelled to agitate against the government. A former army General has even written a letter to the government. To deal with these reactions the government has constituted a secretary level Review Committee. Since the grievances of the military personnel are against the bureaucracy, therefore I am doubtful whether an easily acceptable solution will emerge from this secretary level committee. Therefore, I urge the government that a committee of ministers should analyse the recommendations of the Review Committee before any final decision is taken and it would be preferable if someone from the security forces is also made a part of the Review Committee.

It is my personal opinion that if the government has recommended time bound promotion for the IAS upto the level of Joint Secretary, then the same provision should also be made for the security forces. There should also be an arrangement for "Second Assured Career" for all those officials and military personnel upto 60 years of age after they leave the security forces. I am saying all this because being in the military is not merely a profession but instead it symbolizes a commitment and spirit of sacrifice for the country and in no other profession there is a need to risk one's life to this extent. While the loss of life cannot be compensated in any manner but if the government fails to satisfy our military personnel in terms of salary expectations, then it may lead to long-term implications. Today, given the state of the country's internal and external security environment, the importance of the armed forces has increased substantially. The BJP clearly believes that in such circumstances nothing should adversely impact their spirit. I urge the government to pay special attention to this issue. In addition to this there is also widespread discontent among the teachers and other sections of employees. The government should make arrangements for addressing their objections.

At the National Council Meeting in Delhi I had demanded that keeping in view the salaried class, the government should raise the standard limit of income tax to one and half lakh rupees. The government had to make such a provision in the budget. Simultaneously we had also demanded an increase in the rate of interest on Provident Fund. However, the government has not taken any effective steps on this issue.

Terrorism

On the issue of terrorism, the Bharatiya Janata Party has always stood for a very clear and strong approach. However, after coming to power at the centre, the UPA Government has started viewing this important issue from the point of view of vote bank politics. In a completely unreasonable and absolutely incorrect manner, it has attempted to establish the ongoing actions against terrorism as actions against the minority community and against the Muslim community in particular. That is the reason why among the first steps that this government took after coming to power was the removal of the anti-terrorist law POTA. The government believed that by doing so it would be able to gain the sympathy of a particular community. This has not been done by the Congress for the first time. Earlier also the Congress had criticized the anti-terrorist law TADA for similar reasons. The BJP has continuously opposed this step of the government over the past four years.

Recently, the State Department of the United States of America released a report on the status of terrorism in all the nations of the world. According to this report, India is the worst terrorism affected countries of the world. In the year 2007 alone 22,000 people became victims of terrorism. However in India alone, more than 2300 lives were lost. The issue is not about being the most affected nation by terrorism. The report has also outlined the reasons for this and stated that in India the law enforcement machinery is very ill-equipped and we have a slow and laborious legal system here. This means that in India the law enforcement agency is not equipped with the required laws and the process of dispensing justice is also very slow and cumbersome. Now that even international agencies are indicating that India does not have required arrangements to deal with terrorism then why the government does not still feel the need to create special arrangements.

Speaking at a seminar in Delhi, the Chief Justice of India K.G. Balakrishnan said that though it was not his subject but he believed that in the given circumstances a strong anti-terrorist law in India has become necessary.

Over the last four years all the important cities and national centres have become targets of terrorism. Now terrorism is expanding itself even in the interiors of the country. About six months ago, bomb blasta occured within the court premises of Lucknow, Faizabad and Benares, and in January the CRPF camp in Rampur was attacked, thereafter on 13th May the serial bomb blasts shook the otherwise calm and peaceful town of Jaipur in which 60 people were killed and more than 200 injured. The BJP strongly condemned this utterly dastardly act. Recently, at Indore in Madhya Pradesh, many activists of the banned organisation SIMI were arrested as they were in the midst of planning a big terrorist attack. All these clearly indicate how terrorism is spreading its roots in interior parts of the country. Terrorism is a complex national problem which cannot be pushed over to states by considering it as a law and order problem. The Central government continues to keep pending Acts against organised crimes passed by Gujarat, Rajasthan and Madhya Pradesh legislative assemblies. I would like to question the Central Government about its intention on this issue. If they want to honestly support state governments in their fight against terrorism then they should immediately grant approval to these Acts. Over the last few months, the government pointed out that the share market and nuclear establishments of the country were in the shadow of terrorist attacks and infiltration. Can all these issues be treated as general law and order issues of a single state or states? This is a national problem and Central Government has completely failed in tackling it.

It is amply clear that India requires an effective and strong anti-terrorism law. We have also earlier said that if the government introduces any anti-terrorism law in the Parliament we will support it. Even after being completely exposed within and outside the country, if the government still does not feel the urgency for an anti terrorism law, then this would not only reflect its immaturity but also raises questions about the honesty of the government. The people of the country will not tolerate dishonesty on the issue of national security and will give a befitting reply to the UPA Government in the forthcoming elections.

To highlight the UPA Government's approach on terrorism I would like to present the examples of two highest authorities within the government. The Prime Minister went to the extent of saying that he was unable to sleep throughout the night in sympathy towards Dr. Muhammad Hanif who was arrested in Australia in connection with the attack on Heathrow airport in London. Over 60 people have been killed and hundreds have been injured in the terrorist attack in Jaipur. I would like to question the Prime Minister about what sort of reactions came to his mind after this incident? How restless did he feel? The government should be more sensitive towards the victims of terrorism and on the death of the security forces who are fighting the terrorists than just on the interrogation of a person on charges of terrorism.

The second example refers to the Home Minister Shivraj Patil when he drew a comparison between the cases of Sarabjit and Afzal. We condemn the Home Minister's statement of seekiong to equate a patriotic innocent citizen with a terrorist convicted of attacking the highest institution of the country. The statement of the wife of Sarabjit, Sukhbir Kaur, which came in the media clearly said that "*My daughters and i are not ready to accept the release of Sarabjit in exchange of any terrorist. We are patriots and nothing is above the nation.*" But this government sees one thing over and above the nation and that is vote bank politics.

It is worth mentioning about the recent *fatwa* issued by one of the most prestigious religious centres of the Muslim community Dar-ul-Uloom Deoband which stated that the killing of innocent citizens by terrorists is an un-Islamic act. I welcome this. Deoband is seeking to dissociate Muslims from terrorism. But the Central government wants to equate

Muslims with terrorism and on this very basis is rejecting an anti-terrorism law. Perhaps, the Central government wants to prove itself as a bigger messiah of the Muslims, even bigger than the *Madrassas*.

A government in which the Prime Minister and the Home Minister have such an approach towards terrorism, such a government cannot control terrorism. I want to assure the people that if they vote the BJP led NDA to power at the Centre then we will bring a strong law against terrorism to crush the morale of the terrorists who seek to operate in India.

The Prime Minister has accepted that terrorism is a national problem and it cannot be dealt with at the level of states alone. He has called for a separate federal investigative agency for dealing with terrorism. I am surprised that the Prime Minister feels the need for a federal investigative agency but does not feel the need for a federal law. This means that there is a need for an army but not for arming the military.

The Problem of Bangladeshi Infiltrators

The recent bomb explosions that took place in Jaipur have once again indicated towards the involvement of terrorist outfits operating out of Bangladesh. Prior to this also, in the bomb explosions that took place in the courts complexes of Lucknow, Faizabad and Benaras, there was proof about the involvement of Bangladeshi outfits. The manner in which people are coming into the country from Bangladesh in an unauthorized manner is not a simple problem. While passing a judgement on the I.M.D.T. Act, the Supreme Court said that the infiltration of Bangladeshis into Assam is not a simple problem but amounts to external aggression on the country. Quashing the I.M.D.T. Act, the Supreme Court in December 2006 dismissed the central notification of February 2006 and questioned the intention of the government in expelling the Bangladeshi infiltrators. *"There is a lack of will (on the part of the Centre) in the matter of ensuring that illegal migrants are sent out of the country."* The court further observed that normally it desists from commenting on the issue of national security but despite the decision of quashing the notification of 2005 of the I.M.D.T. Act no action had been taken on the basic spirit behind the court's action. *"Though we would normally desist from commenting, when the security of the nation is the issue as highlighted in the 2005 judgment, we have to say that the bona fide of the action leaves something to be desired."*

Today when not only in Assam but in the interiors of country and in different places in the Hindi speaking areas, when terrorist attacks are taking place and the proof about the involvement of Bangladeshis is being found, even now the government does not feel the need of formulating an effective plan to expel the Bangladeshi infiltrators? The Government of India should seek to identify all Bangladeshis living in the country and make efforts to deport them back to Bangladesh. The BJP will never tolerate vote bank politics to take place at the cost of the common man's life and property.

Today, the problem of Bangladeshi infiltrators has spread throughout the country and become a challenge for national security. The Bharatiya Janata Party is accused of opposing the Bangladeshi infiltrators for communal reasons. But we say that we are opposing them for nationalist reasons. Today's circumstances support our point of view. Today there is a need for all political parties to rise above partisan politics and think about this serious national issue. Vote bank politics can never be more important than the lives of the innocent citizens.

I appeal to all the political parties in the country to reconsider their policies on the problem of Bangladeshi infiltrators with an open mind in the context of the opinion expressed by Supreme Court (on the I.M.D.T. Act) and the Prime Minister should call a meeting in which all the political parties frame a national policy. National security cannot be an issue for politicking.

Neighbouring Countries and Foreign Policy

After the formation of the UPA Government at the Centre, the entire country has witnessed how our basic national foreign policy has suffered over the last four years. One no longer sees the same warmth as earlier with Russia which has been one of our oldest and most intimate allies. The relationship with the United States has been centralized to only one issue the Nuclear Deal and even on that the government has not been able to take a decision nor has answered any of the concerns that we have raised before the people. We are all aware about the peculiar situation with regard to the government's policy on Iran. Over the last four years, there has been no progress on the issue of permanent membership of the UN Security Council.

Even more worrisome is the situation that one sees with regard to foreign policy towards our neighbouring countries. In Afghanistan every other day one hears about cases of kidnapping of Indians who have gone there for employment and some even lost their lives, yet the government has failed to evolve a plan. There has been no improvement in the situation with Pakistan despite a new government coming to power. The tone that the newly formed government in Nepal has adopted after assuming office raises question-marks on our centuries old relationship with them. The government's approach on the Tibet issue has been far from satisfactory. On these very issues, today there will be a detailed discussion on a resolution.

For close to a year, China's attitude on Arunachal has been completely contrary to cordial relations. And a few days ago, China even raised its claim over a portion of Sikkim on which there has never been any border dispute. The government should clearly present the true picture before the country.

It appears that the Central Government is either not serious on the sensitive subject of national security or because of the pressure of its Left Front allies it is willing to ignore China's every activity. I personally feel that given the tone and posture that China has taken over the past few months, it appears that somehow China feels assured that despite its incorrect posturing, the Left parties will not allow the government to adopt any stern stand against it.

Record of Judicial Criticism

Only 15-20 days ago, the court castigated the Central government over the basis on which the Sachhar Committee was constituted. I have mentioned this on previous occasions too that similar to the British system of granting communal awards, the current UPA Government has also sowed the seeds of communal divide and one such measure has been the Sachhar Committee. We have been opposing it from the very beginning. In a way the court also while castigating the Central Government asked how was a survey conducted by keeping a particular community in focus and on what basis did the government decide to do so?

When one studies the details available on the recommendations of the Sachhar Committee, a few interesting facts emerge that some of the members of the Sachhar Committee went on to work beyond its terms of reference. In fact they even suggested that the delimitation of some constituencies should be undertaken in such a manner that the entire Muslim population of a district should come within a single electoral area. They went further to the extent of suggesting that all those Lok Sabha seats which have been reserved for the Scheduled Castes and Scheduled Tribes and in which the Muslim population is over 19%, the reservation on such seats should be removed and in the future also they should not be reserved. On this basis the Sachhar Committee wanted 23 assembly seats each in Uttar Pradesh and Bihar and 17 assembly seats in West Bengal that are reserved for the scheduled castes to be de-reserved. Was it the purview of the Sachhar Committee to decide about delimitation or about the reserved seats for the Scheduled Castes and Scheduled Tribes? All these efforts remind us about the political developments of pre-independence days that went on to sow the foundations for partition.

These indicate that the very basis of the formation of the Sachhar Committee appears to be illegal. From the very beginning we have been saying that the Sachhar Committee goes against the core spirit of the Constitution.

This is not the first instance where the courts have made the central government aware about its crossing the limits or in a common man's language, the government has been castigated by the court.

Prior to this be it the misuse of the office of Governor to usurp the people's mandate immediately after the Jharkhand elections or preventing a majority government from assuming office in Bihar; be it the attempt of reserving government jobs for Muslims in Andhra Pradesh or reserving seats for Muslims in Aligarh Muslim University, be it the issue of making changes in the Act of All India Institute of Medical Sciences or selecting an alternate route on the Setu Samundrum Project, the UPA Government at the Centre has had to face the irritation of the court on numerous occasions. However, it seems that just like an indisciplined person, the government too has become used to this.

Stop the Constitutional Use of the Word "Dharmanirpeksh"

When India's Constitution was written in November 1949, then in the Preamble to the Constitution basically India was declared as a "Sovereign, Democratic, Republic". In context of the Preamble of the Constitution Dr. Bhimrao Ambedkar said that it should be considered as the soul of the Constitution and if there was to be any doubt regarding any Article then the decision should be taken after studying it with reference to the Preamble. Therefore, fundamentally there should have been no change to the Preamble of the Constitution since it reflected India's basic character and was an expression of the public sentiment at the time of independence. Yet, in the decade of the 1970s through the 42nd constitutional amendment, the words "Secular" and "Socialist" were added to the Preamble of the Constitution. And after this change the Preamble of India's Constitution became "Sovereign, Secular, Socialist, Democratic, Republic". It is only after this change that widespread politics began over the word "Secular" which was publicized as *"Dharmanirpekshta"*. However, neither technically nor politically, the true meaning of the word "Secular" can ever be *"Dharmanirpekshta"*. The official Hindi translation of the Preamble of the Constitution published by the Law & Justice Ministry of Government of India, which is also a public document, in that the meaning of the word "Secular" is written as *"Panthnirpeksh"*.

There is a big difference in being *"Dharmanirpeksh"* and *"Panthnirpeksh"*. *Panth* or sect symbolizes devotion towards any specific belief, specific way of prayer and specific form of God but *Dharma* symbolizes absolute and eternal values which can never change like laws of nature. For example one can say *Dharma* is like the earth or land while *Panth* is like different paths built over it. Our mind can choose any path, change from one path to another, we can hold different views about the various paths but how can we ever get separated from the earth?

"Dharmapran Nation" means a nation whose actual consciousness is imbibed in *Dharma.* India is a *"Dharmapran"* nation and this is evident from Amarnath in the extreme north to Sabarimala Temple in the extreme south, and in Haridwar, Nasik, Ujjain and Prayag where one can see *Kumbh Melas* in perpetual occurrence.

India's National Emblem has three lions and carries the eternal message of *"Satyamev Jaytev"* (Truth Always Triumphs) of the *Mundkoupanishad.* Truth signifies *Dharma* and not a sect. India's National Flag has the *Ashoka Chakra* in it. This *Chakra* found in Sarnath is *Dharmachakra* and basically symbolizes the cycle of *Dharma.* In India's Parliament behind the seat of the Speaker of the Lok Sabha *"Dharmachakra Pravartanay"* (for the propogation of the eternal cycle of *Dharma)* is inscribed. Therefore, if *Dharma* is present in the National Emblem, National Flag, and in the supreme seat of Parliament then how can the entire establishment of India be neutral to *Dharma* or be *Dharmanirpeksh?*

Probably by understanding these very sentiments, even in the Constitution the word *Panthnirpeksh* was written. The use of the term *Dharmanirpeksh* instead of *Panthnirpeksh* is not only incorrect, unconstitutional, not only against all the national symbols of India but also against the very basis of the real and perpetual ethos of our great nation. The level of pervasion and confusion created in both politics and among the public by the inappropriate use of the word is unimaginable. This also hurts our identity and traditions. India has always been a *Panthnirpeksh* or sect neutral country. Here from *Shaivism, Vaishnavism, Shakht* to Jainism, Buddhism and Sikhism many sects have flourished. Throughout history there has never been any discrimination with anybody.

However, India was never *Dharmanirpeksh,* is not *Dharmanirpeksh* and till its existence can never ever be *Dharmanirpeksh.* To make this *Dharmapran* nation into a *Dharma* neutral nation is a deplorable attempt to destroy the actual consciousness of this great country. At least after 61 years of independence we should try and come out of this colonial mindset. India needs to come out of the distorted Indianization from the borrowed western thoughts because without appreciating our own identity and also by hurting our own identity India cannot become a proud and powerful nation of the 21st century.

The confusion created by *Dharmanirpeksh* and *Panthnirpeksh* cannot be removed only through an explanation. The only solution is to stop the use of the word *Dharmanirpeksh.* That is why I am announcing that in future we will never use the word *Dharmanirpeksh* and the Government of India should also issue a directive prohibiting the constitutional use of the word *Dharmanirpeksh* so that from the Prime Minister to the common public no one constitutionally uses this term and this will prevent confusion and damage from taking place though its usage.

Scientific Achievements

On account of the wrong policies and intention of the Central Government the overall environment in the country is becoming psychologically extremely pessimistic. At the same time the people of the country also witnessed the achievements of our scientists, who through their tireless efforts and commitment have succeeded in strengthening the country's strategic and technological power.

Recently, the Indian Space Research Organisation (ISRO) by successfully launching ten satellites at the same time marked the dawn of a new era for the country's space science. The strategic power of the country has immensely increased by the successful testing of the Medium Range Ballistic Missile Agni -3. This missile is capable of precisely hitting a target upto 3000 kilometers aways and of carrying nuclear warheads. Our scientists have expressed hope that by the end of this year a missile of 5000 kilometers range would also be successfully tested.

Today in this context, I recall that only twenty days ago marked the completion of ten years of the Pokhran Tests. The nuclear explosions of Pokhran in 1998 marked the declaration of India's pride and power in the international arena. India's international status and ascendance that we witness today was initiated from that point. Today on the completion of ten years, I express my gratitude to the main executer of the operation former President Dr. Abdul Kalam, all his scientist colleagues and our former Prime Minister respected Atalji who displayed exemplary courage in taking the decision.

On the completion of the ten years of the Pokhran Test and for the magnificent success of our scientists for this achievement, the Bharatiya Janata Party salutes them and assures them that on getting the opportunity of being in government, the BJP will provide them every opportunity to develop techniques for the defense of the country in accordance with their capabilities. We will also fulfill our pledge of making India a strong and developed nation by 2020.

Women's Reservation

The BJP Mahila Morcha organised a historic demonstration at the Ramlila Maidan in February 2008 on the issue of 33% reservation for women. In the history of Delhi such a huge gathering of women had never been witnessed before.

I extend my heartiest congratulations to the Mahila Morcha for this most successful rally. In its Delhi session, the BJP carried out the required amendment in its constitution to give one-third representation to women within the organization. Through this the BJP has launched a new chapter in Indian politics. I believe that on account the BJP's initiative and because of the historic decision of the party to give political participation to women, as a direct consequence of the pressure that got created, the UPA Government was forced to table the Women's Reservation Bill in Parliament in the last leg of their tenure.

Forthcoming Assembly Elections

This is a moment of great elation for us. We are in government on our own in seven states. In five states we have coalition governments. Wherever we are in government, people have great expectations from us. Therefore, the BJP ruled state governments will have to make continuous efforts to inspire confidence among the people. I feel happy in saying that our governments in Madhya Pradesh, Rajasthan and Chhattisgarh are leading in the effort of undertaking proper development. While in these states we will highlight the developmental activities undertaken by us before the people, in Delhi and these three states we will also highlight the failures of Congress-led UPA Government at the Centre as election issues. According to my information, our state governments in these three states have undertaken numerous decisions for the benefit of the farmers, labourers, women, youth, scheduled castes and scheduled tribes. I extend my heartiest congratulations to these three state governments for taking historic decisions to help those people living below the poverty line. Simultaneously, I hope that we will form BJP governments in Delhi along with Madhya Pradesh, Rajasthan and Chhattisgarh.

Appeal

The seat of power in Delhi is not far for us. We will need to tirelessly work in the coming days. We will need to awaken India's youth. We will need to use their energy at the organizational level. We all are aware that the youth is always the conduit for change. Youth power is said to be national power. We need to apply ourselves in great detail about how the youth of the country will consider the BJP as their organization, how they will be drawn to our aims and objectives and how they will lean towards our party. I would like to draw your attention to a recent survey conducted on the youth by a leading publication in April on India completing 60 years of independence which also indicates about which direction the country's youth is in reality being drawn towards. When asked about whom did they consider as the most inspiring Indian of the 20th century, a sample survey of 19,000 respondents through sms and website said that their first choice was Shaheed-e-Azam Bhagat Singh and second choice was Netaji Subhash Chandra Bose. This clearly indicates that even today the feeling of nationalism reverberates in the pulses of the youth. Such emotions of the youth can only be represented through the Bharatiya Janata Party. We need to make extensive efforts on this front to ensure that more and more youth come along with us.

Similarly the lead which the BJP has taken in creating leadership of women by giving them one-third representation, in the same manner we need to empower women. The BJP believes in complete social harmony. Every section of society must be developed. On this occasion I would like to appeal to the minorities of the country that they should be wary of those who practice politics in the name of so called secularism. The BJP treats the minorities not as vote banks but as committed citizens of the country.

From the core of their hearts, the people want to hand over power to the BJP. We also want the nation to experience an environment of value based politics. Alongwith Cultural Nationalism, Article 370, Uniform Civil Code and True Secularism, we are committed to preserve the national unity and integrity. We always maintain that power is a means and not an end for us.

I have great hope that our party workers in every village will constitute their teams at every booth and while they will ensure the BJP's geographical, social, political and cultural expansion, they will also ensure that our ideology spreads among our supporters in their respective areas. If we succeed on this front, which I am confident that we will achieve, then that day is not far off when from the ramparts of the Red Fort, our prime ministerial candidate Shri Lal Krishna Advaniji will address the entire country.

□

Lotus Blooms in South

12-14 September, 2008 (Bangalore)

From the time of the foundation of the Jan Sangh in 1951 to 1980 when the BJP was founded, and from then onwards it has always been our dream to see the BJP form a government in the south. That dream has now become a reality and the apex body of the BJP is today witnessing it. There was a time when the Congress used to form the government in all the four states in the south. This change in Karnataka symbolizes the dawn of a new era in the politics of India.

Over the last three months, the biggest event in national politics has been the UPA Government winning the vote of confidence in Parliament. However, the manner in which this vote of confidence has been obtained has shaken the very foundation of our democratic system and parliamentary democracy. The entire country is ashamed by the actions of the Congress led UPA on 22nd July. The Congress has always indulged in acts that turn the administrative setup into a corruption based set up (*Note-Tantra*). But this time, although the government has technically won the vote of confidence by converting '*Lok-Tantra*' into '*Note-Tantra*', it has in the process lost the confidence of the people. This issue would not have been as important if the government had merely lost the confidence of the people, but if the people start losing faith in the very foundation of the democratic process, then such a government will definitely have to be considered guilty of committing a crime. The manner in which the government has attempted to shut its eyes from a fact that has been witnessed by the entire country only demonstrates its complete shamelessness. This act of the government will definitely come before the court of the people who will undoubtedly punish them for it.

That the government has actually lost the faith of the people can be proved by the fact that it has not yet convened the monsoon session of Parliament. Generally, every year the monsoon session is convened in the third week of July. This has probably happened for the first time.

Today the country is facing many important issues such as terrorism, price rise, the prevailing situation in the Kashmir valley, natural calamities like floods, among others. In my opinion, the government does not have the courage to face Parliament. How can an unnatural government after saving itself in an unnatural manner muster the courage to face Parliament?

The BJP has always maintained that the UPA is an unnatural alliance which came into being only to keep the BJP away from power. Earlier this alliance was captive of the left and now it has become captive to the Samajwadi Party. Any government which becomes captive to its allies becomes a 'bonded government'. Probably this is the destiny of the UPA Government.

In the first decade of the 21st century, Bangalore, has twice experienced the turn of history. Firstly, during the time of the Shri Vajpayee government, Bangalore emerged as the most important centre of Information Technology (IT), and now it is also seen as the Knowledge Capital of emerging India. Secondly, some months ago, the Bharatiya Janata Party, which represents pure Indian nationalism, formed the government in the state on its own. The radiant talent of the Indian youth and the nationalist ideology of the BJP are going to play the most significant role in shaping the future of India. Bangalore, by incorporating both, is clearly indicating towards the golden possibilities of the future.

Whenever the turn of history takes place, it also brings with it many types of challenges. Today also we are witnessing something like that. On the one hand, one sees the limitless possibilities of India's economic advancement and development, and on the other hand, we are also witnessing serial terrorist attacks one after the other in important cities and every part of the country.

War in the Form of Terrorism

After independence, from the war of Kashmir in 1948 to the Kargil war in 1999, India has faced many attacks. However, the activities of the enemies were confined only to the borders. Even when terrorism fomented, it remained confined to one or two States or a single region or so. But the manner in which our enemies are attacking each and every part of the country and from the north to south, the common man can become its victim anywhere and at anytime. For the first time such a situation has emerged in the country. For India, this is the biggest challenge of the 21st century.

The manner in which India fought against imperialism in the beginning of the 20th century, today in the beginning of 21st century the same kind of struggle is required against terrorism. At that time even imperialism was a worldwide phenomenon, whether it was British imperialism or Spanish, Portuguese or Dutch; here they not only got permanently eclipsed but with the independence of India, the very concept of imperialism came to an end. Today terrorism is also a worldwide phenomenon and I am fully confident that its decisive defeat will take place from India.

To end terrorism, one will need to understand the very concept of terrorism. It is now dishonest to say that illiteracy, poverty and unemployment are the main causes behind terrorism. The terrorists of today are educated, technically qualified and come from well off families yet they believe in this heinous form of violence. Terrorism is a mindset which has no religion. The only solution lies in vigorously attacking it with stringent laws. That is why we repeatedly keep demanding for POTA or a law equivalent to it.

As karyakartas of the BJP, let us take a pledge, that in the coming elections, if the people give us a mandate, of which we are fully confident, then the NDA Government led by respected Advaniji will embark on an effective campaign to completely weed out terrorism from this land.

Terrorism is a type of war. Throughout history, wars have taken place. In war, in addition to one's capability, confidence and honesty are very important. The incidents that took place in Bangalore, Ahmedabad and prior to that in Jaipur, Lucknow, Faizabad, Varanasi, Delhi, Mumbai, Hyderabad, Nagpur etc. all clearly highlight both the intensity as well as reach of this war against us.

The entire series of events that I have mentioned did not begin in a single day and its seed was sown on the very day the UPA came into power at the Centre. If you recall, one of the first decisions that the UPA took after assuming power, was to repeal POTA. This was the very first signal which was responsible for boosting the confidence of the terrorists. Thereafter, the attempt to grant clemency to Mohammed Afzal, who has been convicted in the Parliament attack case and the Congress Party's Chief Minister of Jammu and Kashmir meeting with the President of India, to personally seek clemency for him, are some of the reasons which further boosted the self-confidence of the terrorists.

Benevolence towards Terrorists: Nature of the UPA Government

Today the UPA Government's soft approach towards terrorism has touched its nadir and this clearly exposes both its faulty policies and also its doubtful intentions. I am not saying this only for the sake of criticism. Only recently a few days ago, we witnessed how the central government failed to defend the ban on SIMI in the High Court. Whereas through the media and other channels, the people of the country can as clearly as broad daylight see to what extent organizations like SIMI are active in expanding and intensifying terrorism in the country. But if anyone fails to see facts that are as clear as the mid day sun, then it is possible that they are blindfolded. The Central Government is blindfolded to such an extent that it cannot differentiate between national interests and national perils.

Not only the Congress but the leaders of its allies the RJD, LJP and Samajwadi Party are also openly giving statements in favour of SIMI. It was shocking to note that despite the admirable manner in which the Gujarat Police quickly apprehended the accused in the Ahmedabad blasts, many senior leaders of the Bahujan Samaj Party, Samajwadi Party and the Congress along with the Imam of Delhi's Jama Masjid went to express sympathy to the home of Abu Basher, who was arrested from Azamgarh in Uttar Pradesh. The people of the country can clearly see whose morale is being boosted by such acts of these political parties.

It is unfortunate that the issue of national security on which there used to be consensus among all the political parties in India, has today also become an element of vote bank politics. While some ministers in this government are trying to define SIMI as a cultural organization, there are others who favour granting citizenship to Bangladeshi infiltrators.

The Supreme Court while giving its verdict on the IMDT Act had said that the problem of Bangladeshi infiltration amounts to the serious problem of external aggression. In the context of the decision of the Supreme Court, if a cabinet minister of this government speaks in favour of granting citizenship to Bangladeshi infiltrators, in a sense should it not be considered a kind of treason? On the principle of the collective responsibility of the cabinet, I would like to ask the government on behalf of the people of this country, that if it is dissociating itself from this statement of its own cabinet minister, then why should this minister not be immediately dismissed from the cabinet? And if it is in agreement with this statement, then should not actions be taken against the entire government in the light of the Supreme Court's verdict?

The approach of the Congress and its allies is not only evident from the passing of a resolution by the Kerala Legislative Assembly in favour of Madani, the main accused in the Coimbatore blasts, to the recommendation of Afzal's clemency by the Chief Minister of Jammu and Kashmir, but also is fueling the politics of appeasement. The hoisting of the Pakistani flag at the Lal Chowk in Kashmir, to the demand advocating the use of Pakistani currency in the valley by a coalition partner, to the voices being raised in favour of SIMI, all indicate towards a nightmarish scenario. Is there any possibility of controversy on these issues? In the interests of the crores of people of this country, we will need to take unequivocal decisions on these issues. But it is not in the character of theCongress to take clear decisions on issues related to terrorism and appeasement.

Soft approach towards terrorism and appeasement have always been a part of the character of the Congress and other so-called secular parties but now it appears that they have also become an integral part of their style of functioning and political culture. We consider this culture a distortion for India. There is a chronic disorder in the government's approach towards terrorism, but with the help of our citizens we will find solution.

Efforts of BJP-ruled States to Control Terrorism

The Central Government has been blinded by the vote bank politics to such an extent that it does not want to even acknowledge terrorists. BJP governments despite their limited resources and without any effective legal mechanism, is admirably combating terrorism. The Madhya Pradesh government was the first to unmask SIMI. The Gujarat government not only foiled the blasts in Surat and was able to quickly arrest the terrorists behind the Ahmedabad blasts. Investigations are also proceeding at a fast pace both in Rajasthan and Karnataka. I congratulate the Chief Ministers of all these four states for leading an effective and responsive administration.

If we ignore the recent achievements of BJP governments, then one finds that no government has been able to arrest even a single person in all cases where terrorist incidents have taken place over the past four years.

And in addition to this, the Central Government is sleeping over the anti-terrorism bills passed by Madhya Pradesh, Rajasthan and Gujarat.

This clearly demonstrates the difference between the BJP and the Congress when it comes to political will and capacity to combat terrorism.

Rising Inflation and Stagnating Economy

The common man has already started feeling the pinch of rising prices. Even if the rate of inflation has crossed 12%, it does not represent the reality. If the prices of the commodities of daily use are taken into account, then the rate of inflation may well cross the 20% mark. This means that the common man is actually burdened much more than what these figures show. We are making efforts to expose the real picture of the economic policy of the government before the country.

During the tenure of the NDA Government, the GDP rate went upto 8.6%. What is even more noteworthy is that we were able to achieve a rising growth rate continuously for 6 years and had created such a momentum that even when the NDA was not in power, this rate of growth continued for the next two to three years. But now, with the passage of time, as the impact of the NDA tenure has begun to wane, the economy has started to reflect the real impact of the UPA policies.

According to the review report presented by the Prime Minister's Economic Advisory Council, the number of non-Budgetary provisions has increased to such an extent that it is expected that non-budgetary allocation could reach 5% of the GDP. This is happening because the government, in order to present a populist budget, kept many important issues requiring funds like fertilizer subsidy, agricultural loan waiver scheme, additional expenditure on rural employment scheme, expenditure on the sixth pay commission etc. out of the purview of the budget. As a result of this, there is a possibility of the emergence of an unbalanced situation. The GDP which was at 9.6% is projected to fall to 7.5% in the coming year and the revenue deficit may touch the 6.5% mark.

The Deputy Chairman of Planning Commission had said that it was not possible to control inflation along with development. However, we do not subscribe to his views, as the Shri Atal Bihari Vajpayee led NDA Government had demonstrated that this was possible. But now even as the prices continue to keep rising, the rate of development is also coming down. Generally inflation is considered to be directly proportional to development, meaning that the increasing rate of development would lead to rising prices, but the economists running this government have even reversed this established principle. Now the rate of development has become inversely proportional to inflation, since despite rising prices, the rate of development is falling. This government has created a bizarre situation. The wrong policies of the UPA Government are not only impacting the pockets of the common man, but also affecting the entire economic structure of the country.

Foreign Policy

The UPA Government's series of failures on the foreign policy front continue unabated. The manner in which cross-border terrorism has been gaining ground, it should automatically become a critical part of our foreign policy. I have already spoken about the government's failure on this subject.

Today, the manner in which the centres of terrorism are being operated from across the border, definitely and clearly reflect the failure of the foreign policy.

Given the continuous failure of this government's foreign policy, now a foreign dimension has been added to the activities of the terrorists. A few days ago, there was a terrorist attack on the Indian embassy in Kabul. This was the first incident of an attack on an institution outside India. It is no secret as to who was responsible for this attack. Even the US government has clearly held the ISI responsible for this attack. But the Indian government has till date not been able to create any effective pressure on the ISI at any international forum.

The approach of the government with regard to China has been very slack and weak. China has tried to create a border dispute even in undisputed areas such as Sikkim. When our External Affairs Minister went to China with relief materials for the earthquake-hit province, he was received not by the Governor of the province but by some junior official. Ever since the UPA has come to power, China has been continuously exerting pressure on India. The Indian Government appears incapable of offering tough resistance on this front. The kind of construction activity that China is undertaking in the Himalayan region and Tibet, could adversely impact the environment. India would definitely be affected by this. But the Indian government is not able to even raise the issue. The Prime Minister is slated to visit China in the coming month of October. I demand that the issue of environment of the Himalayan region should be raised by the Prime Minister during his tour to China.

We have already witnessed the disaster that was perpetrated in the Jaipur, Ahmedabad and Bangalore blasts on account of the activities emerging from the terrorist camps being operated from within Bangladesh. Now even the Bangladesh government has accepted the fact that terrorist camps are operating on its soil and Bangladesh Rifles has assured the

Border Security Force of cooperation in this regard. Despite this, the government is not being able to take any stringent measures against the terrorist camps in Bangladesh.

Nepal has emerged in a new form between the last national executive meeting and this one. Nepal is emerging as a democratic republic. Even in the current power equations in Nepal, one can see reflections of a multi-party system there. We welcome the emergence of democracy in Nepal and hope that the close ties of friendship between India and Nepal would remain as strong and intimate as earlier.

How weak is this government's foreign policy is exemplified by the fact that the US has again denied a visa to Gujarat Chief Minister Shri Narendra Modi. And as far as my information goes, he had not even requested for one. This is not an issue related to any individual or any particular party; the issue is about the Indian government so meekly accepting the denial of a visa to the head of a government elected through the democratic process. Does this not cast questions on the sovereignty of India?

Situation in Jammu and Kashmir

The recent controversy and violence that took place over the issue of granting land to the Shri Amarnath Shrine Board (SASB) by the State government for creating facilities for the pilgrims is truly unfortunate. The Jammu and Kashmir government first granted the land at Baltal for the facilities of pilgrims and then under the pressure of a few separatist political leaders, revoked its own decision. The Central government is totally responsible for the angry response that this incident generated in Jammu and other parts of the country.

Even more shameful than this was how, on 15th August, a few separatists succeeded in hoisting the Pakistani flag in Srinagar. The insult to our national flag on Independence Day is intolerable. Earlier this government could not implement the decision of schools reciting our national song '*Vande Mataram*'. Now it is unable to protect the sanctity of our national flag. The sanctity of our national symbols is not safe under this UPA Government.

There may be difference of opinion among the so-called intellectuals on the incidents that are taking place in Jammu and Kashmir. But if I see it from the eyes of a nationalist, then i cannot fail in distinguishing between the ones who hoist the Pakistani flag and those who raise the slogan '*Bharat Mata ki Jai*' with the tricolour in their hands.

The message of the recent problems in Jammu and Kashmir is that it is a fight between the nationalists and the anti-nationals. When the green flag of Pakistan is brought before the Indian flag, there cannot be any two opinions over the solution. From this perspective, some of the solutions in the given situation could be as follows:

- It is imperative to resolve the complaints of discrimination in the allotment of developmental funds and remove regional disparities between Jammu, Kashmir and Ladakh.
- New opportunities of employment should be proportionately created for all the regions of Jammu and Kashmir.
- I demand that the government should mark a special area in the Kashmir Valley for the rehabilitation of the Kashmiri Pandits.
- The Amarnath yatra is not only a religious pilgrimage but also signifies the vibrancy of relations between the far off Kashmir valley and the rest of India. During the two months of pilgrimage, the interior parts of the Kashmir valley get emotionally linked with the rest of India. Therefore, this pilgrimage symbolizes national integration. That is why I consider this yatra to be of national importance.
- It is in this context that I am demanding that the Central Government should nationalize the road leading to the Amarnath Yatra so that, in the future, no attempt is made to disturb the social harmony for political reasons.

Whatever has happened in Jammu and Kashmir for over so many days is a condemnable example of the government's insensitivity. Shri Amarnath Sangharsha Samiti while struggling for the resolution of the dispute displayed exemplary patience. For the first time, voices could be heard throughout the country against the noise being made by separatists in the valley. We express our condolences to the families of all those who sacrificed their lives in the struggle.

We should learn from this incident as to how a handful of people were able to create tension in the entire country. When this movement was at its climax and the anti-national voices were being raised, even then the Central Government was unable to do anything. I remember that after the disputed structure in Ayodhya came down, to control its possible use/misuse by the State government, the Central Government had acquired the land. At that time the Central Government had argued that the sensitivity of that land was influencing the entire country. The condition with Shri Amarnath Shrine Board issue is also somewhat similar to that. But the Central Government was unable to do anything due to Article 370 despite understanding the gravity of the situation. I appeal to all the political parties of the country that in the light of the recent controversies in Jammu and Kashmir, should they not once again reconsider their policies regarding abrogation of Article 370? Would they ever want that such a situation, where on account of a problem in the valley that is affecting the entire nation, the Central Government finds itself unable to take any action? In my opinion if all political parties honestly reflect on this issue, then it might be possible to create a consensus for abrogating Article 370. I congratulate the people of Jammu for keeping the spirit of nationalism alive amid the grave threats of the anti-nationals.

Sri Ram Setu

From Shri Amarnath in the north to Sri Ram Setu in the south, this government is continuously attacking the very symbols of Indian culture. It has attempted to destroy Sri Ram Setu to erase the very existence of Bhagwan Ram one year ago. Apart from objectionable comments on Bhagwan Ram by its allies, it is condemnable how this government has tried to misinterpret the Kamban Ramayana in the Supreme Court, to legitimize the destruction of Sri Ram Setu.

Sri Ram Setu is not only an ancient symbol of India's culture or a centre of faith of the Hindu religion, but also symbolises India's identity and definition since times immemorial. In the Puranas, the geographical boundary of India is mentioned as 'Aasetu Himachal' (From the Setu to Himachal). The manner in which the Himalayas cannot be segregated from India's identity, in the same way Sri Ram Setu also cannot be dissociated from it. The destruction of the Setu is a conspiracy to change the identity of this country. The BJP will never allow this to happen.

I declare that if our government is formed, the Sri Ram Setu would be declared as a national heritage monument. And if any problem arises in declaring the Sri Ram Setu as a national heritage monument, then we will amend the rules and regulations accordingly and also try to get it listed among the world heritage sites of the UNESCO.

While not a single step could be taken to find a solution for solving the Shri Ram Janam Bhoomi dispute, on the contrary, the undisputed Sri Ram Setu is being sought to be destroyed. I find it strange how such a deliberate attempt to destroy the undisputed Sri Ram Setu and to drag into controversy the symbol of our composite culture Shri Amarnath Yatra and Shri Amarnath Shrine Board which looks after its arrangements has taken place. I would like to ask as to why do controversies arise only on matters of our faith and belief?

We condemn the incident in Kandhmal, Orissa, in which Swami Lakshamananand and his disciples were assassinated. I offer our homage in the memory of Swamiji and his disciples. We hope that the Orissa Government will apprehend and punish the culprits at the earliest. We also strongly condemn the attack on the convoy of Yogi Adityanath in Uttar Pradesh and hope that action will be taken against the guilty. In a civilized society, such life taking incidents are not only condemnable but also are shameful.

Changing of the 'Kamal' Logo of the Kendriya Vidyalaya Organisation

Recently, the government has taken a decision to change the logo of the Kendriya Vidyalaya organization because the lotus flower is inscribed in it. The lotus flower is considered to be linked with our culture. I would like to remind the government that the lotus is not only considered sacred by the Hindu, Jain and Buddhist religions but is also the national flower of India. Is the national flower a communal symbol in the eyes of the Government of India? Why would any sect or religion have objection on any flower? I would like to remind about the objection that I had raised in my last speech about using the word '*Dharmanirpekshata*'. I would like to reiterate that any objection on a flower can only be made by confusing secularism with '*Dharmanirpekshata*'. In '*Panthanirpekshata*' no one can have any opposition to any flower because the lotus flower is symbolic of Indian culture. Only by trying to understand secularism as '*Dharmanirpekshata*' can make the lotus appear communal. I would like to ask the government as to how many national symbols would have to be changed because of its misplaced understanding of secularism. Along with the logo of the Kendriya Vidyalaya would it also change sentences like the one inscribed in the Supreme Court, '*Yato Dharmastatojayah*'; or the term '*Shannohvarunah*' inscribed on the Indian Navy logo; or '*Nabha Sparsha Diptatama*' the sentence of the Air Force because it highlights the Wind God? All these Dharmic words are inscribed in the numerous symbols of the Indian nation because these symbolize the fundamental character of India. To change them would be a misguided attempt to change the fundamental character of India which we will never allow to succeed.

Indo-US Nuclear Deal

The revelations made in the letter written by US President George Bush have now clearly proved the apprehensions that the BJP had continuously raised, that by signing the agreement India's nuclear sovereignty would be undermined. It has also proved that the concealing of facts was not done by the US government but by the Government of India. The Prime Minister consciously misled the country, all the political parties and the Indian Parliament on the issue. Does a minority government have the moral right to commit itself to an international treaty that involves issues related to national security and sovereignty? For the sake of the nuclear deal, the government has completely twisted the truth and engaged in various acts of misdemeanor that include the purchase of votes during the vote of confidence to misleading the country.

The revelations in a section of the media that the United States of America is now of the view that "assured fuel supply" is not a legally binding agreement but merely a political assurance has shaken every Indian. Assurances die with men and regimes, binding agreements bind nations. India must now ponder as to what the deal means for us. Our testing options appear to have been eliminated and there is no legally binding agreement on "assured fuel supply". Does this deal mean differently to different people or is the nuclear deal intended to be breached by the more powerful party to this deal. There are many reasons for opposing this deal. For instance, one of the main newspapers of China, the People's Daily, has recently published an article that China does not intend to limit its nuclear power. According to this newspaper, China needs to conduct further nuclear tests. If this kind of thinking is taking place in China and if in such a situation the Government of India surrenders its right to conduct a nuclear test, then it could be dangerous for the country. And such a surrender will impact the autonomy of our decision making ability.

Also by agreeing to the terms of the NSG, have we not willfully converted our unilateral moratorium on nuclear testing into a multi-lateral international commitment? Moreover, if either Pakistan or China conducts a nuclear test that might threaten the balance of our regional strategic and security arrangement, then would not our right to conduct a nuclear test in response be seriously compromised?

We once again want to make it clear that our opposition to the Indo-US Nuclear Deal is different from the opposition of the Left parties. We are in favour of better relations with the US and other countries. We are also in favour of nuclear and political cooperation with the US. Our opposition is limited only to those unbalanced provisions in the deal that endanger the nuclear sovereignty of India.

Calamity of Floods in Bihar and other regions

Over the last one month we have witnessed the natural calamity of floods in many parts of the country. Its severity has been seen in Uttar Pradesh, Bihar, Bengal and Assam. Particularly in Bihar, the flood situation became very grim due to the Kosi's flooding on account of the breach in the dam across the Nepal border. The Bihar government despite limitation of resources has tried to sensitively deal with the situation. All BJP Chief Ministers have contributed in this effort. The BJP also directed all its state units to give financial and other kinds of assistance. I also wrote to the Prime Minister that after the earthquake in Gujarat and Tsunami, the manner in which MPs from outside the state were allowed to make contributions from their funds, a similar provision should also be made in the context of Bihar. I am happy to note that my suggestion has been accepted.

Prior to this, many parts of the country have witnessed drought and farmer suicides are continuing unabated. The government should make a long term plan to deal with farmers' suicides in Vidarbha on the one hand, and the problem of floods in various parts of the country on the other hand. I once again request the government to consider implementing the ambitious river linking project that was conceived during the tenure of the NDA Government, so that to a large extent the country is saved from floods and droughts and farmers in large areas are able to get water for irrigation.

Congratulations to the Medal Winners at the Beijing Olympics

India is one of the largest countries of the world but till now, apart from hockey, we had not been able to win a gold medal. In the 112 year history of the Olympic Games, individual medals were won only on one or two occasions. At the Beijing Olympics, India won the largest number of medals so far. On behalf of the Bharatiya Janata Party, I congratulate Abhinav Bindra for winning the gold medal in shooting, and Vijender

Singh in boxing and Sushil Kumar in wrestling for winning bronze medals. They have displayed the constructive energy of the Indian youth on the international forum. The youth of our country will feel highly encouraged by these achievements.

But I would also like to raise the question whether this success is satisfactory for us? No, certainly not. If we desire to reach a high position in the medal tally list at the Olympics, then we will have to identify talented players right from the schools, and provide them with facilities of international standards.

Along with the physical efficiency, the players should also have a high national spirit. I was surprised to learn that in the government text-books from the primary to the secondary levels, nowhere it is written that we are proud to be Bharatiya. Perhaps, such a situation does not prevail anywhere else in the world.

In my opinion, if the government does not in a proper manner make our children feel proud of their being Bharatiya, then how would they be instilled with the spirit to compete for the sake of the country, be it in their normal day to day life or upto the international forums.

North-eastern States

Many north-eastern States are victims of the shortsighted policies of the Congress. In addition to trying to resolve the Bangladeshi problem in Assam, the Central Government is not able to take any effective steps for improving the conditions in Manipur, Mizoram and Nagaland. We are part of the coalition government in both Meghalaya and Nagaland. The north-eastern States account for a total of 26 Lok Sabha seats. Given the misrule of the Congress in the other States of the north-east, I am hopeful, that in cooperation with the various political parties there, we would be able to perform well.

Forthcoming Elections

Friends, the festival season will begin in about 18 to 20 days. In India, many festivals are celebrated during the months of October-November. Alongwith them, the celebration of democracy i.e. time for elections is also approaching. Elections in Jammu and Kashmir are before us. After that in the month of November, elections in many important States would take place, and thereafter within a few months, elections to Lok Sabha are slated to take place. We should collectively try and make the results of these elections similar to our festivals.

Today, in seven States the Bharatiya Janata Party is in power on its own and has coalition governments with its allies in five states. The BJP has the largest number of scheduled caste, scheduled tribe and woman legislators in the country. On the one hand, while we are expanding politically, on the other hand, our social and political responsibilities are also increasing. The people no longer have any expectations from the Congress.

The forthcoming elections of the legislative assemblies in many States are of importance to us. In three states, Chhattisgarh, Madhya Pradesh and Rajasthan we have our own governments. The governments of Shri Shivraj Singh Chauhan in Madhya Pradesh, Smt. Vasundhara Raje in Rajasthan and Dr. Raman Singh in Chhattisgarh have done many important public welfare works which have benefited the people. The need of the hour is to ensure that these developmental activities reach the people. For this, all the karyakartas and leaders of the party should work with full dedication and commitment.

We often recite the song, '*Desh hame deta hai sabkuch; hum bhi to kuch dena sikhen*' (The nation gives us everything, we should also learn to give back something to the nation). Today there is lack of people who can give back to the nation. This is a matter of concern. Today there is an urgent need of people who can give back to the country. In such a difficult situation, people only have hope from the BJP. They want to see the BJP different from other parties. Therefore, our primary concern has to rise to the expectations of the people.

Organisation

It gives me pleasure to say that the work of the organization is fast spreading throughout the country through the various Morcha's and cells. The State units are also fully active. Particularly in those states where elections are due in the months of October and November, awareness programmes are continuing both at the levels of the government as well as the organisation. Be it the issue of the destruction of Sri Ram Setu or the Shri Amarnath land dispute or the purchase of MPs during the trust vote in Parliament, through the organizational setup we have been able to run nationwide programmes. The BJYM's *Yuva Kranti* Rally, *Bhandaphor* Rally in the various states, *Yuva Jodo Abhiyan* in Madhya Pradesh and Chhattisgarh were successfully organised. In context of the *Vijay Samkalp* Rally, effective programmes were organised at Raurkela in Orissa and at Kanpur in Uttar Pradesh. In Chhattisgarh, the *Vikas Yatra* has been successful while in Madhya Pradesh the *Jan Aashirvad* Rally is successfully proceeding. In Rajasthan also there have been many successful rallies and programmes at the booth level. The *Satta Parivartan* Rally in Jammu and the successful *Mahila Sammelan* of the Minority Morcha were in the news. Be it the Traders Cell, CA Cell, Medical Cell, Media Cell, Ex-Servicemen Cell, Investors Cell, NGO Cell or the Kisan Morcha have all been organising effective programmes in their respective areas. Even though the Central government has not yet convened the Parliament session in its attempt to evade the people, the BJP is however, with the support of the people, continuing with our struggle on the streets. The karyakartas of the party have played an important role in the expansion of the BJP and will also do so in the future. That is why we are considered as a party of Karyakartas.

Booth Committees

The process of constituting booth committees is continuing. Many States have already sent the CDs of their booth committees. By further expediting this process, we need to complete the formation of booth committees in all the States before the elections.

Appeal

The manner in which the UPA has lost the faith of the people over the last four and a half years, clearly indicates that the people have made up their mind for change. We all have to be ready to contribute our offerings in this *Yagya* of change. Our goal is clear. Our resolve is to win. Therefore, I am fully confident, that the future will be ours, and the great personality, who stands before us and the entire nation, with the consent of respected Shri Atal Bihari Vajpayee, as the prime ministerial candidate, Shri Lal Krishna Advani will definitely become the Prime Minister of the country. Advaniji is not only a ray of hope for all of us but the entire country is also expectantly looking at him. Let us all collectively move ahead towards establishing a golden future and prosperity of India!

Immediately after the elections to these States, the environment will be for the Lok Sabha elections. Therefore, the time has now come to prepare ourselves to tirelessly work in the coming months with the resolve that we will rest only after forming our governments in these States and at the Centre. I am well aware of your capabilities. You have the capacity to achieve even the most difficult of tasks.

□

Call for Lok Sabha Elections

7-9 February, 2009 (Nagpur)

After celebrating the Karnataka victory in Bengaluru, we have assembled in Nagpur for the one day National Executive Meeting and the two day National Council Meeting. The 2009 Lok Sabha election is ahead of us. We are all aware that in the forthcoming Lok Sabha elections, the people will take into account the work undertaken by the Atalji led NDA Government and led UPA Government.

All the Lok Sabha elections that have taken place after independence, have been contested between various political parties. In 1999 and 2004 also there was only one alliance – the NDA. The UPA was constituted after the elections. The Congress, for the first time in the history of the country, accepted the importance of an alliance. The Congress, which a few years ago at Panchmarhi had claimed to form the government on its own, has now accepted the politics of alliance. It is for the first time in the country that a direct contest is going to take place between two alliances. On the one hand, the UPA in its present form has emerged as a result of the diminishing base of the Congress. On the other hand, the BJP led NDA, in its present form, has emerged with the increasing political expansion of the BJP. In terms of party politics, starting as a small party, the BJP has been able to increase its stature higher than the Congress'. In the politics of alliance, the BJP emerged as a pioneer and Congress had to follow. While the UPA is the crumbling fort of the past, the NDA under the leadership of the BJP is the rising sun of future.

Both the alliances differ radically. While the NDA is positive, the UPA is based on the negative concept of opposing the BJP. One more difference between both the alliances is that the UPA has begun with doubts about its leadership. The BJP led NDA has already decided that respected Lal Krishna Advani ji will be our prime ministerial candidate. Now the people of the country want to know as to who will be the prime ministerial candidate of the UPA.

The country is now awaiting to see as to who will hoist the tricolour at the Red Fort on the coming 15th August? Keeping in mind the inclination of the BJP *karyakartas*, supporters and the inclination of the people of the country, I can say with complete faith that the people of the country will elect our senior leader Lal Krishna Advaniji as the next Prime Minister of the country. We had dreamt of making Atalji the Prime Minister of the country. That dream was realized through the untiring efforts of the people, *karyakartas* and our supporters. We again have a dream that Shri Lal Krishna Advaniji will be the next Prime Minister of India. I have full faith that this dream of ours will also be realized with the support of the people and dedication of workers

Over the last five years, elections to 17 state assemblies have taken place. The Congress has been able to win only 4 state assemblies on its own. This clearly exemplifies that the Congress has lost ground all over India. From being a very large political party, a situation has now come whereby the Congress cannot survive without an alliance. In this era of alliances, the people will surely compare as to whether they want the NDA or UPA. We will discuss this issue in detail tomorrow at the National Council Meeting.

Assembly Elections

In the six states where assembly elections were held in last November-December, the BJP won 294 seats while the Congress could win only 244. We had an unprecedented success in Madhya Pradesh and Chhattisgarh. We came back to form the government in both these states. I take this opportunity to congratulate the Chief Ministers of Madhya Pradesh and Chhattisgarh, Shri Shivraj Singh Chauhan and Dr. Raman Singh, State Presidents Shri Narendra Singh Tomar and Shri Vishnu Sai, the state organization, leadership, *karyakartas* and the people for this success. Madhya Pradesh and Chhattisgarh have created history in real terms. We could not form our government in Rajasthan by a very slender margin. Our performance in Delhi was not on expected lines. But I would like to mention that despite our less than satisfactory performance, we still remain at the centre of the people's hope. The Bharatiya Janata Party has always moved ahead by overcoming hurdles. I have total faith that we certainly will be able to emerge victorious in the Lok Sabha elections by overcoming all challenges. Recently, we increased our strength from one to eleven in the Jammu & Kashmir assembly elections. I congratulate the state leadership of Jammu & Kashmir, all the *karyakartas* of the organization and the people for the success of the BJP.

The UPA's Tenure

The country has seen from close quarters the tenure of the Congress-led UPA. It has neither direction nor vision; neither ideas nor wisdom. An atmosphere of lawlessness and extreme despair has been created in the entire country. To serve vested political interests, many mindless decisions have been taken and there was a time when it appeared that the country was being forced in the direction of yet another partition. In the post independence era, never before has the policy of appeasement been so recklessly practiced on the chessboard of politics.

What has not taken place? The Sacchar Committee report, repeal of POTA, communalization of the budget, reservation of government's jobs in Andhra Pradesh on religious lines, reservation in Aligarh Muslim University on religious lines, the Prime Minister saying that Muslims have the first claim over the country's resources, discriminating students on the grounds of religion while distributing scholarships; in what direction does the UPA want to take the country? As an opposition, we tried to warn the UPA even as it continuously tried to disturb communal harmony.

Terrorism

While there should have been efforts to keep the country united on the issue of terrorism, the opposition was not even consulted on the issue. Today, the entire country is facing an explosive situation. There is not a single corner in the country where terrorist attacks have not taken place. Terrorists kept challenging the establishment of the country. They kept on expanding their network. The lives of innocents were continuously sacrificed. But the UPA Government kept turning a deaf ear towards this.

The terrorist attack on the Taj Hotel in Mumbai, actually was an attack on the 'Taj' of self respect and pride of India. The BJP never played politics on the issues of terrorism. The NDA enacted POTA to facilitate capturing terrorists and to easily bring them to book but God alone knows what kind of message of appeasement the UPA intended to give by repealing POTA. In fact, terrorists were emboldened by the repeal of POTA.

The nation wants to fight terrorism. For a nation which has defeated

Pakistan on four occasions, can terrorism be a factor against it? But if the UPA Government itself decides to surrender before it, then with whom will the self respect of the entire country stand?

In the last session of Parliament, the anti-terror law was passed. Even though its provisions were not adequate, we supported the Central Government. The BJP will continue to support all kinds of measures against terrorism. We are committed to this. Similarly, even though the UPA Government has formed the National Investigating Agency, but still no concrete initiatives have been taken to equip the police and security personnel with modern weapons and latest technology.

The results clearly show the kind of policies that were pursued by the government over the last four years. Today, the flame of terrorism is engulfing every part of the country. A few days ago, a new and unusual dimension was added to terrorism when comic actors started receiving threats and warnings that they should not make fun of the underworld dons and terrorists. This proves the extent to which the terrorists have been emboldened. One has to contemplate as to how such a situation has been created.

Immediately after assuming power at the Centre, the UPA softened the government's approach against terrorism. Not only POTA was repealed, but such political policies were also implemented which consequently emboldened the terrorists. Today, the kind of sentiment being displayed throughout the country, from the common people to government staff and traders, from actors to intellectuals, and from politicians to lawyers and judges, every section of society is expressing anger against the policies of the UPA policies over the past four years.

Neighbouring Countries

Under the tenure of the UPA, there has been an increasing build up of anti-India environment in the neighbouring countries. But the kind of atmosphere that exists in Pakistan, not only generates concerns but also exposes the short sightedness and incompetence of our foreign policy.

During its tenure, the UPA Government has committed not one but four strategic and diplomatic blunders with respect to Pakistan.

- On January 6, 2004, at the time of Vajpayee government, Pakistan had in a joint statement committed that it would not allow its land to be used for anti-India terror activities. However, in 2005, in the joint statement that was released, there was not even a mention about Pakistan's this commitment.

- In 2006, at the Non- Aligned Summit in Havana, the Prime Minister by declaring Pakistan a victim of terrorism, gave it an escape route to defend itself.
- The joint statement released by India and Pakistan stated that terror incidents would not be allowed to become an impediment in the path of the peace talks. As a result of this, the opportunity for creating diplomatic pressure in the wake of terrorist attacks has been lost.
- The biggest blunder by the government was to agree to form an Indo-Pak joint anti-terror mechanism. Under this mechanism, there is an arrangement that India and Pakistan will share terror related information and evidence with each other. Taking advantage of this, on the basis of media reports, Pakistan has demanded the handing over the Malegaon accused Lt. Col. Purohit in the Samjhauta Express incident.

It pains me as I am forced to say that the steps which the Indian government has taken after the Mumbai attack, further actions will have to be taken far beyond them. As part of such steps, India should dissociate itself from the joint terror mechanism which was declared on 16th September 2006 in Havana, Cuba's capital, by Prime Minister Manmohan Singh and the then President of Pakistan Pervez Musharraf. This is because Pakistan's approach is not of cooperation but of treachery. Instead of showing dependence on any country, the central government should act strongly against terrorism on its own.

On the other side, the war between the LTTE and the Sri Lankan army is reaching a decisive end and its far reaching impact will be felt in India. According to the Sri Lankan army's claim, about 95% of the LTTE's power has been exhausted. Even though India considers LTTE a terrorist organization, but we also believe that the Tamil problem of Sri Lanka cannot be resolved only through the use of military force. Therefore, while the power of the LTTE is decisively coming to an end, the Sri Lankan government must also create a new environment far from that of military struggle. Time has come for the Government of Sri Lanka to present a new solution to the Tamil problem.

For this, the government of Sri Lanka will have to first clearly distinguish a common Tamil from the LTTE. The Government of Sri Lanka should undertake necessary steps to ensure the security and self respect of around one and half lakh to three lakh Tamil citizens trapped in the conflict zone.

In my opinion, the government of Sri Lanka should take new initiatives to begin the peace process by involving all Tamil groups. A proposal based on the Indo-Lankan Peace Accord of 1987 should be brought forward to bring about a political solution of the problem.

In Nepal, despite the formation of a new government under democracy, the situation has not yet returned to normal. The influence of such elements that are naturally inclined towards violence, has increased in the Government of Nepal. Over the last few days, many incidents of violence perpetrated by organizations associated with the government, have taken place. This is not in accordance with the core principle of democracy. The aim of establishing a democratic system is to create a liberal system free of violence and oppression and not to create a violent atmosphere through misuse of power. The Government of Nepal should immediately stop giving support and patronage to those elements who are involved in perpetrating any kind of violence. This is a test of faith for the Government of Nepal under the democratic system. And this is also necessary for ensuring that the peace process of Nepal reaches its logical conclusion.

The Terror of Price Rise

The Congress enjoys an old relationship with price rise. Unchecked price rise has been a feature of close to five years of Congress led UPA rule. The life of the common people has become a hell. The Congress claims that it is with the "*aam admi*" but in reality it has hit the "*aam admi*" the hardest during its tenure. The rate of inflation continuously increased during its rule. In the election year, however, there is some relief in terms of statistics but that too it is a by product of the recession. Despite this, the prices of food grains are still zooming. For the last five years while prices kept on increasing and the people were restive, the Congress remained inactive. But now the Congress has begun showing some activism. It has realized that people are very agitated and the elections are close. The Congress which takes every decision keeping only elections in mind and ignoring public interest, has now lost its balance. They should be prepared to face the consequences.

Today the rate of inflation is decreasing. The decrease is not because of the government's efforts but due to the economic recession. That is why the prices of the items of daily use are not coming down. The price of food grains is high even today. It causes a heavy burden on poor families. According to an estimate of the National Sample Survey, in villages 52% of the income of the poor is spent on edible items while it is 26% in the case of urban poor. What I am trying to say is that the economic recession is affecting the poor in urban and rural areas and they are not getting any benefit from the decline in the rate of inflation.

Economic Crisis

Approximately over the last five years, the economic crisis has intensified on account of the policies pursued by the UPA Government. The "dream team of talented economists" – Prime Minister Dr. Manmohan Singh, P. Chidambaram who remained Finance Minister for four and half years and Deputy Chairman of the Planning Commission Montek Singh Ahluwalia – kept misleading the country. Their developmental plans were not in sync with the ground realities. The impact of the economic crisis was being felt in almost every sector. The rate of industrial development remained negative. The share market kept crashing on repeated occasions. Small investors were cheated. The rupee increasingly got devalued. The foreign exchange reserve which during the time of the NDA was a strong point of the country, has declined under the UPA. Not only this, during the tenure of this government, a number of scams have taken place. The economy of the country has been severely hit by scams like the wheat import scam, NREGA scam, DDA scam, Spectrum scam, Satyam episode, Balu episode among others.

India is presently passing through a phase of economic recession and unemployment. Lacs of people are losing their jobs every month. Lacs of artisans whether they are linked to the textile industry of Tirupur (in Tamil Nadu) or in the diamond industry of Surat, are on the verge of starvation and many incidents of suicides are also coming to light. After all why has such a situation emerged?

The UPA Government cites global economic recession as the reason behind this sorry state of affairs. I want to remind them that on 9th January when the BSE Sensex index touched the mark of 21000 points, the then Finance Minister declared that, "this is the result of our policies and India will not look back. Now we have reached the double digit figure of the rate of development". On 28th February 2008, when the UPA Government presented its last budget, the troika of these economists, Dr. Manmohan Singh, Shri P. Chidambaram and the Deputy Chairman of the Planning

Commission Shri Montek Singh Ahluwalia had spoken in a similar vein. Once again the then Finance Minister Shri P. Chidambaram said that, "This is our internal growth, our fundamentals are strong. Now we will not look back." Only after ten months when the economic crisis started taking its toll, the government dissociated itself from its earlier claims citing the crisis to be on account of the global economic recession. If the policies and fundamentals of the UPA Government were so strong, then how did they crumble down within ten months?

In reality, the policies of the UPA Government were fundamentally wrong. During the UPA rule, the kind of policies that were pursued, intensified the impact of the global recession on India instead of restraining it which led to the worsening of the situation.

The government slowed down the infrastructural projects continuously for four years adversely affecting the development and employment. The UPA Government's mismanagement of the economy led to price rise, and then perturbed by the rising prices, it altered the policies of the financial institutions in such a way that a liquidity crisis was created. For instance, the government changed the CRR of Banks from 4-5 percent at the time of the NDA to 9.5 percent in October 2008. In the same period, the prime lending rate was doubled to reach 14 percent. It led to the decrease of one lac crore of rupees that was available for industrial loans. This resulted in making the situation from bad to worse. After October, the government agreed to change its policies but by that time it was too late.

The Plight of Farmers

The Congress led UPA has been completely anti-farmers and anti-workers. During the tenure of this government, I can recall how the cycle of farmer suicides began in such a manner that the entire country was shocked. The entire country was ashamed to witness incidents of the food providers committing suicides. At that time, I told Prime Minister Manmohan Singh that agriculture is the main basis of economy. If the neglect of agriculture and farmer is not immediately halted, the pace of development in the country will get arrested. In this context, I had demanded that a Special Session of Parliament be convened on issues related to agriculture and such non-partisan policies should be framed and a concrete plan for the coming ten years be prepared, to ensure that the problems of the farmers are resolved. The Congress led UPA never paid any attention to our demand.

We all know that during the time of the NDA, many decisions in the interest of the farmers like reduction in the interest rates on agricultural loans, Kisan Credit Card, agricultural insurance etc. were undertaken. With the coming of the Congress led UPA Government, all developmental plans were placed in cold storage. Led by the partisan politics of not wanting to give credit to the NDA, the UPA government worsened the condition of the farmers.

Such policies were made for the development of India by the UPA government that the villages, the poor and farmers were kept on the margins of these policies. Today the farmers have to face a situation in which the cost of agriculture is increasing while the land for agriculture is decreasing. Presently, on an average, a farmer in the country has 1.4 hectares of land. More that 80 per cent of the farmers have less than two acres of land. One can imagine as to how constrained are the financial resources of the farmers.

In such a situation, it is necessary to make available cheap agricultural loans to the farmers. The Vajpayee government had reduced the long continuing interest rates by 50 to 60 percent. The BJP governments in Karnataka, Chhattisgarh and Madhya Pradesh have reduced the interest rates on agricultural loans to less than 4%. But I believe that the farmers will not be benefited in real terms by only reducing the interest rates or declaring loan waivers at the time of elections. This is because even today 84% of the poor people inhabiting the rural areas take loans from non-governmental sources like the local money lenders. This large section fails to get direct benefit of the loan waiver scheme. Therefore, I believe that to improve the economic condition of the farmer, we need to increase their purchasing power.

In addition to this, due to the lack of transportation and storage facilities, a large part of the agricultural produce gets destroyed. For the fear of their produce getting destroyed, smaller farmers are compelled to sell their produce at lesser prices. According to an estimate, 25 to 30 percent of the crops in India are destroyed due to lack of proper storage facility, the estimated cost of which stands at around 1.5 billion dollars. If proper facilities for storage and selling are created, the income of farmers can adequately get improved. But the UPA Government has taken no steps in this direction, and the food crisis that took place last year, mismanagement in storage was one of the main reasons for it.

Development Work Stopped

Throughout the tenure of the UPA Government, the country has witnessed political instability every day. The UPA which came into power by accident, has committed many political accidents in the country. During these years, the prestige and stature of India has been severely undermined. We all know how the country's position was enhanced at the time of the NDA Government led by Atalji. The doors of development were opened from all sides. But as soon the UPA came to power, the pace of development not only got stunted, but in some cases development was also stopped. A new dimension in the development of the country was added by the Prime Minister Gramin Sadak Yojana and the Golden Quadrilateral project. Employment opportunities were created. Investors chose India as one the best places to invest. The Pokhran test and victory in the Kargil war at the time of the NDA led by Atalji, etched a golden history for India. POTA was enacted to end terrorism. Not only were such decisions like the Sarva Shiksha Abhiyan, Pradhan Mantri Rojgar Yojana, Indianisation of education, Kisan Credit Card, farmer insurance scheme undertaken for the welfare of the people, but these decisions were also implemented on the ground ensuring positive results. The Congress led UPA Government virtually stopped these schemes as soon as it assumed power. Why? Change in government does not mean that whatever decisions were taken by the earlier governments should be changed.

Ideology based Constructive Opposition

We are in opposition for the last five years. In politics, the opposition should be based on ideology and not be against development. We opposed the UPA Government on the grounds of ideology. We opposed the policy of appeasement for votes. We opposed the soft and slack approach of the UPA on terrorism and Naxalism. We opposed the repeal of POTA. We expressed our opposition to rising prices. We never opposed the development works and welfare measures. The problem was that Congress led UPA Government took most of its decisions with an eye on votes. Even though the bill that was presented in Parliament after the Mumbai attacks was not clear, yet in the national interest we supported it. We supported the UPA despite many shortcomings in the National Investigating Agency. The BJP clearly believes – country first, then the party.

UPA has No Faith in Democracy

The incidents of committing fraud with the basic spirit of the Constitution in Bihar, Jharkhand and Goa, the nefarious act to purchase MPs at the time of the trust vote in Parliament, are well known to the people. These have been witnessed by everyone. The conspiracy to transform "*Lok Tantra*" into "*Note-Tantra*" itself exposes the faith of the UPA in parliamentary and democratic values. What kind of ideals do we propose to present before the future generations? Today, when common citizens are getting disenchanted by the political system and feeling a lack of faith in them, our responsibilities increase. The entire country was ashamed by what was done by Congress led UPA and its ally the SP to win the trust vote in Parliament. Therefore, the government which came to power by default and continues to hold it by "*Note-Tantra*" has no right to continue.

Worldwide Economic Recession and the Future of India

The manner in which the crisis of economic recession is getting intensified, it appears as if it has engulfed the entire theoretical as well as practical aspects of the economy. Some intellectuals are even hinting towards the same kind of crisis in future with the capitalist economy as has been experienced by the communist regimes around 1990-91.

At this hour, I remember two great visionaries of this country. One of them propounded the ideological legacy of the BJP and whose death anniversary we are going to observe on 11th February. And the other is *Rashtrapita* Mahatma Gandhi whose death anniversary we have observed a few days ago.

I recall that one hundred years ago in 1909, *Rashtrapita* Mahatma Gandhi had written a book *Hind Swaraj*. In this he had said how the Indian model of development can be based on our traditional knowledge and experience. Gandhiji had said that the idea to develop India on the basis of the western economic model is contrary to Swaraj. Gandhiji believed that this model of development was neither good for India and nor for the world.

The fall of communism and now the crisis of capital in the entire world reminds us of what Bapu said 100 years ago. Perhaps for India, the time has come to act in accordance with the ideas of Bapu.

We will have to think of a new model for India which imitates neither the USSR nor the US so that while India develops, it also shows to the world the path of development - one which was thought by the thinkers like Mahatma Gandhi and Pandit Deen Dayal Upadhyaya.

Though I am not an economist, even then I believe that in extremely centralized and capital intensive models of economic development, there always remains doubt that in the wake of recession in any of its important centres (for example the US), it will also immediately impact the entire world. The basic Indian model as propounded by Mahatma Gandhi and Pandit Deendayal Upadhyaya was based on decentralization of industries and compatibility between capital and labour. It was based on local requirements and systems. Contrary to the marketing rules of today, it is based on controlled use and not on unbridled consumerism. This is because the model of maximum consumption of the resources can be profitable for a country but it cannot be good for the entire world.

It is based on giving a special place to agricultural and village industries. The *Gram Swaraj* of Mahatama Gandhi and *Gramodaya* of Deendayalji are its examples. This concept may today be linked with highly technical industries. For example by decentralizing electronics, IT and entertainment industries, a huge contribution to the economy can be made. Coordination among all the centres may be established by using communication means and modern resources. By explaining the ideas of Gandhi in accordance with the current age, the economists can present Indian economic model of development before the world.

Young India

The recent global recession has created a crisis for the youth of India. Unemployment is rising continuously. In foeign countries, people are continuously losing their jobs. According to an ILO report, around 5 crore people may lose their jobs in 2009.

Today India has a majority of youth living here. 70 percent of the country's population is less than 35 years of age. Today it is required that the constructive energy of the youth is used by the country so that a new phase of development is witnessed in the nation.

The real development of the constructive energy of the youth can only be undertaken when, instead of blindly following the western model, we have such a model of development, which is not based on material development alone. In addition to material growth, the energy of the youth needs to grow on all aspects including emotional, social, moral and spiritual. The cognitive intelligence which the thinkers in US want to develop among the youth today, is based on these values.

In *Hind Swaraj*, Mahatma Gandhi also thought of creating such a youth one hundred years ago. One who can herald the new age of material progress in the world while being rooted in the spiritual basis of the eternal Indian values. The youth of India should not become followers of illusionary ideologies of the past. He has to become the torch-bearer of a new age of development of the future. How can the youth of India make the India of the future which will provide leadership to the entire world without the elements of Indianness? Mahatma Gandhi had realized this a hundred years ago.

Today there are discussions on the clash of civilizations while in *Hind Swaraj* Gandhiji has spoken about a dialogue between civilizations. If such complete and perfect development of the youth of India takes place, then India can take over the role of dialogue in place of clash.

If the self-proclaimed inheritors of Mahatma Gandhi, that is the people of the Congress, are themselves involved in creating internal bickering in the country, then how can India bring an end to the clash of civilizations?

In my opinion, Gandhian values are becoming more and more relevant today at the social, diplomatic and economic levels.

Call for Change

Through the *Vijay Sankalp* rallies, the Bharatiya Janata Party is engaged in a public awareness campaign throughout the country. The plan of the "BJP on every booth" is already in progress at the organizational level. We have clearly witnessed the gain from these unique plans during the state assembly elections that were held a few months ago. We all know that pre-planned attacks are being made on nationalist forces from all sides. We will have to be constantly alert and prepared in this situation. The BJP is the voice of democracy and nationalism in the country. Our opponents are indulging in conspiracies to malign the image of our party. We will have to suitably reply to them. Under all circumstances, we need to remain unshaken from our ideology. And we must remain dedicated to the values of the party. We will have to constantly make people realize that we are different from other parties. We will have to give primacy to the national interest and the interest of the party by rising above our own self interests. Our elders have presented examples that are worth emulating. We will have to continue this tradition unhindered. We should always keep in mind that our discipline and conduct becomes an example for others. Our sensitive conduct should always make the people feel that we are with them in all circumstances. Politics is a mission for us. It is a medium to bring about change in the society. Our source of inspiration, Pandit Deendayal Upadhyay has repeatedly said that we have taken up the work of serving society and we desire social change in a wider perspective.

This is possible only when we dedicate ourselves in preparations for the forthcoming Lok sabha elections that are expected to take place in April-May. We should engage ourselves at all levels. In democracy, the path of change is paved forward through elections. Therefore, the forthcoming Lok Sabha elections are both a challenge as well as an opportunity for us. Our desire is that in May 2009 once again the BJP led NDA returns to power. We will have to work hard in our Lok Sabha constituencies to convert this opportunity into our goal. People will need to be made to realize that the future of India is safe in the hands of the BJP led NDA and our leader Lal Krishna Advaniji has the capability to take India to the epitome of glory.

The people are disturbed by the policies of the Congress led UPA. People want to uproot the UPA. In such a situation, if we falter a bit, the people will never forgive us.

□

Reflections over Current Scenario

08-09, Feb.2009 (Nagpur)

I can clearly recall when, on January 20th 2006, I took over the responsibility as President. Three years have passed since then. And today being in Nagpur again after three years, bears a special significance for me. The reason is that right from my childhood days as a *bal-swayamsevak* in a small village in Uttar Pradesh, I have in my heart always felt a deep reverence and faith for Nagpur even though I had not even seen the city. In this context I feel highly elated in Nagpur as the Party President.

Geographically, Nagpur is said to be located in the centre of the country. In my opinion, Nagpur is not only a geographical centre but has also been the centre of many social, cultural and other nationalist movements dedicated to the nation. 84 years ago in 1925, a light of nationalism was ignited here which continues to illumine and influence the entire India till date. The sacred memorial of *Pujya* Dr. Hedgewar and *Pujya* Shri Guruji even today shines like a lighthouse guiding nationalists. The Nagpur region has also been the *karmabhumi* of the immortal forebearer of social harmony and the author of the Indian Constitution Dr. Bhimrao Ambedkar. Let us solute these tall symbols of India's national and social development.

Not just Nagpur and Vidarbha but for centuries the entire land of Maharashtra has been the flag bearer of nationalism in India.

Whether it was the establishment of the Hindu *pad-padshahi* by Shivaji Maharaj during the darkest moments in the history of India; or Nana Saheb Peshwa inspiring the first war of independence; or Lokmanya Balgangadhar Tilak launching the freedom struggle by declaring *Purna Swaraj*; Swatantrya Veer Sawarkar lighting the lamp of staunch nationalism; the land of Maharashtra has always contributed towards strengthening the struggle for nationalism.

In accordance with their glorious past and the possibility of a golden future, I am confident that the people of Maharashtra will choose development with nationalism and in the forthcoming Lok Sabha and Vidhan Sabha elections and extend full support to the BJP-Shiv Sena alliance. A development oriented and nationalist government will come both in the Centre and Maharashtra.

This is our last National Council meeting before the Lok Sabha elections and neither will a National Executive Meeting be held prior to the polls. This is our last collective meeting before the elections. It is natural that this meeting should also symbolize a pledge for victory for the BJP led NDA alliance in the forthcoming Lok Sabha elections. We all should leave this meeting with the resolve and confidence that when we meet again, it will be after establishing a BJP led NDA Government.

Prior to this, our National Council Meeting had taken place in Nagpur on 27th and 28th August 2000. At that point of time, we were in power at the Centre and by the time of the next meeting, we will again be in power at the Centre under the leadership of respected Shri Lal Krishna Advaniji.

Results of the Assembly Elections

In November and December, assembly elections took place in six states - Madhya Pradesh, Chhattisgarh, Rajasthan, Delhi, Mizoram and Jammu & Kashmir. For us the election results have been a mixed outcome. While we could not return to power by a small margin even after running a good government in Rajasthan, the results in Delhi were surprisingly contrary to our expectations and would have impacted the mood of our *karyakartas* across the country.

In Jammu & Kashmir our performance was magnificent and we increased our strength from one to eleven. The impressive victory of the BJP in Jammu has hoisted the flag of nationalism in this separatism inflicted northern state. This remarkable victory has also proved that even today people can support us on our ideological issues. We will play the role of an effective and strong opposition on all issues of public good including the Shri Amarnath Shrine Board and rehabilitation of Kashmiri Hindus.

These election results have also added some glorious chapters to the BJP's history. I remember that on January 28th 2008, when we had met at the National Council meeting in Delhi, we were filled with excitement after the splendid victories in Gujarat and Himachal. Similarly, the victories in Madhya Pradesh and Chhattisgarh enthused us. The victory in Madhya

Pradesh and Chhattisgarh has shattered the myth that the BJP does not come back to power. Prior to this, in Gujarat, which has remained our stronghold for the last 15 years, we have repeatedly been returning to power and as an exception, in Jharkhand in 2005 and Rajasthan in 2003 (with a brief interregnum of President rule) we have not returned to power in any other state. From this point of view, our victory in Madhya Pradesh and Chhattisgarh symbolizes the entry of the BJP into a new era. For the first time in the history of the BJP and Jansangh, we have successfully returned to power in two states at the same time. For this, on behalf of the National Council, I congratulate the people, all BJP *karyakartas*, leaders, State Presidents Shri Vishnu Sai and Shri Narendra Singh Tomar, the incharges and election incharges Shri Dharmendra Pradhan, Shri Ravi Shankar Prasad, Shri Anant Kumar and Shri Venkaiah Naidu. Also especially to the Chief Ministers, Dr. Raman Singh and Shivraj Singh Chauhan.

If we look at the election results of all the states in totality, then we are far ahead of the Congress. We have got more MLAs elected. But we should also learn from this experience that we need to establish stronger bonds with the people. Greater sensitivity and efforts are required to tackle the people's problems.

Today's Situation

Today we cannot remain satisfied by saying that while some countries in the world are moving towards a negative growth rate, if our rate declines by 3-4 percent, it is not a matter of concern for us. I would like to convey to the policy makers of the Government of India that given the great size of India and the basic developmental level of our economy, even a 1% decline in the growth rate affects the bread and butter of millions of people. According to an estimate, around one crore people will lose their jobs in the near future. In Tamil Nadu's Tirupur alone, due to the decline in exports, about ten lac workers are now facing problems of livelihood. A similar problem is also being faced by lacs of workers in the diamond cutting industry of Surat.

If such a crisis is visible across the entire world, why has the government not initiated effective and timely steps in India? I would like to repeat that even in 2001-02, a difficult situation had emerged when the NDA Government was in power, but we did not allow its effect to be felt on India.

I would like to remind the UPA Government, which is using the international economic crisis as a pretext today, that during the NDA rule, the international economic situation for India was far more critical than this. Immediately after forming the government, we faced economic sanctions in the wake of the Pokhran nuclear tests, and thereafter, we had to face the Kargil war under such circumstances. Despite all this, we neither allowed the growth rate to decline nor allowed inflation or the rate of unemployment to increase. During the time of the NDA, interest rates on home loans and agricultural loans were reduced and the share market marched ahead steadily. I would like to ask the government that today the country is neither facing any sanctions nor any war. Yet the country is facing economic problems. Why unemployment is continuing to increase? The only reason is that this government completely lacks a longterm economic vision.

This government not only lacks a long term vision for the economy, it is also incapable of keeping an eye over all the scandals that are happening literally under its nose. The nature of the recent financial scam that has been unearthed in Satyam, one of the country's reputed IT companies, proves that the government is also incapable of controlling problems that are arising out of the fast emerging and expanding corporate world.

The tenure of the UPA Government, which came to power in the name of the *aam admi,* is now coming to an end. If we take the UN Development Report into account, then even today 80% of India's population earns one US Dollar or less than Rs 50 a day. 25% people have a spending power of less than Rs. 15 per day. About 38% people do not have a source of water close to their homes. Half of the population still lives in mud houses or such inappropriate housing conditions. Around 43% villages are still not connected with proper roads. Is this what we can call economic development?

The common man remained continuously burdened by price rise during the four and a half years of UPA rule. Today the government claims that prices are coming down. Are prices declining due to the efforts of the government? Prices are coming down due to the global recession and neither is it yielding any relief to the common man as unemployment is also continuously increasing simultaneously. According to a joint survey conducted by the reputed American think tank Heritage Foundation and the Wall Street Journal, in 2008 India ranked 115th in the Economic Freedom Index.

Despite all this, the UPA Government, on coming to power, virtually put all the important infrastructure related projects started by the NDA Government into cold storage. The National Highway Project launched during the tenure of the NDA Government was regarded as a milestone in the development of the country. According to the original plan, this project would have been complet by now, but in reality it actually stands far from complete. The reason behind this is that while during the tenure of the NDA 11 KM of road was being constructed everyday, under the UPA Government less than 1 KM of road is being constructed daily.

Not only has the pace of projects slowed down, one can also see a decline in the allocations of funds. According to an estimate, today hundreds of crores of rupees for infrastructural projects is entangled merely on account of administrative procedures.

At a time of economic recession, can the country bear the burden of slowdown of infrastructural projects and hundreds of crores of rupees being stuck because of red tapism? The country is being compelled to suffer all this. The UPA Government feels that since these were the projects of the NDA Government, so even if the roads remain in poor condition or are incomplete, the NDA should not get credit for them. Is it not dishonesty with the nation?

I am not saying this merely for politics. In fact this is the opinion being expressed even by foreign economists as well as economic experts from communist China.

A few days ago, a senior Polit Bureau Member of the Communist Party of China who is also the head of the Shanghai unit of the party, met me. While discussing the economic recession, I said that if India pushes infrastructure projects for which there is immense potential in the country, then many companies looking for new projects will be attracted to come here. India will in the process benefit from standard projects at lesser costs and this will also help the country emerge out of the recession. While agreeing with this, he added that they were also doing the same thing in China.

However, the UPA Government wants to keep all these projects in cold storage merely because the NDA's name is associated with them.

The people of the country have now understood about this dishonest game being played against development. Now the NDA Government will again come to power, then all these mega developmental projects will again be speedily implemented to help the country recover from the current recession.

Terrorism

I clearly recall that after the UPA Government came to power and when Prime Minister Dr. Manmohan Singh went to Mumbai, then he had said that he would ensure that Mumbai becomes like Shanghai. The manner in which terrorists created a war like situation between the 26th and 29th November at railway stations, hospitals, hotels, roads and everywhere else, made me wonder whether this was the face of the same Mumbai which the UPA was claiming to make like Shanghai.

Now, finally the government has passed an anti-terror law. It is worth remembering that among the first steps which the UPA Government took after coming to power was to repeal POTA. Now in the last phase of its tenure, it had to finally pass an anti-terror law again. This proves that during its entire tenure, the government, which was blinded by vote bank politics, has now accepted the same point that we have been demanding for the last five years.

However, over the last four and a half years, the country has had to pay a heavy price for this. Over the past four and a half years of UPA rule, more than 40 terrorist attacks have taken place. This means that on an average, not even one and a half month could elapse without a terrorist incident taking place. Hundreds of people have been killed in these terrorist attacks and every nook and corner of the country has been affected. I would once again like to remind you that even the US State Department had in its report for the year 2007 ranked India as the most terrorism affected country after Iraq. The manner in which the incidents took place on the streets of Mumbai between 26th and 29th November, it appeared as if they were taking place in Iraq's Baghdad and not in Mumbai.

The government has now also accepted the need for a central investigating agency. The realization for having a new anti-terror law and an agency dawned upon them only after the entire country was literally burning in the flames of terrorism. The government's policy of tackling terrorism reminds me about the famous "*Niti Shatak*" by the great scholar Bhartrihari who had said – *"Proddipte Bhavane, Cha Kupa Khananam"* – meaning the person whose vision is akin to digging a well only after the building is on fire, leads the entire society towards destruction. The policy of the UPA Government is like this.

False Resolve to Fight Terrorism

Over the past few years all the main cities of the country have faced terrorist attacks. In addition to the terrorist attack a few months ago in Mumbai, serial bomb blasts took place in Delhi in September 2008 in which 25 persons were killed and more than 100 were injured. On 19th September the brave inspector Mohan Chandra Sharma was martyred in the Batla House encounter and on 30th October 2008 serial bomb blasts shook four districts of Assam in which 83 persons died and more than 400 were injured. This was the biggest terrorist incident in Assam till date.

Even as all these incidents were taking place across the country, the people need to recall what kind of statements the ministers of the UPA Government were making:

- One Central minister was speaking about granting citizenship to Bangladeshi infiltrators.
- Another Central minister was declaring SIMI as a cultural organization.
- The leaders of the Congress and its allies rushed to the village of a terrorist accused and made statements about the so called injustice being meted out to him.
- While one leader of the government's alliance partner was demanding an inquiry into the Batla house encounter, another important Congress leader in Parliament raised a question mark on the martyrdom of the STF officers.
- A Communist Party Chief Minister used derogatory language for the family of the Major martyred in Mumbai terror attack.
- And the sleep of the Honourable Prime Minister was disturbed on account of the investigations that were carried out against a terror suspect in Australia.
- The Prime Minister advocated the first claim of the Muslim community on the country's resources. The first claim should go to the poor irrespective of their religion or caste.
- The Prime Minister on his tour to Cuba declared Pakistan as a victim of terrorism.
- And all these activities should be seen in context of how nothing has moved over the past three years in executing the sentence announced by the Supreme Court against the Parliament attack accused. While on the other hand, by creating the hoax of "Hindu Terror" to serve its political interests, the investigation was carried out at such a fast pace that literally every day a new revelation was being made.

- These two examples of the government's delaying and fast paced tactics expose the two aspects of its approach towards terrorism and also proves its questionable intentions.
- then a government having such policies and intentions speaks about dealing with terrorism then it not only comes across as ludicrous but also anguishes one.

Neighbouring Countries

Many important developments are taking place in the countries neighbouring India. Today our internal security and our foreign policy towards our neighbouring countries have become two aspects of the same coin. That is why in the last National Council Meeting, I had demanded that the government should formulate a separate foreign policy for our neighbouring countries. The current situation with Pakistan proves the necessity of this.

The facts which have come to light after the terror attack in Mumbai clearly point towards the active involvement of many organisations in Pakistan and also some parts of the government machinery in perpetrating the ongoing terror attacks in India. I would like to ask the Government of India as to whether this is the same Pakistan which the Prime Minister said was a victim of terrorism?

After the terror attack in Mumbai, some statement or the other emanates from the government on a daily basis as if war is about to take place. Then the statement is contradicted only for another statement to appear again after two or three days. The government wants to divert the attention of the people by making such statements. We have already said that in this situation Pakistan will have to take some concrete measures and for this and the Government of India should take the international community into confidence and create diplomatic pressure on Pakistan and if there is no outcome even after this, then the alternative of direct action should be resorted to.

I want to ask this government another question – It's two and half months since the Mumbai attack and the government is continuously raising questions about the terror-network in Pakistan. However, the UPA Government should also inform as to how many terror-modules has the Central Government destroyed within the country over the past two and half months? The government should update the people of the country about the status of investigation of every terrorist attack that has taken place over the last four and a half years, the situation as of now on each case and the details of the success achieved in punishing the perpetrators of these terror acts.

The Bharatiya Janata Party is completely with the government in its attempt to fight terrorism. The leader of the Opposition in Lok Sabha and the future Prime Minister of the country, respected Shri Advaniji has clearly said that we are united with the government in its fight against terrorism. I have also publicly declared the BJP's support to the government. But the central government has till date not been able to take a single effective step within the country what to speak about outside. It would not be inappropriate to say that the government's so-called fight against terror is like an empty vessel only making noise.

Afghanistan

In Afghanistan, the influence of the Taliban is continuously increasing. The activities taking place in the frontier regions of Afghanistan and Pakistan are definitely a matter of concern. The influence of the Taliban is now not only limited to the North West Frontier and FATA Provinces but has expanded deep into other parts of Pakistan. In this manner it is also coming closer to the Indian border. The Taliban has already made a declaration that in time of war, it will support the Pakistani army against India. The Government of India should take effective measures to deal with this situation.

Sri Lanka

The LTTE in Sri Lanka is on the verge of a decisive defeat. In this changing scenario, the Sri Lankan government, in a sensitive manner and through dialogue, should work out a political solution to the ethnic conflict keeping in mind the problems and sentiments of the Tamil people. The Government of India should extend full cooperation in this effort to ensure that permanent peace is established in Sri Lanka.

We respect the sovereignty and integrity of Sri Lanka. However, permanent peace and stability in Sri Lanka can be achieved only if the Sri Lankan government devolves power to the Tamil areas according to a federal structure as envisaged in the 1987 peace accord. Moreover, according to the 1987 peace accord, the Tamil people should also be provided power according to the 13th Constitutional Amendment of the Sri Lankan Constitution.

Bangladesh

The Bharatiya Janata Party welcomes the return of democracy in Bangladesh. After a gap of seven years including two years of military rule, a new Awami League government led by its president and former Prime Minister Sheikh Hasina Wajid has come to power in these parliamentary elections. I extend my congratulations to Sheikh Hasina and her new government. We hope that the new government will ensure an end to the terrorist centres operating from Bangladeshi soil against India and pave the way for better bilateral relations. Sheikh Hasina has expressed a commitment for fighting terrorism in South Asia. If Bangladesh honestly and effectively cooperates in this direction, then we can free the entire region from terrorism and herald a new age of peace and prosperity.

Nepal

The Maoist government in Nepal after assuming power through democratic means, in our opinion has tried to harm the country's social and cultural set up in an inappropriate manner. Recently, despite court instructions, the manner in which the centuries old system was attempted to be forcibly changed in the world famous temple of Bhagwan Pashupatinath, a major centre of faith for the Hindus across the world, raises doubts about the commitment of the government towards Nepal's democracy and culture.

The issue is not just about Indian priests but refers to the common cultural heritage between India and Nepal spanning thousands of years and such attempts can inflict damage to these relations. Understanding the gravity of the issue, I immediately spoke with the Prime Minister of Nepal Shri Pushpa Kamal Dahal 'Prachanda' and the President Shri Rambaran Yadav over the phone. Having made them aware of my sentiments, I requested them to intervene and immediately restore the status quo.

India never links cultural and religious issues with politics. If Sister Alphonsa or Mother Teresa are declared as saints by the Vatican, we would never oppose this on the ground that such processes should be undertaken only by Indians. The government of Nepal is seeking to lay down an indigenous Nepali procedure for appointment of priests in Pashupatinath Temple, so that the appointment and the recognition of priests can be decided within Nepal. I would like to ask the Government of Nepal, whether they will oppose the appointment of the Archbishop and Cardinals of Nepal by the Vatican, and will they lay down an indigenous Nepali procedure for appointment and recognition of Archbishops and Cardinals as they are trying to do so in the context of Pashupatinath Temple?

China

The manner in which China has been constantly raising the question of Arunachal Pradesh, has now become a matter of concern for us. The central government which claimed good relations with China throughout its tenure, has not even once been able to adequately respond diplomatically everytime China has summarily rejected India's claim.

The NDA Government under the leadership of Atal ji:

- Established India in the league of global superpowers.
- Resolved the issue of Sikkim.
- Isolated Pakistan on the issue of Kashmir.
- Rendered ineffective Pakistan's anti-India propaganda in the western countries.
- Did not allow a single opportunity to any third country to interfere in our internal affairs be it the Kargil war or the attack on Parliament.

Foreign Policy

Between the last National Council Meeting and this one, the Indo-US Nuclear Deal has been approved. The Central Government has claimed that India has become a strategic partner of the US. We are in favour of good relations with all countries including the US. I had demanded that if the US is indeed a strategic partner of India, then it should stop all financial aid to Pakistan until Pakistan effectively acts to control all the terrorist outfits operating from its territory.

The President of the United States Mr Barack Obama immediately after taking his oath, in a foreign policy directive said that it would not be possible for the US to continue providing aid to Pakistan if it failed to stop terror activities from its soil. However, the US has increased non-military aid to Pakistan. In my opinion any kind of aid to Pakistan strengthens the terrorist elements there because the line dividing state and non-state players vis-à-vis terror activities is becoming increasingly unclear.

The Defence Secretary of the United States has also recently said that there is a possibility of a big al Qaeda network in Pakistan and if this is proved to be correct, then the US army can even consider a direct attack on Pakistan. Is this situation appropriate for giving additional aid to Pakistan? In my opinion certainly not. Even though, the US administration has slightly reduced the amount of the additional foreign aid to Pakistan, in my opinion the government of India should persuade America that it should not give any additional financial aid to Pakistan.

The new President of the United States has assumed office. On behalf of the Bharatiya Janata Party, I extend my best wishes to President Barak Obama for his tenure and hope that Indo-US relations will get stronger and play an effective role in establishing peace in the world.

Another incident during the oath ceremony of the US President filled every Indian with a sense of pride. From the time of the first US President George Washington, it has been a convention in the US that various religious leaders pray for the President. This time, a lady priest of Indian origin and a respected doctor in America, Dr. Uma Mysorker officially participated in the prayer ceremony. This is yet another indication of the continuously increasing respect for India's culture in the US and other parts of the world.

The respect and reputation which India enjoyed at the international level during the tenure of the Vajpayee government, has been completely lost under the UPA rule.

The manner in which the Union Home Minister says that he will visit the US to once again show the evidence against Pakistan, illustrates as if India has become helpless under the UPA Government.

At the meeting of the Chief Ministers, the Prime Minister said that the government machinery of Pakistan was involved in the Mumbai attack. However, the British Foreign Secretary David Miliband said that Pakistan's government machinery was not involved. He also said that proceedings against the accused should be undertaken in Pakistan whereas the Indian government wants the action to be undertaken in India. And if this was not enough, the British Foreign Secretary went to the extent of saying that the Kashmir issue was the root cause of the problem and with its resolution, terrorism would get completely controlled.

Despite this statement being fundamentally in contravention to India's foreign policy, even then the Government of India has failed to register any effective protest.

The situation in Jharkhand

In the Jharkhand elections of 2005, the BJP emerged as the single largest party and other parties could not even win half the number of seats won by us. We formed the government, but the manner in which the Central Government misused the constitutional machinery and abducted the people's mandate, initiated a tragic political drama that even today has not yet ended. The defeat of Shibu Soren clearly demonstrates the people's anger against the policies of the Congress and its allies in Jharkhand. I am fully confident that the people of the state, fed up with this kind of ugly political drama, will give a thumping majority to the BJP in the forthcoming assembly elections.

Northeastern States

The northeastern region of India is one such area that has not been given due importance by the mainstream political parties. The 26 Lok Sabha seats in the entire region are more than any medium sized state. The area has distinct circumstances and therefore unique problems. The BJP has always been committed towards developing the northeast. Recently, the Asom Gana Parishad, the main opposition party in Assam, the largest state in the region, has declared its alliance with the BJP. I am confident that in the forthcoming Lok Sabha elections, the BJP-AGP alliance will record an impressive victory. In addition to this, in other states like Arunachal, Nagaland, Mizoram, Manipur, Sikkim and Meghalaya, many political parties may come forward to cooperate with us.

Bangladeshi infiltration is a huge problem in the northeast which has led to demographic changes in many districts of the region. The governments in Assam and the centre have completely failed in resolving this problem.

Today the Home Minister is speaking about scrutinizing the visas granted to Bangladeshis and tightening legal measures. For the last five years, in fact not just five years but for the last 30 years, ever since this problem started, the approach of the Congress governments at the Centre and in the state has not only been soft but one that actually encouraged infiltration.

The Supreme Court even passed strictures against the government in its decision on the IMDT Act. The Assam Governor's report has described in detail the unhindered infiltration that is taking place from across the border. Yet the government instead of checking infiltration has helped it by adding provisions of the IMDT Act in the Foreigners' Act.

Not only this, a minister in the government has spoken about granting citizenship to Bangladeshi infiltrators.

Given this background, the talk by the Congress about taking strong measures against Bangladeshi infiltration is nothing more than a charade.

Farmers

Today India has emerged as one of the important, largest and fastest growing economies of the world. Yet around 60% of the population is still dependent on agriculture for their livelihood in one way or the other. Therefore, in the absence of proper development of agriculture and the farmers, it would be futile to contemplate about a bright future for India. The land in India is among the most fertile lands of the world and is full of natural resources. In such a situation, any development model that only focuses on the industrial and service sectors while neglecting the agricultural sector, cannot do justice to the real potential of India. That's why I believe that the actual future of India is embodied within the future of the farmers.

Today, when the salary of top officials of multinational companies has touched lacs of rupees, the average income of the farmer in India is Rs. 503 for his monthly expenses, which is close to the poverty line and of which more than half is spent on food.

According to a report of the National Commission for Enterprises in the Unorganised Sector, 83.6 crore people in the country are not capable of earning even Rs. 20 a day. According to the official figures in a report of the National Sample Survey, the loan on an average farmer family has doubled in the last few years.

For this very Vidarbha region, the Prime Minister had announced a relief package with lots of hype but according to a report by the Government of India's Comptroller & Auditor General of India (CAG), even after the announcement of the relief package, the suicides by the farmers in the Vidarbha region have increased. It is clear that farmers have not benefitted from this relief package and loan waiver.

As a result of the UPA's policies, a situation has emerged over the last few years whereby undertaking agricultural activity is increasingly becoming more expensive. For example, in the Telangana region, the farmers having 5-7 acres of land are also living below the poverty line. Even in a prosperous state like Punjab, 60% of the farmers are burdened with loans. In the Vidarbha region, where the per acre cost of cultivating cotton 15 years ago was Rs 2500, today it has become Rs. 13,000. It is as a result of this that farmers are committing suicide in large numbers or are being compelled to abandon agriculture despite the absence of any alternative employment opportunity.

The tenure of the UPA Government has come to an end. It saddens me to note that my demand for a special session of Parliament to discuss the condition of the farmers and the entire agriculture sector which is passing through its worst phase in independent India, was finally not accepted by this government.

We should not think that the problems which are emerging in the agriculture sector will remain confined only to the farmers. If these kinds of policies are allowed to continue, then we may have to face a situation of food crisis in the coming days. Last year we had witnessed a glimpse of shortage of food products. The shortsighted policies of the government are endangering our food security.

Youth

There are three main national parties in India –Congress, Communists and BJP. Among the three, the BJP is the youngest party. The BJP was founded after independence. Our ideology and vision are based on the vision of a new young India which was dreamt by young ascetics like Swami Vivekanand and Sri Aurobindo and for which many youth like Bhagat Singh, Chandrashekhar Azad, Bagha Jatin and Vasudev Balwant Phadke laid down their lives.

Today 70% of the country's population is less than 35 years of age. Who will address this section, who will take care of the youth? During the tenure of the NDA, we created impressive employment opportunities and development. According to many reputed international institutions, during the last phase of the NDA Government, in the year 2003-04, the highest amount of employment opportunities were created. This provided the youth an opportunity to display their ability and talent in totality.

When former Prime Minister respected Atalji envisioned making India a developed country by 2020, it was a resolve for young India. Because the youth of today will become the policy makers of India in 2020 and thereafter.

Be it the issue of using new technology or launching a website or connecting the entire party through Information Technology, among all political parties, the BJP has always been in the forefront in relating to the technologically savvy youth.

However, even today, three fourth of the country's youth is either living in the rural areas or in urban slums earning livelihood through petty means. While speaking about the youth, we often tend to forget this huge section of youth. We need to pay more attention to this section of the youth.

Today one can see two conflicting expressions of young energy in the country. While young software engineers and scientists in Bangalore, Chennai and Hyderabad are earning laurels for India in the international arena, in Jammu and Kashmir and many parts of the country, they are creating problems by indulging in terrorist activities.

The creative energy of the youth helped establish India as an IT superpower at the international level in the closing years of the 1990s and in the early years of 2000. This path was further paved during the tenure of the NDA government. On the other hand, the seeds of terrorism were sown in the decade of the 1980's when the Congress of Indira Gandhi and Rajiv Gandhi ruled the country with two-third and three-fourth majority.

This clearly exemplifies that only the BJP has the ability to enlighten the youth of the country in the right direction.

Today's Congress and Gandhi

In the previous National Executive Meeting, I had mentioned that the developmental model for making India's future glorious should be based on that power of the youth which was envisaged by great thinkers like Mahatma Gandhi and Deen Dayal Upadhyaya and inclusive of economic, social, intellectual, emotional, moral and spiritual development of the youth.

I had also said that 100 years ago in his famous book *Hind Swaraj*, what kind of development model that Mahatma Gandhi had spoken about for the future of India.

Gandhi in his philosophy has categorically said that for the future of India, the principle of *"Karma-vaad"* is of utmost importance. Only this alone can take the youth of the country in the right direction. The Gandhian concept of *karma-vaad* is totally based on the principle of the Gita's *nishkaam karma.* Tilak, who pioneered the entire political journey of India's freedom struggle by giving the call for total independence (*purna swaraj),* has also given the concept of *Karmayog Shastra* in his famous book *Gita Rahasya.* In politics, Mahatma Gandhi carried forward the legacy of Tilak. For the fear of being called communal, probably the Congress of today will shy away from even taking the name of the Gita what to speak about the *Karmayog Shastra* of Tilak and *karma vaad* of Gandhi.

Today's Congress does not reflect any of Gandhi's values and thoughts. I would like to ask my Congress friends, to what extent they have implemented the Gandhian thoughts in their policies while ruling this country for around 50 years? The policies of Congress reflected more the elements of British Raj while the element of Gandhi's *Hind Swaraj* was missing. Is there any Gandhian thought left in the conduct of the today's Congress? In today's Congress' thinking neither is there any *Hind Swaraj* nor *Gram Swaraj;* no place for villages and no respect for the farmers; no *swadeshi* cottage industries; no section living a simple life of sacrifice is connected to them; neither is there a *swadeshi style* nor *swadeshi* language. And if this not enough, then the very symbol of Gandhian *karma vaad,* the *Srimad Bhagwat Gita* is communal and the very basis of Gandhi's vision of *Ram Rajya Bhagwan Ram* is also communal. Gandhi's favourite prayers be it *Raghupati Raghav Raja Ram* or *Vaishnav Jan To Tene Kahiye* are totally communal by today's parameters. If one is to seek any of these aspects of Gandhian ethos in India today, then it can only be found in the ideology of the BJP and in the simple and dedicated lifestyle of several organizations of our *parivar.*

I would like to ask what does today's Congress have that was Gandhi's ? Today probably no leader even wears the *khadi* of Gandhi. Today's Congress has nothing related to Gandhi except a family name. All the works associated with Gandhian ethos, if at all are visible, will not be found in that *parivar* of the Congress but in our *parivar.* They are only a name while we are the ones who are carrying forward his actual work.

Women

The BJP is serious about providing adequate representation to half of the country's population. Instead of *"Nari-Mukti"* (women's liberation), the party believes in *"Nari Shakti"* (women's empowerment). Even today women have to face numerous problems. Over the last six decades, even though literacy among women has increased, it cannot be considered satisfactory. The participation of women in politics today is not to the extent as it should be. We are committed towards providing 33% reservation for women in the legislature. During the tenure of the NDA, we presented this Bill on two occasions, but due to opposition by some political parties, it could not be passed. The participation of women in politics is not just an intellectual exercise. We have expressed our commitment by ensuring 33% participation by women within our organizational structure. The BJP has displayed its credibility of having no difference between what it speaks and practices. In BJP ruled states, we have also implemented 50% reservation for women at the panchayat and municipal levels.

Scheduled Castes

The Bharatiya Janata Party and BJP Scheduled Caste Morcha have always made efforts for the development of the scheduled castes. Our governments have implemented many welfare plans for the benefit of the scheduled castes.

In addition to development, self respect is the other feeling that constantly remains in the minds of the people belonging to the scheduled castes. The Bharatiya Janata Party has always accorded top priority to the self respect of the scheduled castes. On every important post, be it ministers, chief ministers, governors or central ministers and even the Lok Sabha Speaker, we have ensured adequate representation to the scheduled castes.

Shri Ram Janambhoomi and Ram Setu

Five years of the UPA Government's tenure have elapsed, and I feel pained in saying that during these last five years, the government has failed to spare even five minutes for initiating dialogue to resolve the Shri Ram Janambhoomi dispute. No effort, direct or indirect, has been undertaken by the government. On the contrary, in the affidavit filed by the government on the issue of Sri Ram Setu, the government denied the very existence of Maryada Purushottam Bhagwan Ram, something not even the foreign rulers had dared to do.

During the tenure of this government, the kind of contempt that has been displayed towards our cultural symbols, has perhaps never taken place throughout our history.

On January 20th 2006 in my Presidential Address at the first National Council Meeting in Delhi, I had cited the example of the Wailing Wall in Israel. Today I will cite another example. If you visit Bangkok, the new airport there is called Swarnabhoomi Airport, and on entering the airport, one can see a beautiful mural depicting the scene of the *"Sagar*

Manthan" as enumerated in the Vishnu Purana and Devi Bhagawata. Just imagine if such a proposal comes for any airport in India, then all the so called secularists would see communalism in it. Prior to this, the government of Sri Lanka authenticated places associated with Bhagwan Rama and the Ramayana.

It is painful to note that our cultural symbols are respected outside India but to seek respect for them within our country is considered communal. After 60 years of independence, at least now we should come out of the colonial mindset that sought to instill an inferiority complex within us.

Successful launch of Chandrayaan

Over the last few days, with their expertise and perseverance, our space scientists made history when India successfully launched its first unmanned space craft to the moon. With this, India has become the sixth nation of the world to send its mission to the moon. For this historical achievement, I extend my felicitations and greetings to the Chairman of ISRO, G Madhavan Nair and his entire team of scientists and engineers. For the BJP, it a matter of even more pride since the project was initiated under the leadership of Atalji during the tenure of the NDA.

NDA versus UPA

Today in the country one witnesses a political polarization between two broad alliances. One is the Congress led UPA and the other is the BJP led NDA alliance.

The UPA alliance is an opportunistic, self-centered and full of internal contradictions alliance which has severely harmed the interests of the country during its tenure. On the other hand, the NDA over the last 10 years has been working as a stable and positive alliance. Our allies have a long history of cooperation with the BJP. Our alliance with the Shiv Sena is more than 20 years old. Our alliance with the JD(U) has been for the last 14 years. The Shiromani Akali Dal has been our ally for twelve years and we have been working with the Biju Janata Dal for the last 10 years. Has the Congress been able to keep its allies together for such a long period of time?

Recently, some more allies have joined the BJP. In Haryana, the Indian National Lok Dal led by Shri Om Prakash Chautala has announced their joining the NDA. In Assam, the Asom Gana Parishad has declared that it will be contesting the forthcoming Lok Sabha and Vidhan Sabha elections in alliance with the BJP. In the coming days, we will see a further expansion of the NDA.

The examples of the better condition of the country during the tenure of the NDA and the deteriorating condition of the country under the UPA are given below:

Economic

- The NDA continuously kept price rise under check for six years. Price rise continuously increased under the UPA in the last four and half years.
- The NDA reduced the rates of interest on agriculture and housing loans. The UPA increased it.
- Under the NDA, food stocks were overflowing. Under the UPA, there has been a problem of foodgrains.
- Employment increased under the NDA. Unemployment has increased under the UPA.
- No economic scam took place during the time of the NDA. During the tenure of the UPA, many scandals like the food scam, spectrum scam and Satyam scam have taken place.
- We provided a development oriented economy of plenty. The UPA has given an economy of recession and deficit.

Security

- The NDA on forming the government implemented the anti-terror law POTA. The UPA repealed it.
- The NDA established India as a military power through the Pokhran tests. The UPA surrendered this position by signing the nuclear deal.

Political

- The NDA gave justice to all. The UPA has displayed the height of appeasement politics.
- NDA preserved the dignity of constitutional values. UPA destroyed it (as in the case of Bihar, Jharkhand Goa etc.).
- The Parliament functioned only for 322 days during the entire tenure of the UPA Government. In the history of Indian Parliament, this is a government which throughout its tenure has faced

Parliament for the least number of days.

- NDA enhanced the international status of India. The UPA diluted it.
- The NDA never gave political support to the corrupt. Under the UPA even Quattrochhi was given an opportunity to run away with the country's money.
- NDA allowed its government to fall by a single vote. The UPA purchased votes by distributing notes to win the trust vote.

Development

- NDA started huge infrastructural projects. The UPA either slowed down these projects or dumped them in cold storage.
- NDA established India as superpower in the field of atomic energy, space science, communication and information technology. UPA could not initiate any such measure.

Cultural

- NDA deleted the derogatory remarks against great religious personalities from the text books. UPA added such references.
- NDA respected the cultural values. The UPA has shown disrespect towards the key cultural symbols (for example Vande Mataram, Ramsetu and Amarnath controversies etc.)

If we study the UPA Government's entire tenure, one finds that development has fallen, employment opportunities have reduced, international stature has declined, security got destroyed, the entire economy is in shambles, and above all, the government has even denied the existence Lord Ram. In a single sentence it can be said that "*UPA sarkar ne kiya kaam tamam; aam admi ko na maya (economy) mili na Ram*".

After comparing the two, the people of the country can themselves decide as to under which alliance the future of the nation will be secure. I challenge the UPA Government to name even a single task undertaken by it which will have a significant positive impact on the future of the country. The people's anger against the UPA has been witnessed clearly over the last few years. In the last two years, out of the 17 state assembly elections held, UPA lost 11 and Congress on its own managed to win only 4.

The NDA has unanimously declared senior BJP leader respected Lal Krishna Advaniji as its prime ministerial candidate. Respected Advaniji is not only one of the most experienced and senior leaders of the country, but the kind of commitment and dedication that he has displayed by retaining a clean image in over 50 years of his political life, is a lesson for us to emulate and follow. Without doubt no other alliance or party has a leader of such maturity and vision as the NDA has in respected Shri Advaniji.

Karyakarta

Over the last few years, we have jointly steered the BJP through various situations, and marching ahead we have effectively strengthened our position throughout the country.

We have not only geographically and politically expanded but also added a new chapter in terms of organizational expansion. For the first time in history, booth committees have been constituted. Today, throughout the country, we have constituted our units on more than 65% of the booths. In many states like Gujarat and Himachal, more than 90 to 95% booth committees have been formed.

Today the electoral process for the Lok Sabha elections has commenced. In the BJP's history, the forthcoming Lok Sabha will be the most significant and extraordinary. After our formation, we did not have any significant role to play in national politics in the elections that we fought in the decade of the 1980s. Between 1989 and 1999, we contested elections either on ideological issues or on the plea that Vajpayeeji should get a chance to be the Prime Minister of the country. In 2004, we contested the elections on the issue of development. The 2009 elections are important for us from all the three perspectives. This means that we will have to formulate an integrated strategy for the forthcoming elections. By integrating our ideological base, capacity to offer good governance (*sushashan*) and the strength of alliance and organization, we will definitely be able to get the people's mandate.

Today India is facing challenges from within, challenges from across the border, the economy is in difficulty, capital is in shortage, and in addition to all this, there is a crisis of credibility among the political parties. As a result of globalization, there is also a cultural crisis in the country in terms of social and family values. This year, on the birth anniversary of Netaji Subhash Chandra Bose on 23rd January, I read in a newspaper that there is a large section of such children who are not aware about Netaji. One child said he was a cabinet minister while another said that he was a police officer.

I am trying to say that in the post independence era, today we are passing through a really critical phase. At the time of elections, such a situation can be both a challenge as well as opportunity for us. The entire nation is looking at us to find answers to these challenges. If the BJP fails to respond to these challenges, then rest assured, no other political party will have a solution for them. If by galvanizing our organizational powers we are successful in this election, respond to all these challenges and take the country out of these crises, then we will be considered as architects of history in the years to come.

I am fully confident that all of us as BJP *karyakartas* will eventually do well in our efforts and be successful in this election, and on the coming 15th August, respected Advaniji will address the nation from the ramparts of the Red Fort.

"Senani karo prayan abhay, bhavi itihas tumhara hai.
Sab nakhat ama ke bujhte hain, sara akash tumhara hai."

□

Epilogue

20-21 June, 2009 (New Delhi)

We fought the 15th Lok Sabha elections with our full political strength. I would like to personally thank each and every one of the millions of supporters and voters as well as our Karyakartas who supported us in the recent Lok Sabha elections. The results were not upto our expectations. The people have once again given us the mandate to sit in opposition. We accept the verdict with humility and will once more resume our work. While we may be surprised by the results, we are certainly not demoralized by them. Why have such results come? This is definitely a subject of serious introspection and analysis for us. At every step we will undertake introspection and analysis. The conclusions that emerge from this process of churning of ideas will become our guiding light, and keeping that in mind, we will untiringly proceed further on our path by taking everyone along. We will neither stop nor get tired. I am fully confident that in the end, we will be victorious. But in order to realize this dream of victory in the true sense, it is incumbent on our part that we should have a feeling of *Nishkaam Karma* and dedication. In my opinion, there might have been some shortcomings in our dedication and action. With time we need to do away with these shortcomings.

The Results of the Lok Sabha Elections

The results of the Lok Sabha Elections have not been upto our expectations. We accept these results. However, there is a widespread propaganda that the BJP has been defeated nationwide. I do not accept this, because if we analyze the results regionally, then the results are varied and not uniform from state to state. At some places our performance has been spectacular, in some places we have substantially improved as compared to earlier, in some places it has been as it is and in some states our performance has been disappointing.

Yet the reality is that in totality we have lost 22 seats from what it was in the previous Lok Sabha.

We are all aware that over the last five years we emerged victorious in the maximum number of states that went to the polls across the nation. We defeated the Congress in Jharkhand, Bihar, Punjab, Himachal and Uttarakhand. In Gujarat we got elected once again. Not only this, by forming the government in Karnataka, we hoisted our flag in the south. This was a historic day in the political journey of the country.

No doubt we were unsuccessful in Uttar Pradesh, Rajasthan and Delhi. But we once again formed our governments in Gujarat, Madhya Pradesh and Chhattisgarh. On account of the BJP's increasing strength and the UPA's unpopularity, the atmosphere appeared becoming favorable for us. No one can deny this that even one day prior to the election results, the Congress leadership was in search of support from allies. Even the leaders of the Congress were not expecting so many seats. In any case, the political situation favoured them and the Congress was successful in getting over two hundred seats.

The Meaning Behind the Results

If we analyze the Lok Sabha results not from the point of victory and defeat, then one can find some intrinsic positive indications in them. The results have given a big jolt to those parties that used the politics of pure opportunism and had made it a fashion to unnecessarily pressurize the government to display their strength. All such parties who followed this type of unprincipled politics that had emerged over the last 15-20 years, suffered heavily in these elections.

On the one hand, the dreams of those parties who pursued caste based politics got shattered, and on the other hand, several candidates having the image of musclemen were also badly defeated. So at least on this account, the results of the 15th Lok Sabha have given an indication that our democracy is becoming more mature.

This election has virtually demolished the politics of despotism and absolute opportunism. In West Bengal and Kerala the people have not only taught a lesson to the communists by defeating them, but have also put a stop to their political blackmailing.

In this Lok Sabha, not only has the Congress emerged as the largest party and the BJP as the second largest party, but the parties which are at the third position like the Communists, SP, BSP and DMK, their strength is about 1/5th (around 20 seats) of ours. The big difference between the second largest and third largest parties clearly indicates that the people's confidence in the country is increasing towards bi-polar politics.

That is why we can claim that if in the forthcoming years we properly expand our organization and take effective steps to get the people's mandate, then tomorrow will definitely be ours.

In contrast to many political parties who never hesitated in taking the help of caste, creed and religion for the sake of votes, there we placed greater emphasis on the nation over votes. Not only me but all of you believe that for us the nation is bigger than votes and we can draw satisfaction from the fact that the issues that we have raised was our national duty. We are not burdened by guilt. How can any nationalist support reservation on religious lines? How can one justify the allocation of budgetary support on religious lines? Politics and backwardness should not be viewed on communal angles, rather it should be viewed from a humanitarian angle. Be it the Sacchar Committee recommendations or the headcount of Muslims in the armed forces, all these are a blow to the secular fabric of the nation. Even today, I believe that constitutionally and morally, we are on the correct side. Eventually, even the country will accept that like social justice, National Justice is a concept and politics cannot be above the national interest. In my opinion, the BJP stands for national justice, and in the future we will present this aspect in a more effective way before the people and get their support.

Emphasis on Nationalist Policies

This time in our election manifesto we reiterated, our commitment for building a grand temple on the Shri Ram Jananbhoomi, our clear views for abrogating Article 370 and our appeal for implementing the Uniform Civil Code. Even today we are firm on these issues because we believe that they are the core issues for the unity and integrity of the country. All these issues are in national interest. In the coming years we need to more effectively convince the people about these issues.

Our Role as an Effective Opposition

The responsibility entrusted upon us by the people is not ordinary. I would like to make it clear that the Congress now cannot shirk from its responsibilities. It can no longer take the alibi of its allies. We will continue our fight for the cause of India's poor, farmers, labourers and the common man.

Here I would also like to make it clear that on all issues of national interest and those connected with the welfare of the average citizen, we will fully support the government. However, for this, the government will also have to step forward. As is expected in a democracy, it will be the responsibility of the government to show that it is continuing with the tradition of building consensus on all important issues.

Hindutva/Bharatiyata/Cultural Nationalism

After the results of this Lok Sabha election, some people have started to give us this advice and in many newspapers it is being propagated that the BJP should now leave the issue of Hindutva, because the BJP has for the second time not won the election.

Firstly, Hindutva has never been a political issue and the BJP has never made it an issue that now it should discard Hindutva. A propaganda is being made that the defeat of the BJP symbolizes the rejection of the ideology of Hindutva by the people of India. I would like to ask whether this election was a referendum on Hindutva? If not, then how can the adverse results symbolize the rejection of our ideology? Since we have emerged as the main opposition party, how can it be said that we or our ideology has been totally rejected by the people?

Whenever anyone questions the BJP as to what we have to say about Hindutva, in this context I would like to state that Hindutva is not only ours but is an eternal way of life. In its famous judgement of 1995, the Hon'ble Supreme Court had ruled that Hindutva is not a religion but it is a way of life.

Hindutva is such a geo-cultural concept which has a sense of respect and a place for everyone and it is a concept of co-existence. It is this cultural consciousness imbibed with the concept of coexistence which has made Hindutva so benevolent and flexible. That is why Hindutva is eternal. Hindutva is the national essence of India. It is the natural flow of India's national consciousness. Hindutva has not emerged out of a political resolution from the parliamentary board or executive of a party or organization; it is the national identity of India. On account of this very identity, the political nature of India is inherently democratic.

When we won, then also these people had propagated that Hindutva is behind the BJP's progress and expansion. To associate a vast concept such as Hindutva with the politics of power, is nothing but one's own lack of understanding. That is why we should not be confused by any such talk. Ideology is a perpetual flow. This flow can reduce or increase but it can never stop. Therefore, only those who are confused should think about this, we need not ever be confused about Hindutva.

Many reasons behind the defeat in the elections are being identified. We are analyzing them. We are not conservative in a negative sense. We welcome advice from society as "Amrit Prasad". However, if someone advises us to sever ourselves from our very roots and remain attached only to the stem, in my opinion they are themselves confused and have not been able to understand the basic core of the BJP.

Any political party has four dimensions – ideology, organization, leadership and strategy. In my opinion, organization, leadership and strategy play a more significant and immediate role in determining victory or defeat in elections. Ideology is a constant which is a perpetual guiding force for a party over and above victory or defeat in elections.

Hindutva/Bharatiyata/Cultural Nationalism occupies the same esteemed space in the politics of the BJP as the Constitution of India occupies in the politics of the country.

Our political power emerges out of both, the policies and programmes of the party. Though we may not have got the expected success in the elections, but even today I am not willing to accept that our policies based on the feeling of stanch nationalism are faulty. Even today we are firm on all the issues raised by us, be it related to external and internal security of the country, foreign policy, terrorism, appeasement or disrespect to the cultural symbols or those related to the plight of the common man or farmers, as these issues are relevant for the country.

Yes, I accept that we may not have been able to disseminate our position on these issues among the people as effectively as it was required in the present context. Perhaps we need to present our views in a better and more contemporary context.

For this, it is necessary that we evaluate our organizational structure, campaign and strategy.

As the President of the party I would like to make it clear that as per the BJP's tradition and ideology, success is a collective credit and failure is a collective responsibility. Therefore, we must collectively find out the solution. Yes, if anyone feels that any person should take the responsibility, then as the President of the party, I am willing to take this responsibility.

Today, the manner in which the comments and propaganda is being made about the defeat of the BJP, it can create confusion in the minds of our workers and supporters as to what were the reasons that we were unable to get the requisite support. According to one theory, we were unable to get the requisite support because we were unable to maintain our character. According to another theory, we were unable to get the requisite support because as per the political terminology in fashion, we remained right wing and could not emerge as moderate as was required today.

Even though many learned persons have commentated on this,

nevertheless a clarification on this subject is required to create clarity in the minds of our workers, voters and supporters.

Direct and Indirect Effect of Hindutva on Politics of India

The ideology of staunch nationalism, which is also termed as the ideology of Hindutva, has always played a decisive role in the politics of independent India. The rise of the BJP in the decade of the 1990s was not only due to this but if we analyze it then the great popularity of Indira Gandhi after the 1971 Bangladesh victory was also a subtle expression of this staunch nationalistic ideology. At that time the people of India attached this ideology with Indira Gandhi. If we analyze carefully, the uninterrupted support which the Congress enjoyed for about one full generation after 1947, basically originated from a reaction in the sub conscious psychology of the common man due to partition in which the Congress emerged as a symbol of nationalism in contrast to the Muslim League.

If we delve into the history of the country, the politics of the so called right wing as described by today's political analysts always had a definitive space not only in the politics but also history of India. This space never got vacant though it's context kept on changing.

At the time of the freedom movement, in the eyes of the British rulers, the Congress was a right wing party. After independence, the Congress became more centrist and the Bharatiya Jan Sangh and today's BJP subsequently occupied this space in Indian politics and ultimately changed the political configuration of the polity in independent India by making it bi-polar.

When we study the pre-independence Congress, then the division of the Congress in 1907 into "Naram Dal" and "Garam Dal" actually germinated the seeds of a full fledged freedom movement. In 1905 when Tilak demanded total freedom, then he was termed as a right wing leader and the Britishers considered him as the cause behind the discontent in India. But from here itself the seeds of the freedom movement were sown which ultimately led to our independence.

Even when we read the views of the Viceroy of India Lord Dufferin at the time of the establishment of the Congress in 1885, it reflects that the formation of the Congress at that time was a right wing thought. The moderate thought at that time was to see more rights and concessions from the Viceroy and not the formation of a separate party.

Prior to this, in the first war of independence in 1857, which actually laid the foundation of our struggle for freedom, its architects Nana Saheb Peswa, Rani Laxmi Bai and Mangal Pandey who are considered hero's by the nation today, at that time symbolized the right wing staunch nationalist thought in the politics of the kings and princes of that period.

Even before this, the rise of Guru Gobind Singh in the north and Chhatrapati Shivaji in the south of the Vindhyas against the despotic rule of Aurangzeb, who at that time had the most powerful army in the world, also symbolized that staunch nationalism could never be suppressed by might.

Prior to this, the diplomatic politics of Akbar under the influence of which most of the Rajput kings at that time opted for a moderate path, then Maharana Pratap raised the flag of nationalism. By doing so, he became immortal in the history of India. If one views him through the eyes of modern analysts, the politics of Maharana Pratap would be today's so called right wing nationalist or Hindutva politics.

What I am trying to say is that what is called right wing today, its context has kept on changing not only over the last 40-50 years but actually over the last four or five centuries, and the historical changes were brought about by this. From Maharana Pratap to Shivaji, Guru Gobind Singh, Nana Saheb Peswa, Tilak and India's independence emerging out of their efforts, the entire history is a proof of this. I am giving you these examples of history because without understanding the politics of the past, the foundation of future politics cannot be laid down.

The past indicates that this so-called right wing positions in Indian polity never left vacant. We are the natural flag bearers of this legacy. In this is imbibed our pride of past, the strategy of the present and achievement in the future.

Political Reality of Today

Leaving aside the historical facts, if we look at the hard political reality of today then in the states where we are a political power, where we are in government on our own, where the chief minister belongs to BJP or where we have had a BJP chief minister earlier, in all such states like Gujarat, Madhya Pradesh, Chhattisgarh, Rajasthan, Himachal, Uttarakhand, Delhi, Jharkhand and Karnataka, if we are in a direct fight with any single party then it is the Congress. In Uttar Pradesh also we had our government earlier and in these elections if any party which has registered the maximum success then it is Congress. It means that our political power would be assessed in standing on the pole opposite to Congress. Therefore, the political reality of today indicates that we should be seen clearly on the pole opposite and different to the Congress. Otherwise any kind of confusion not only in principle but also in political terms would be detrimental to us.

If we look at the results of this election for instance, then indications are that the political parties relinquishing their basic character in Indian politics had to bear losses.

In Indian politics there are mainly two political parties with respect to ideology, first the Bharatiya Jansangh / BJP considered to represent right wing ideology and second the Communist parties considered to be representing left wing ideology. In addition, the Congress as a third stream is considered to be representing a centrist ideology. To a certain extent socialists represented socialist ideology and BSP the dalit.

In this election the Leftists had to bear the maximum damage. The Left Front government was seen acting contrary to their basic character on issues related to Singur and Nandigram. Not only they compromised for power but also gave an impression of enjoying the power by practising the politics of convenience which is in complete contravention to leftist ideology.

The result of the BSP trying to change its character by posing to be harbinger of social harmony through the slogan of sarvasamaj in the form of the so called Dalit-Brahman alliance is very much evident. Its dream of taking a big leap forward stands shattered.

Therefore, whether it is the past or present, political or ideological, in every aspect the conclusion is that changing the basic character or ideology proves to be fatal for any party. Therefore any such idea would be fatal for us in future. We should free ourselves from any such illusion.

Former US President Ronald Reagan had once said that – *If you have to choose between character and strategy in politics, then, leave the strategy but be with the character - because you can survive without strategy but cannot survive without character.*

Therefore we should keep in mind the eternal words, *"swadharme nidhnam shreyoh, pardharmo bhayavaha"*, said in Bhagwad Gita by Bhagwan Krishna.

When we talk about the basic character of the party we should keep in mind that we are not an ordinary political party which has the sole aim of forming the government. But we are a representative party of such an ideology the goal of which is to establish a new era and civilization. Our thinking has a civilizational parameter. Therefore, defeat in one or two elections cannot deviate us. Senior leaders like respected Atalji and Advaniji are symbols of this before us. Through a major part of their political life while working for the party with dedication, they might have never thought about coming to the power within their lifetime.

Most of us have ourselves seen Atalji, Advaniji and before them

Deendayalji and Dr. Shyama Prasad Mookerjee and numerous symbols of the great tradition of dedicated activists like the late Sunder Singh Bhandariji and late Kushabhau Thakreji. All of them used to work with the clarity that they will never come in power in their life. When we did not deviate at that time then can defeat in one or two elections deviate us? If we want to change history then we will have to possess an extremely strong will to stand against the tide of time.

Foreign Policy

In the present time, many important changes are taking place in the neighbouring countries of India. A few months ago, in Nepal the Maoist government has fallen and a new government under the leadership of Shri Madhav Nepal has been formed. On behalf of the Bharatiya Janata Party, I congratulate Shri Madhav Nepal and his new government and hope that in coming days the Indo –Nepal relations will become normal and close as per the centuries old traditions.

Even now in Nepal attempts are being made to use violence and force in the political system. BJP believes that the change of system in Nepal should take place in a democratic manner and not through use of force. Even now the Maoists do not appear to be ready to leave the policy of using force. In Nepal the constituent assembly ably enforcing the new constitution through democratic means and strengthening the roots of democracy are not only in the interest of Nepal but also of India.

With the fall of LTTE in Sri Lanka, the politics based on violence has in a way come to an end and along with this a responsibility of presenting a stable political solution to the problems of Tamils by taking the advantage of a violence free atmosphere has come on Sri Lanka. We completely respect the sovereignty of Sri Lanka but it is necessary that proper representation to Tamil sentiments is given in a united Sri Lanka. I believe that long term solution of this problem may be reached only by giving proper representation to the Tamils in the political system of Sri Lanka.

But, the kind of violence used in the course of operations against LTTE and the kind of news that have been received, it appears that common Tamil citizens had to face heavy violence. Thousands of deaths have taken place and Tamils have to live in an atmosphere of pain and fear. The Indian government has not taken any effective measures for its resolution. We believe that the government of Sri Lanka should initiate such measures to see that Tamil people are free from fear and an atmosphere of confidence is built, so that mutual confidence is established between the Tamil and Sinhalese people.

Government of India should take initiative in this direction.

Whatever is taking place in Pakistan today has at least shattered the myth created by certain intellectuals in India and the international community who used to cite Jammu & Kashmir as the main reason behind worsening relations between India and Pakistan. The kind of internal situation that exists in Pakistan shows that the basis of poor relation with India is inherent in the ongoing internal radical politics of Pakistan. All those countries who want to help Pakistan should understand that it is not prudent to do so without changing the basic system of Pakistan. As long as the army in Pakistan doesn't accept the system of working under the democratic government, the resolution of the internal problem of Pakistan is not possible.

The situation in Pakistan is deteriorating continuously. I have been saying it for the last two years that the Central Government should keep a watchful eye on the condition in Pakistan as Pakistan is seen as moving towards disintegration. The extent to which the influence of Taliban has reached, it may definitely have an impact on our internal security. The kind of slackness which the UPA showed in its last tenure on the internal security front, if it keeps moving in the same direction the future may be grim.

The Government of India should make it clear that no formal dialogue with Pakistan is possible until Pakistan reiterates its commitment to its promise made to the Vajpayee government on January 6th 2004 that it will not allow its soil to be used for anti-India activities. The Atalji led NDA Government had extracted this promise from Pakistan but the UPA has failed to get it implemented. Now terror attacks like 26/11 in Mumbai and the peace process cannot go on simultaneously. I would also like to tell the international community that whatever is taking place on the western borders of Paksitan, nothing less is happening on its eastern borders. If the Pak activities on the Afghanistan border are grave then India can also now not remain a mute spectator to the activities on its borders. The Indian government should take effective diplomatic steps in this direction.

The incidents of racial violence against Indian students in Australia have risen over the last few days. The BJP expresses concern over this. Even before this, in Malaysia, the manner in which oppressions against people of Indian origin were carried out, the Central Government failed to respond suitably. Today violence is taking place against Indian students in Australia. As long as the Central Government does not make a clear and strong policy vis-à-vis Non Resident Indians (NRIs) and People of India Origin (PIO), such kind of problems will keep cropping up. We expect the Central Government to make a strong policy in this regard so that not only in Australia but in the coming time NRIs and PIOs are not harassed in any other country.

Our Working Method – All Embracing Principle of Coordination and Progress

We are passing through a difficult phase. We have all the possibilities. People are also not denying the possibilities present in us. But we will have to kindle trust in their minds. Only those who have the capability to sacrifice themselves can kindle trust in society. The basis of our working method is trust and coordination. These are not two words but represent the basic spirit. The work of the organization cannot progress without them.

We will have to expand ourselves organizationally, ideologically, socially and on the political plane. Somewhere limits of our expansion have stunted or we have not reached upto it. We will have to gear up for entering into a new horizon of expansion and progress. We will have to start making efforts collectively. In fact coordination is the all embracing philosophical perspective which would help us in finding answers to our all questions related to life and politics. We will have to keep chanting the basic mantra of BJP ideology to meet the challenges facing the country and the organization. While treading on this path we should be free from all doubts in our mind that coordination is a formula of compromise and therefore a path meant for weak people. No, it is a path of the strong. In fact it is an important component of the leadership and we will have to move ahead in this direction. The tradition of "Not me, but you" will have to be revived.

Developing Youth Leadership

I have no doubt in saying that the Bharatiya Janata Party gives maximum importance to youth in the state and national level politics. We have many young MPs, MLAs and Chief Ministers. Even then we should definitely develop youth leadership at the district, state and national levels. We believe that the work of identifying and grooming youth leadership should be done speedily.

On the national and state levels, such public programmes should be organized which attract the youth and the Morcha should link them to the ideology. The youth have the power to change – there is no doubt about it.

Scheduled Castes and Scheduled Tribes

Scheduled Castes and Scheduled Tribes have been associated with the BJP for years in comparison to other parties. We always say with pride that the BJP has the largest number of SC / ST MPs. But this time the situation is not as per our expectations.

We all know that in our organisation, both SC and ST Morchas have been active. We will have to undertake an intense and well thoughtout plan of expansion in this direction. Along with this, we will have to carry social campaigns through these Morchas. In the states where we are in government and wherever we are in opposition we will have to take effective measures among these sections and we will have to expand our efforts in the seats we have lost and also by identifying the other seats as well.

Activate the Ground Level Units of the Party at all Levels

Even after constituting the organization upto the booth level, we will have to make plans and organize programmes to keep them always active. We also feel the need to monitor and take care of the efforts of these units at our levels. We will have to keep in mind that only our activists at the ground level units move among the people in villages and towns. The strength of our organization increases by his ideological commitment, activism and his personal contacts.

I feel that in every state, District Presidents and Mandal Presidents should compulsorily tour upto ground level units. Not only for election results, but for organizational expansion and activism of the ground level units it becomes necessary to establish continuous links with them. They should also be linked with social and other constructive works along with party works. If we succeed in doing so then I feel that in coming five years the strength and hold of our organization will increase.

People's Representatives

I have been informed that out of all the MPs that we had in the 14th Lok Sabha only 37-38 have been re-elected. This is a matter of concern for us. I also remember that in the 14th Lok Sabha too the number of MPs getting re-elected from 13th Lok Sabha were less.

In the first National Executive Meeting after the election of 2004 Lok Sabha, respected Advaniji had expressed his concern about our MPs and MLAs not caring properly for their parliamentary and assembly constituencies. He had expressed grave concern over whether the ideologically motivated voters who form our constituencies were getting reduced. I feel that elected representatives should take care of his constituency at all levels. Along with this there should be close relation between the elected representative, organization and the core activists. After being elected, the representatives mostly get engaged in various other works leaving their constituency.

I believe that the image of the party is built through the representatives. When I am talking about the image of the party then I should make it clear that the people's elected representatives have the larger responsibility in building the image of the party and the society. When a representative goes among the people like one of them, takes the people along and struggles continuously and actively for the resolution of even smaller problems in a positive manner, then not only the reputation of the representative but the reputation of the party from which he is elected increases in the society also.

I feel that the people's representatives should understand their double responsibility. Party and the representatives themselves will have to take effective measures in this direction. Society never bears with the neglect of the people. And the era in which we are working politically is completely based on image. Therefore, as a people's representative we should get our image assessed from time to time by different sources. At the party level also arrangements will have to be made so that image of the people's representatives is improved instead of registering a decline. The party will have to make some concrete and effective plan in this direction. We all know that today common people want easy availability of the elected representative. The expectations of the common people from the elected representative also increases which is normal. I have no doubt in saying that an elected representative by his personal behaviour improves the image of the party and expands the party work among different sections of the society and by taking keen interest he may help win the nearby seats which the party might have not won earlier.

Expectations from State Governments

The Bharatiya Janata Party has plenty of expectations from its state governments; the governments of Gujarat, Madhya Pradesh and Chhattisgarh have proven themselves hundred per cent upto expectations therefore people in these states returned the BJP to power again. One of the biggest reasons of the BJP coming back to power in these states is that these governments were successful in building an image among the people that these governments are their own. Common people in these states felt that these governments were meant for them. I feel pride in saying that the popularity and humility of our Chief Ministers of these three states had a big role in bringing back the governments.

It is not simple to create a sense among the people that the government is doing exactly what the people are expecting. In Karnataka and Himachal

Pradesh, the BJP government is gaining popularity as the governments of the common people. In Bihar we have our government in coalition and people in Bihar not only believe but say that after years a government working for development has been formed.

There is a huge responsibility on these governments. Whether the government in alliance in Punjab or the BJP government in Uttarakhand. Wherever our government is there or where we are in government, we have to create history. By creating history we have to try to win people's affection and goodwill. Every section of society should feel that the government they have elected is their own and it is the duty of the common people to defend and cooperate with the government. Our state governments should establish close and deep relations with the people.

Discipline

I want to say a few words with regard to party discipline. We should keep in mind that the people who have built this party kept the organization above everything else. What we are today is just because the interest of the organization has always been kept above the interests and aspirations of individuals. The BJP has been known for a different kind of party. It is a party which gives primary importance to its commitment towards discipline, principles and programmes of the party. All the state units of the party will have to ensure that the disciplinary mechanism and its principles are upheld with full commitment so that in the coming years the party may move forward with better coordination and unity within party organization in the states.

Some Recommendations for Important Organizational Initiatives

- Activists should be made to participate in the decision making process, programmes and in the implementation of policies.
- More coordination between units at all levels and Morchas in the centre and state and with its constituent parts should be ensured.
- Difference of opinions and complaints should be quickly sorted out. Disciplinary actions should not be delayed but should be taken immediately.
- Party units should be made active and effective at the ground level. We should not limit ourselves upto the mandal level alone. We will have to ensure that these units continue to be active and work at all the time.
- Regular training camps should be organised for both new entrants and existing activists at all levels.
- New curriculum for the training of activists should be prepared and

should be carried out in sessions.

Lastly, I would like to say that we should not have doubts or apprehensions of any kind with regard to the future. In this context I would like to recall an important incident in the history of the world when the US was passing through a phase of grave economic recession in the 1930s. The faith of the people of the US was shaken. At that time, Franklin Roosevelt, whose both legs were affected by polio and was himself unable to stand on his feet said in his historical speech on March 4th 1933 instilling faith across the entire US, "The biggest fear of ours is the fear itself–that our actual fear is based on the existence of fear. Roosevelt moved ahead with these words, brought the US out of the era of recession and made it play an effective role in the Second World War. He became US President for four terms and this was the time when the US got established as a world super power. Therefore we should also keep in mind the following lines from two poems of Atalji:

"Har me ya jeet me, kinchit nahi bhayabhit main"

And another famous poem –

"Kadam mila kar chalna hoga"

The essence of our present and future are implicit in these two lines of Atalji.

□□□